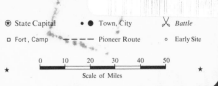

Ken

D1062574

⊛ State Capital   ●● Town, City   ✕ Battle

□ Fort, Camp   ----- Pioneer Route   ○ Early Site

0   10   20   30   40   50

Scale of Miles

𝕲𝖗𝖊𝖊𝖓𝖛𝖎𝖑𝖑𝖊 𝕮𝖔𝖑𝖑𝖊𝖌𝖊
𝕷𝖎𝖇𝖗𝖆𝖗𝖞

GREENVILLE COLLEGE

ILLINOIS

917.69   C54

Drennon's
Springs

RIVE

OHIO

s of
hio

Area of

Simpsonville

le   MIDLAND

Taylorsville

ld Station ○

● Cox's Creek

rdstown

Chaplin R

Harro

Springfield

Danv

hertonville

ville   Lebanon

pring   Loga

a Lincoln's   (St. A

lace)

● Campbellsville

Green

Columbia ●

Lake
Cumberland

Wolf Creek Dam

Springs

sville ●

kinsville   ● Albany

Pineville

Cumberland Gap ●

Middlesboro

ville

Tug Fork

● Pikeville

NTAINS

Breaks of
Sandy

A

P

Cumberland

APP

● Evarts

Powell R.

ROAD

WILDERNESS

Clinch R.

Holston R.

Kentucky: *Land of Contrast*

REGIONS OF AMERICA

*A series of books that depict our natural regions,
their history, development, and character*

Edited by Carl Carmer

KENTUCKY: *Land of Contrast*
by Thomas D. Clark

Already Published

FLORIDA: *The Long Frontier*
by Marjory Stoneman Douglas

TEN FLAGS IN THE WIND:
The Story of Louisiana
by Charles L. Dufour

STATE O' MAINE
by Louise Dickinson Rich

PENNSYLVANIA: *Seed of a Nation*
by Paul A. W. Wallace

THE HEARTLAND: *Ohio, Indiana, Illinois*
by Walter Havighurst

LOVE SONG TO THE PLAINS
by Mari Sandoz

YANKEE KINGDOM: *Vermont and New Hampshire*
by Ralph Nading Hill

VIRGINIA: *A New Look at the Old Dominion*
by Marshall W. Fishwick

BOOKS BY THOMAS D. CLARK

Kentucky: Land of Contrast
The Emerging South
Frontier America
The Bluegrass Cavalcade
The Rural Editor and the New South
The Southern Country Editor
Pills, Petticoats, and Plows
The Kentucky (Rivers of America series)
The Rampaging Frontier
The History of Kentucky

A REGIONS OF AMERICA BOOK

917.6
C54

Kentucky: *Land of Contrast*

By Thomas D. Clark

HARPER & ROW, PUBLISHERS

NEW YORK, EVANSTON, AND LONDON

To

J. Winston Coleman, Jr.

LEWIS & CLARK LIBRARY SYSTEM

P. O. BOX 368

EDWARDSVILLE, ILL. 62025

KENTUCKY: LAND OF CONTRAST. *Copyright © 1968 by Thomas D. Clark. Printed in the United States of America. All rights reserved. No part of this book may be used or reproduced in any manner whatsoever without written permission except in the case of brief quotations embodied in critical articles and reviews. For information address Harper & Row, Publishers, Incorporated, 49 East 33rd Street, New York, N.Y. 10016.*

LIBRARY OF CONGRESS CATALOG CARD NUMBER: 67-28804

Contents

117316

Preface

Kentucky has almost as many faces as there are sectional divisions of the state. Whether it be the colonel with his goatee and julep or the mountaineer with his hog rifle and jug of moonshine, the image seldom if ever is an accurate one. Blazing a path into the heart of the first trans-Appalachian frontier, pioneer Kentuckians were apprentices to the westward movement along the western waters. Out of the stirring early years of international conflict, Indian wars, and pioneering arose heroes like George Rogers Clark, Daniel Boone, Simon Kenton, Benjamin Logan, and Isaac Shelby. There were also rascals like James Wilkinson and his hired men. Behind the heroes were yeomen settlers who were less heroic in opening farms, building villages and towns, and opening the rich trade downriver to the southern markets. The mixed reputations of the "Kentucks" were established both aboard flatboats drifting south and in the salons of plush steamboats as much as in the mountains, Bluegrass, and Pennyroyal.

Because it played so important a role in the expansion and settlement of the West, Kentucky became involved in every national and international issue which was raised in the formative years of the Republic. Whether it was an attempt to expand constitutional government or to engage in international intrigue there were some Kentuckians ready to play an active role on either side of the issue. Virginia in time hustled many a frustrated politician over the mountains into its western counties, and these in time bred Kentucky political personalities who played central roles in shaping the Kentucky tradition.

No part of the Kentucky story is more meaningful than the fact that its people have been isolated by geography, provincial at all times, and submissive to political influences which oftentimes have handicapped them in broadening their views of the world. In social relations their reactions have been translated into terms of intensive personal values. Folk literature, mores, and behavior were shaped by this fact, and still are. Much of the history of the state has been colored in terms of personalities and the commonplace. Even the sophistication of towns and cities like Ashland, Covington, Louisville, Lexington, Owensboro, and Paducah is tinged sharply with the coloration of the rural mind.

Until the middle of the twentieth century the unyielding rock of agrarianism has shattered campaigns to revise the old ways of life. In recent years, however, traditional rural Kentucky is being overwhelmed by an industrial-commercial invasion which most surely will obliterate much of the old rural tradition. Kentucky farmers still raise loud hues and cries against change, but they now get fewer responses than in the past. Every time a new industry locates in the state rural Kentucky has to retreat. Hearts of the older cities show signs of decay. At the moment considerable areas of downtown Louisville resemble their virginal state, and Lexington is troubled and puzzled by the coming of industry, crowding of its roads and streets with traffic, and the migration of business to the suburbs.

Most important of all, Appalachia stands befuddled in its present suspension between the past and the future. It never shed its old folkways, nor did it fare well in the first wave of industrial exploitation of folk and resources. Part of the Appalachian problem at the moment lies in the inability of the reformers to distinguish between genuine poverty, the stubbornness of people, and the chaos created by social change.

This book is not a history of Kentucky. It is an exploration of parts of Kentucky's past with an attempt to identify some of the historical forces which have made the state a distinct entity in the Union.

No people have ever faced harsher realities at times with more complacency than have Kentuckians. Few people have revered their past more for the sake of relating themselves to the historical experience. Their memories, however, are short, as any politician can tell you. They are ready to believe that the past was benevolent; to them it involved family histories, the rise of colorful political figures, and the time of struggle. The past supplies the Kentuckian a basis of comparison of his own condition, and is a rich source of nostalgia. It would be difficult to imagine a people embraced by a single set of political boundaries who presented sharper contrasts than have Kentuckians. Sectional and social boundaries within the state have ever been separative influences.

I am grateful to Colonel J. Winston Coleman, Jr., to Joe Creason, and to Burton Milward for their generous reading of this text.

Table of Events

1750: Thomas Walker's party enters Kentucky through Cumberland Gap, April 13.

1751: Christopher Gist crosses Kentucky from the Big Bone Lick on the Ohio to Pine Mountain near Harlan.

1752: Lewis Evans issues first map of the Kentucky country.

1760 (*approx.*): John Swift, the silver miner, comes to Kentucky.

1765: George Croghan is at the Big Bone Lick, May 30.

1766: Captain Harry Gordon, Chief Engineer for Western North America, at the Falls of the Ohio, June 18.

1766: The long hunters arrive in Kentucky from the Yadkin Valley in North Carolina.

1769: A survey party from Virginia reaches the Falls of the Ohio.

1769: Daniel Boone and John Finley arrive in Kentucky with their hunting party, June 7.

1774: James Harrod and his men arrive at the site of Harrodstown, May.

1775: Daniel Boone and his party blaze the Wilderness Trail and begin building Fortress Boonesboro. That same year George Rogers Clark arrives in Kentucky.

1777: Clark plans Northwest campaign.

1778: Daniel Boone and the saltmakers captured at the Blue Licks; September that year Boonesboro besieged by De Quindre and Black Fish.

1780: Transylvania Seminary chartered.

1782: Battle of the Blue Licks; last major Indian attack, August 19.

1792: Kentucky becomes a state June 1, and on June 4 the state government is organized at Lexington.

1811: First steamboat arrives at the Falls of the Ohio, November.

1819: The great financial panic, and the Kentucky upheaval over debt relief.

1825: General Lafayette visits Kentucky, May.

1830: George D. Prentice begins publication of the Louisville *Daily Journal*.

1831: First railroad construction begins, October 21.

1839: Great four-mile race between Wagner and Grey Eagle in Louisville, September 30.

1855: "Bloody Monday" riots in Louisville, August 6.

1861: Kentucky declares position of neutrality in the Civil War, May 24.

1861: Confederate forces under General Leonidas Polk violate Kentucky neutrality by invading the state at Columbus, September 3.

1862: Battle of Mill Springs, January 19.

1862: Morgan invades Kentucky at Tompkinsville, July 8.

1862: Morgan at Midway, July 15, and the Battle of Cynthiana Bridge, July 17.

1863: Battle of Perryville, October 8.

1865: University of Kentucky founded, February 22.

1865: Sue Munday captured at Webster, Breckinridge County, March 12.

1865: Quantrell, the guerrilla, captured at Wakefield, Spencer County.

1875: Price McGrath's Aristides wins the first Kentucky Derby, May 17.

1883-1887: J. Proctor Knott Governor of Kentucky.

1891: Fourth Constitution adopted.

1894-1900: Tollgate war in Kentucky.

1894-1911: Hargis-Cockrill feud in Breathitt County.

1895-1899: William O. Bradley Governor of Kentucky.

1899: Music Hall Convention in Louisville, June.

1900: William Goebel assassinated in Frankfort, January 30.

1905-1909: Tobacco war in western Kentucky.

1915-1919: A. O. Stanley Governor of Kentucky.

1919-1923: Edwin Morrow Governor of Kentucky.

1927: Alben W. Barkley becomes United States Senator.

1937: Great flood.

1938: Hotly contested senatorial election between A. B. Chandler and Alben W. Barkley.

Kentucky: *Land of Contrast*

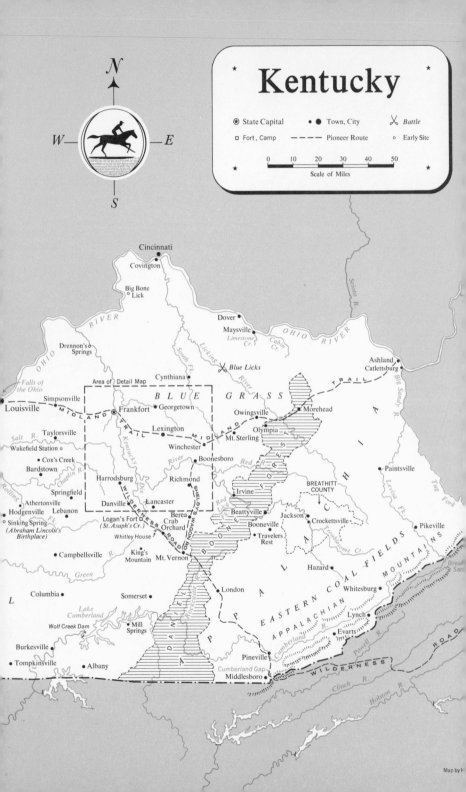

N
W — E
S

Kentucky

⊛ State Capital • ● Town, City ⚔ Battle
□ Fort, Camp --- Pioneer Route ○ Early Site

0   10   20   30   40   50
Scale of Miles

Cincinnati
Covington
Big Bone ○ Lick
Dover
Maysville
Limestone Cr.
⚔ Blue Licks
Drennon's Springs
OHIO RIVER
Ashland
Catlettsburg
Scioto R.
Cabin Cr.
Licking River
South Fk.
Cynthiana
Area of Detail Map
BLUE GRASS
Falls of the Ohio
Louisville
Simpsonville
MIDLAND TRAIL
Frankfort
Georgetown
Owingsville
Morehead
TRAIL
Big Sandy R.
Salt R.
Taylorsville
Lexington
MIDLAND
Olympia
Mt. Sterling
Wakefield Station
Winchester
Boonesboro
Irvine
FOREST
Paintsville
Cox's Creek
Kentucky River
Red Lick
BREATHITT COUNTY
Bardstown
Chaplin R.
Harrodsburg
Richmond
Levisa Fk.
Springfield
Athertonville
Danville
Lancaster
Beattyville
Jackson
Crockettsville
Pikeville
Tug Fork
Logan's Fort (St. Asaph's Cr.)
Berea
Booneville
Hodgenville
Lebanon
Dix R.
Crab Orchard
Travelers Rest
Sinking Spring (Abraham Lincoln's Birthplace)
Whitley House
WILDERNESS ROAD
King's Mountain
SHELBY'S WAGON RD.
Tygers Cr.
Campbellsville
Mt. Vernon
Hazard
Whitesburg
Green R.
London
Lynch
APPALACHIAN MOUNTAINS
Columbia
Somerset
BOONE
EASTERN COAL FIELDS
Evarts
Break Sar.
Lake Cumberland
DANIEL
Rockcastle R.
Powell R.
Wolf Creek Dam
Mill Springs
Cumberland R.
ROAD
Burkesville
Pineville
Tompkinsville
Albany
Cumberland Gap
Middlesboro
WILDERNESS
Clinch R.
Holston R.

Map by H

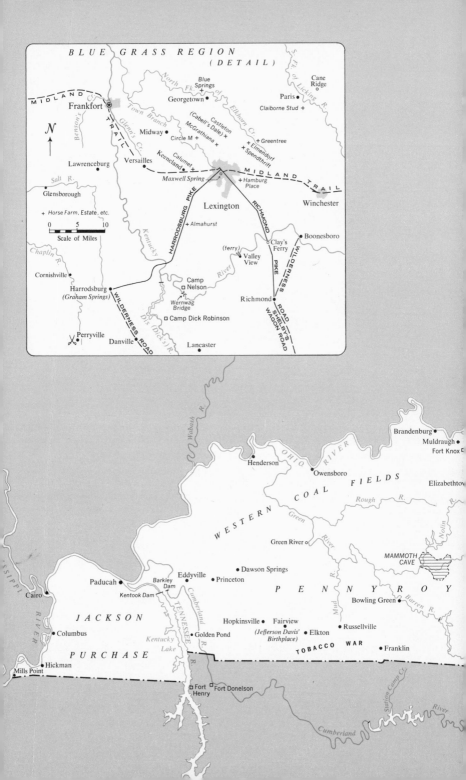

BLUE GRASS REGION (DETAIL)

Cane Ridge
Blue Springs
Georgetown
Paris
Claiborne Stud +
MIDLAND TRAIL
Frankfort
North Fk. of Licking R.
North Fk. of Elkhorn Cr.
Town Branch
Benson's Cr.
Glenn's Cr.
(Cabell's Dale)
Castleton
McGrathiana +
Midway
Circle M +
+ Greentree
+ Elmendorf
+ Spendthrift
N
Lawrenceburg
Versailles
Calumet
Keeneland
MIDLAND TRAIL
Maxwell Spring
+ Hamburg Place
Winchester
Salt R.
Glensborough
+ Horse Farm, Estate, etc.
Lexington
RICHMOND PIKE
HARRODSBURG PIKE
0   5   10
Scale of Miles
+ Almahurst
Chaplin R.
Kentucky R.
Boonesboro
Cornishville
(ferry)
Valley View
Clay's Ferry
WILDERNESS PIKE
Camp Nelson
Harrodsburg
(Graham Springs)
Wernwag Bridge
Richmond
WILDERNESS ROAD
SHELBY'S WAGON ROAD
WILDERNESS ROAD
Dix Dick's R.
□ Camp Dick Robinson
Perryville
Danville
Lancaster

Wabash R.
Brandenburg
Muldraugh
Fort Knox
OHIO RIVER
Henderson
Owensboro
WESTERN COAL FIELDS
Elizabethtow
Rough R.
Green River o
Green River
Nolin
MAMMOTH CAVE
SSIPPI RIVER
Cairo
Paducah
Barkley Dam
Eddyville
Dawson Springs
Princeton
Cumberland R.
Mud R.
PENNYROY
Kentook Dam
Bowling Green
Barren R.
JACKSON
Columbus
Kentucky Lake
Hopkinsville
Fairview
(Jefferson Davis' Birthplace)
Golden Pond
Elkton
Russellville
PURCHASE
TENNESSEE R.
TOBACCO WAR
Franklin
Mills Point
Hickman
Station Camp Cr.
□ Fort Henry
□ Fort Donelson
Cumberland
River

Springing the Latch

With its back to the great Appalachian wall and its face to the Ohio and Mississippi rivers, Kentucky stretches out into an elongated tongue of land which separates the mountaineer of the Big Sandy from the swamp dweller of Mills Point by almost four hundred miles. Centuries before the first European set foot in this sweeping green forest land Indians of two or three layers of civilization wandered here. Corn-growing and basket-weaving ancients built their villages here and left in evidence of their having passed this way burial and ceremonial mounds which have occupied the interest of modern archaeologists and anthropologists for the past half century.

Angry red invaders from above the Ohio and from the Appalachians of the east met in the Kentucky forests and meadows to hunt and fight it out with their enemies. They and the plodding American bison pawed out trails from one patch of grass and cane to the other, and they connected the numerous salt licks with a webwork of traces. A great warrior's trace sliced the eastern highlands from Cumberland Gap to the mouth of the Scioto on the Ohio. The historian can only guess that hunter and warrior alike glided along this trail, which like an upraised arrow was pointed at the heart of the Cherokee country, or conversely at Shawnee and Wyandotte villages above the river.

Stringing out in weaving herds the American bison wandered southward as far as the Yadkin Valley in North Carolina, but its anchorage was in the middle-western forests and fields. This animal

1

was as masterful at trailmaking as was the Indian. He never climbed a rise when he could find a level grade or a decline. With a seasoned engineer's certainty he located good fording places across streams and he stayed away from laurel brush and storm-tousled fallen timbers. For this lumbering beast and his fellow grazing neighbors there was plenty of grass and cane in Kentucky and enough salt to make life pleasant.

Water flowed abundantly. Behind every ridge there ran a creek or major river. Six arterial streams slashed deep passways through lime and sandstone cliffs to feed the omnivorous Ohio in its push to join the Mississippi. The account of the passage of time and the powerful forces of nature was chiseled inerasably upon the face of towering palisades along these streams, and from many a rock-lined perspective the earliest white visitors were to spy out the land.

Towering above mountain and stream stood one of the most magnificent virginal forests in North America. Giant tulip poplars shot up from riverbank and cliff shoulder with the precision of an arrow shot. A hundred and fifty feet in the air they spread their graceful branches and sent forth their almond-colored blossoms. These monarchs often measured ten and twelve feet in diameter at the height of a man's chest. Crowded about these erect sentinels were centuries-old white oaks containing enough tough close-grained wood to launch a conquering navy or to build enough charred kegs to age bourbon whiskey for generations to come. On the ridge monstrous chestnut trees spread their limbs to shed a rich mast each fall, and to yield fence rails enough to glorify politically half the male population of the continent as rail splitters. Towering walnut, maple, and buckeye contained enough handsome lumber to build fine furniture for most of Western civilization.

Not all primeval Kentucky was buried beneath a heavy bank of forest trees. Rolling hills in the central bluegrass area and western barrens broke the spell of the woods. Indian fires annually fought back brush and shrub to keep bluegrass land and the barrens open and grass succulent for grazing animals. Whether or not these pleasant savannas of central Kentucky were carpeted in bluegrass still remains in doubt. Maybe they were, but it also may be true that bluegrass was imported from Europe, no one knows. Certainly there was grass, and there was lush, tender, trim cane that fattened herds of meat- and skin-bearing animals.

This was the land beyond the mountains, or the "land on the western waters" of Indian and hunter-trader legend. From a dim and uncertain moment in the sixteenth century fame of the western mountain and valley country began to excite European newcomers. In the south along the Gulf, along the St. Lawrence to the north, and in the settlements hugging the Atlantic, Latin and Englishman alike listened attentively to stories of the Ohio country. By word of mouth the great legend was fabricated so that by the latter part of the century the fame of the west had almost become that of a New World Cathay.

In recent years authors have made much of the legend of the Eden of the West. Early hunters and, later, Kentuckians were entranced with the idea that their land inside the river-mountain triangle was a garden of plenty locked behind the narrow gates of the Ohio and Cumberland Gap. The edenesque gossamer was quickly swept away once settlers faced the realities of a hard land making unrelenting demands of men and their trail-bound families. A sweep of the vast horizons revealed a most pleasing country, but a more detailed view brought into focus the realities of snatching the land away from Indian, animal, and woods.

Kentucky was a natural extension of the undefined boundaries of spreading Virginia. No political delineations either in royal proclamation or in land survey determined where Virginia left off and Kentucky began. Only the stony face of the Appalachians and distance itself set the two regions apart. The rocky spine of the eastern mountains did more than rear a frowning geographical barrier; in time to come it formed a psychological dividing point beyond which Virginians became Kentuckians.

Penetration of the Ohio Valley before the first quarter of the eighteenth century was more easily undertaken from the Great Lakes and river frontier. French trader, priest, and explorer from Canada and Louisiana in time were to reach the Ohio Valley. Some Kentucky historians have persistently maintained that Robert Cavelier, Sieur de La Salle came along the Kentucky shore on his first visit in 1668. There are even accounts which give in some detail his visit to the Falls of the Ohio. These claims are groundless. La Salle saw Kentucky all right, but it was from the gunwale of his canoe that swept past its tip along the Mississippi.

In those years in the eighteenth century when Englishmen were being acclimated in the coastal Virginia littoral, they were not without curiosity about the western country. The London Company grant was so sweeping in its land descriptions that it was only natural for England to expand westward. The English, however, were not alone as masters of all-embracing gestures toward huge blocks of geography. At the Sault Sainte Marie, before an amazed Indian audience, Daumont de Saint-Lusson in 1671 claimed the land also. There he not only laid claim for France to all the country within immediate view, but to all lands, rivers, and lakes adjoining. This was about as inclusive a claim as could be imagined.

As the passage of time was to prove, Saint-Lusson was late in laying claim to the Ohio Valley west. Virginians were already astir. Governor William Berkeley cast an eye westward, and in 1646 Colonel Abraham Wood led a party up the James to establish Fort Henry. It mattered not that this first serious penetration of the back country got no farther than Petersburg, the Virginians had begun their trek toward the far-flung Blue Ridges. From Fort Henry before the close of the century other adventurers, including Colonel Wood himself, were to push on to the beckoning hills. They collected a good body of information about the back country, and bit by bit they were able to establish the outline of its geography.

By the third quarter of the seventeenth century, Virginians had become excited about the frontier. Legend, casual hunter gossip, and a couple of pamphlets had developed in the public mind a concept of a body of rich land lying beyond the mountains. The author of the tract *A Perfect Description of Virginia* not only stimulated the imagination about the primeval Appalachian frontier but he held out hope that beyond the mountain ranges was the possibility of a quick passage to China.

Of far more practical meaning to westward expansion was the opening fur and skin trade with Europe. Once English merchants entered the market for skins and furs they encouraged traders to brave the wilderness hardships with more fortitude than men heretofore had pursued a legend. At the same time the Lords Proprietors in securing the Carolina charter added a second incentive to explorer and hunter activities. Never again was the westward movement to be free of insatiable land hunger.

Abraham Wood had a rival in that strange adventurer John Lederer. This expansive German physician was persistent in three attempts to sweep away the mystery of the Virginia hinterlands in the

1670's. Accounts of his exploits were as farfetched as if they described imaginary journeys. Lederer did, however, help to bring the Appalachian frontier into clearer focus. He also recorded some interesting encounters with upriver Virginia Indians. Later Thomas Woods, Robert Fallam, and Thomas Batts were to encounter Lederer's natives on their journey up to the headwaters of the James.

Governor Berkeley was determined. To the west lay rich and exciting territory. There were mountains, and beyond these was a river. In 1671 Robert Fallam and Thomas Batts reached the divide where they could gaze through the New River gorge into the western piles of hills which drained their waters into the Ohio. Standing on this divide between east and west the explorers were to feel one bit of frustration. Carved on a nearby tree were the initials M.A.N.I. Though they were denied the privilege of being the first Europeans to reach that place, they still had the satisfaction of being first to record existence of the divide. By this crossing they brought Kentucky country a step nearer discovery and exploration.

Two years after Batts and Fallam clambered down from the New River passage, James Needham and Gabriel Arthur set out from Fort Henry on an ill-starred journey westward. Traveling southward through the western Carolina ridges and valleys they were captured by Indians. Needham was heartlessly murdered, but the illiterate Arthur was taken captive to visit Florida, and later he may have passed through Cumberland Gap, and certainly he visited the Kanawha Valley.

For the next half century trader, hunter, land viewer, and adventurer penetrated the west. In the late summer of 1717 Governor Alexander Spotswood led a party of mounted gentlemen westward to a lofty peak of the Blue Ridge Mountains to gaze off into the azure Shenandoah Valley. This expedition was more famous for its company and equipage than for accomplishments. Spotswood, much in the manner of Saint-Lusson, suffered a stroke of grandeur there atop his Blue Ridge pinnacle and made sweeping proclamations of ownership of the view before him.

Less well-equipped and not so numerously accompanied was humble John Peter Salling, who traveled up the James in 1730 to hunt and explore. Before he set foot in the Virginia settlements again he was taken by his Indian captors across Kentucky to the Ohio and on to Kaskaskia, and back by way of Canada.

Already the west was alive with hunters and explorers. The Baron Longueil had descended the Ohio, and legend had it that three years later, 1742, John Howard, an Englishman, had traveled down this stream.

By 1740 most of the cobweb of mystery had been swept from the western country. The flow of many of the rivers was known, and the relationship of the Ohio to the Mississippi had been established. Frenchmen, beginning with La Salle, had produced this information. The leading issue now was who would claim the land and its rich resources? Both French and Anglo-colonial traders competed for Indian favors and goods. Pathways were being opened from the Potomac to the Ohio and from the James to the Appalachians. After 1745 George Croghan's traders, with others, paddled canoes down the Ohio and its lateral streams. One party had gone as far south as Indian Oldfields in Kentucky to establish a trading post.

In time the back country was to be rocked by a hot three-way rivalry. Frenchmen and Englishmen struggled both in the backwoods and at the diplomatic table to control the region. A parade of Latin explorers and traders pressed along the streams from Canada and Louisiana. Paul Céleron de Blainville came southward from Quebec on orders from Governor La Gallissonnière to lay tangible claim to the Ohio Valley. Burdened with tin shields and engraved leaden plates to plant at the mouths of the rivers, he dodged hostile tribes of Indians and traders alike. The Indians feared loss of their homeland, while traders sought to stave off competition. On the larger scene two powerful nations were beginning a worldwide struggle to determine mastery of the North American continent and the high seas.

Though Frenchmen disturbed colonial officials and traders alike, not all the rivalry was of international origin. New Yorkers, Pennsylvanians, Marylanders, Carolinians, and Virginians sought to enrich themselves by exchanging cheap British goods for prime furs and skins. About the headwaters of the Ohio and downstream Pennsylvania and Virginia traders ranged widely. Along the eastern rim of the Blue Ridge Virginia traders sought to crowd out Carolinian competitors coming inland from Charleston. The western country was now a rich prize.

The latch to Kentucky had been sprung but the gate was not yet opened. The land on the western waters was known. Companies of men plotted to possess the land for speculative purposes just as others were to monopolize the rich Indian trade. In 1748 a company of gentlemen, including Thomas Lee and George Washington's half brothers, Lawrence and Augustine, organized the ambitious Ohio Company which proposed to lay claim to 200,000 acres in the Ohio Valley. A year later a rival group, the Loyal Company, set out to claim 80,000 acres of land west of the mountains.

Dr. Thomas Walker of "Castle Hill," Albemarle County, a graduate of William and Mary and a physician, was employed to lead an exploring party westward early in the spring of 1750. Dr. Walker's party was to follow known trails down the inside rim of the mountain frontier, and at some point cross over into the western country. Crossing from the New River headwaters to those of the Holston, Clinch and Powell, Walker and his men came to face a solid rock wall which towers for miles down the mountain spine. From far to the east there is visible a gap in this wall, and to this point the Virginians came on April 13, 1750. They had learned in some way that it was called Cave Gap. Like Batts and Fallam at the New River passage, Walker discovered initials carved on trees along with signs of the cross. Some nameless white man had passed that way before.

Beyond the gap, which Thomas Walker named for the "bloody" Duke of Cumberland, his party was confronted by a maze of valleys and passages which led generally down the Cumberland Valley. None of the land which Walker saw in this area conformed with descriptions of land which his employers sought. In fact the doctor did little good for the members of the Loyal Land Company. His path lay over the most rugged parts of what is now eastern Kentucky, and it was hard to conceive of an eighteenth-century land company profiting from the sale of such territory. Worn and saddle-galled, Thomas Walker and his men rode up to Andrew Johnson's house at Augusta Courthouse in the Shenandoah Valley on July 11. Their condition was graphically described in the journal entry of the 8th in which Walker said:

Having shaved, shifted, & made new shoes we left our useless raggs at ye camp & got to Walker Johnston's about noon. We moved over to Robert Armstrong's in the afternoon & staid there all night. The people here are very hospitable and would be better able to support Travelers was it not for the great number of Indian warriors, that frequently take what they want from them, much to Their prejudices.

Hardly had Dr. Walker unsaddled his nag at Castle Hill in Albemarle before the Ohio Company's agent Christopher Gist was off to explore the Ohio Valley. This famous woodsman had moved from Maryland to the Yadkin Valley in western North Carolina where he was brought closer to the great mountain west. Instructions from the Ohio Company ordered him to go by the headwaters of the Ohio River to search out a likely claim in that fertile valley. His was to be an exciting journey, but it was not to be without its treacheries. Like de Blainville, he was forced to obscure the purposes of his mission from Indian and trader alike; he even had to take his compass readings in secrecy. Gist traveled westward across Ohio to the Miami Valley, and then moved down to cross the Ohio River into Kentucky. His destination was the falls of the great river, but friendly Shawnees persuaded him not to go there because treacherous French Indians would kill him. He collected two huge teeth from the massive skeletons lying about the Big Bone Lick and set off across country for the Yadkin. Gist had traced the route to Kentucky by way of the Ohio, as Walker before him had opened the pathway through Cumberland Gap. Neither of their journals gave the impression that they had crossed an Eden land in their wanderings.

II

Hunter's Interlude

Although Thomas Walker and Christopher Gist helped to open Kentucky's gateways, their visits did not set off an immediate inrushing of settlers. Before the land could be secured there were still international decisions to be made in the French and Indian War and the Treaty of Paris in 1763. This conflict all but checked the appearance of traders and explorers in Kentucky. After 1763 this movement west was further checked by the royal proclamation which sought to hold settlers on the eastern watershed until an Indian policy could be devised.

In these beclouded years an occasional and unwilling visitor crossed the Kentucky country as captive of war parties. One such person was Mary Ingles, who had fallen victim to her captors on the Virginia frontier. In the early 1750's almost every cabin dweller in the Valley of Virginia had a tale of awe to tell of the Indian raids which swept the back country like wildfire in a high wind. On July 8, 1755, skulking Shawnee warriors raided the new-found settlement at Draper's Meadow, killing several men and taking women and children captive. Among these were Mary Draper and Mary Ingles and the Ingles children. They were hustled off to be displayed as prizes of war in the villages beyond the Ohio. On the way the Indians stopped along the Kanawha to make salt. Mrs. Ingles ingratiated herself with the chief and his warriors to the extent that she was permitted to go at will into the woods to search for herbs to treat Mary Draper's

9

injuries. In these sorties she contemplated escape, but to have done so would certainly have brought death to her children, and each time she returned to camp.

In the villages the Shawnees celebrated victory by displaying scalps and forcing all the prisoners except Mary Ingles to run the gantlet. Early that fall she further cemented Indian trust in her by making gaudy heel-length strouding shirts for the entire male population of the village. Later her children were sent off to die in other villages and Mary Ingles was taken below the Ohio to make salt at the Big Bone Lick in Kentucky. Here she met an aged Pennsylvania German woman who also had been taken captive in a border raid. Armed with tomahawks and knives, the two women began their desperate journey to Virginia. The story of their grueling adventures was one of hunger, fatigue, mental derangement, and loss of heart. Fortunately they made their way home. They brought firsthand knowledge that Kentucky was a hard and treacherous land. Bushes and thorns riddled their clothes, treacherous streams barred their way, and food was scarce.

The year before Mary Ingles fled Big Bone Lick, John Finley came to Kentucky to hunt. He had paddled downstream in a canoe, had shot game about the salt licks, and had viewed what he conceived to be a veritable promised land. Here a hunter could take a stand and game came into rifle range.

Finley, like numerous other visitors in the sprawling wilderness, no doubt assumed that he was alone in the country. That same year, however, James McBride, a Scotch trader, passed the mouth of the Kentucky River, and there in humbler fashion than Céleron de Blainville carved his initials on a tree. Except for the unwilling visit of Mary Ingles and the German woman, and the visits of the mysterious John Swift, silence fell over Kentucky for the next decade.

In 1760 John Swift was said to have come to Kentucky. This was John Swift the silver miner, and there was such a person and he was in the western country despite the fact that his name long ago was associated with an intriguing legend of fleeting riches. Swift kept a journal of his adventures which was entrusted in 1790 to the widow of Joseph Renfro of Bean Station, Tennessee. She was said to have had personal beauty and a large inheritance of land, both of which appealed mightily to Swift. The journal described its author's wanderings in the mountains of Kentucky and Tennessee and the discovery of a fabulous silver lode. There were veiled directions for relocating these riches and an accompanying map which proposed to give more precise instructions, but since Swift knew no landmark names it is well-nigh meaningless.

Every hunter and trader knew about Kentucky's rich store of skins, furs, and the endless tracts of land, but now John Swift added the lure of silver. Geologists have repeatedly searched for silver outcroppings, but none have been found. The Swift legend survives, and in almost every hill county there are persistent people who had rather seek fortune by searching for nebulous silver than by plowing corn. Swift's journal has been copied countless times with each transcriber writing into it his own beliefs and secret desires. Owners of copies of the journal, and there must be hundreds, are forever making discreet inquiries as to their worth, but they coyly refuse to part with their manuscripts because somewhere in their wordings may be the magic key to riches. Historically John Swift may have been a liar extraordinary, but his legend has been a part of Kentucky folklore since 1770. As late as July, 1961, a group of mountaineers appealed to the Kentucky Parks Commission to establish a state park in their county, partly on the grounds that it was there that Swift discovered his silver mine. In this case exuberant local citizens placed far more confidence in silver tourists would spend there than in their ability to uncover the mother lode.

The Kentucky wilderness offered more to the hunter of game than to the amateur mineralogist. Its fruits, however, were not to be plucked without danger. Every sound and every movement had to be identified. The hoot of an owl or the call of a familiar bird might in fact be that of a lurking warrior in search of a scalp. Spring and fall hunting parties crossed Cumberland Gap to spend weeks and months along the Cumberland River or to wander deeper into the central canelands. Among them came Gaspar Mansker, Elisha Walden, Jack Blevins, Benjamin Cuthbirth, Henry Skaggs, William Newman, and William Pittman. These men were more than hunters, they were the forerunners of Anglo-American civilization who searched out the courses of streams, tested the quality of the land, learned the location of salt licks, and spied out Indian and game trails. East of the mountains their stories stimulated burning desires to claim the land.

Yet in the sprawling Eden of the West there was frustration. Man was ready to do injury to his fellows. A tattered and time-stained sliver of paper in the University of Kentucky Archives records a moment of intense disgust and disappointment. Jesse Bledsoe and his long-hunting companions who had roamed the Kentucky wilderness during an extended hunting season returned to their skin cache near the Cumberland River to find it robbed. This was too much for the impetuous Bledsoe, who stepped aside and 'suaged his wrath on a tree by carving, "2300 deerskins lost, ruination, by God." It was startling enough for Carolinian long hunters to lose the fruits of a season's hunt, but it is more startling to modern Kentuckians to realize that these woodsmen had slaughtered 2,300 deer.

Successful hunting stories were honored in the Yadkin country of Western North Carolina by their repetition. Early people learned that the land beyond the mountains was out of the immediate reach of the hostile Cherokees, but there were the Shawnees, Delawares, and Wyandottes. In a country where almost every boy divided his time between corn planting and hunting, the long green ranges to the west beckoned.

Among the restless men of the Yadkin was Daniel Boone. In earlier years he had made the long move southward from Bucks County, Pennsylvania, by way of the Valley of Virginia. Five years after arriving in North Carolina he appeared on the Monongahela with Major Dobbs's North Carolina militia as a part of Braddock's army and a companion of John Finley. In the disaster at Little Turtle Ford, Boone and Finley had cut horses loose from their wagons and ran for their lives. Daniel's enlistment was short, and he returned to the Yadkin to marry that most patient of frontier women, Rebecca Bryan.

Long hunting was not an unknown pastime for Daniel Boone. He had hunted with such seasoned woodsmen as Benjamin Cuthbirth for game and land along the Watauga in eastern Tennessee. In 1767 he and a companion or two set out for Kentucky, but they turned too far north inside the Gap and were landlocked on the rugged Cumberland Plateau along the Big Sandy River. There was a lack of salt licks and game trails, but plenty of bad weather and perplexing mountain ridges. This unfortunate journey left Daniel Boone with less enthusiasm for Kentucky than had Gaspar Mansker, Henry Skaggs, and others who had gone down the Cumberland on their hunts.

Daniel Boone's name might never have been inseparably linked with Kentucky had it not been for John Finley, his voluble peddler friend of Braddock's Road days, who was to lead the famous woodsman across the mountains straight into the heart of Bluegrass Kentucky. Today a modern traveler flying from North Carolina toward Cincinnati can see the old Boone-Finley route unroll below. From the Yadkin across the headwaters of the eastern Tennessee rivers, across the rearing Cumberland wall, over the headwaters of the Cumberland River, leaping the narrow land gap to the south fork of the Kentucky, and down that stream to the mouth of Station Camp Creek, the country glides by in minutes. There beneath the plane is the tawny Red River tumbling down from its oxide-laden headwaters, off to the right towering over the Indian Old Fields, a glacier-leveled tableland, is Pilot Knob, and then Boonesboro on the south bank of the Kentucky River. Weeks and months of long-hunter wanderings slip by in the twinkling of an eye. One hardly has time to focus on one landmark before another has pressed into view. Deep coves are slashed into the bulging sides of hills, rock-bound peaks and wind-blown points heave up in all but impassable ridges. Streams tumble down between shrub- and brush-bound banks. All of these had to be negotiated by the hunters. From high points they could view the haze-blue hills sweeping away in endless waves of rock and forest.

Such was the land through which Boone and Finley traveled in 1768, ranging widely over central Kentucky. The hunting was good, the cane and grass were fresh, and the land was rich and promising. As they went through the country they planted some identifiable landmarks. Station Camp Creek, a vigorous little stream which plowed its willful way down between rock-bound shoulder ridges in present Estill County gained its fame because the long hunters stopped along its banks to camp. Nearby the carmine waters of the Red pushed down from a multitude of wind-eroded topknot cliffs and land arches. On top of one of these towering domes Boone's party was said to have stood and gazed into the heart of the Bluegrass. In reality they saw the table-level Indian Old Fields.

The men of Yadkin brought with them a copy of *Gulliver's Travels,* and about their campfires in this exciting virgin country they read of the startling world of Samuel Gulliver. So impressed were they by Jonathan Swift's stories that they left behind the name Lullbegrud Creek, and in later years a church honored this literary invasion of Kentucky in its name.

For two years Daniel Boone wandered about Kentucky, dodging

the Indians, sleeping in caves, and living a thoroughly unhurried and unpestered life. His most industrious acts seemed to have been carving his name and records of his bear-killing exploits on beech trees. But of greater importance was his spying out the land. His dreams may have been colored with the desire to see the wilderness turned to farmsteads and the trees wrought into houses. A distillery advertised in July, 1961, that Daniel spent a part of his time making moonshine liquor. This sophisticated corporation and its slick-haired Madison Avenue boys no doubt charge Kentucky's most famous frontiersman with carrying on an activity for which he lacked pot, corn, and talent to perform. If in those lonely years he engaged in such an unlikely business he no doubt horrified his Baptist preacher-brother Squire who twice crossed the mountains to visit Daniel.

An interest greater than moonshining occupied the attention of Daniel Boone. Like Dr. Thomas Walker, he was a land scout. In a somewhat vague arrangement he was acting as land agent or spy for Judge Richard Henderson of North Carolina, as he had done previously along the Watauga, Clinch, and Holston. Too, like all long hunters, he gathered bins of skins, one of which Squire took back to North Carolina. This was Daniel Boone's time of seasoning for the moment when he would lead settlers through Cumberland Gap.

Once during his wanderings along the Cumberland Boone sprawled flat on his back in the sun and sang to his dogs. This ungodly sound in the silent wilderness startled a party of long hunters, and Gaspar Mansker, believing it was made by treacherous Shawnees, dodged from tree to tree to get a look and a shot at him. Instead of a redskin there lay his old Yadkin neighbor taking life on the first bounce without a momentary care in the world.

Materially two years in the wilderness yielded Daniel Boone almost nothing. A patient wife back in North Carolina had kept his family together and thriving. She tended the crops, kept the cabin, and waited faithfully for Daniel's return. Boone's gains were not measurable in tangibilities. He had established an enduring reputation as a woodsman, and his knowledge of western lands was unexcelled. If only he could use his knowledge in establishing a settlement in Kentucky his fame would be assured.

Odds were indeed great in 1773 against a settlement being planted in Kentucky. It was still too far in advance of the spreading line of civilization for safety. Indians hunted and battled through its valleys at will. They were jealous guardians of their rich hunting ground as they made clear to Boone and his companions when some of them were captured in the summer and early fall of 1769. John Stewart and Alexander Neely lost their lives in this first hunting adventure. Daniel Boone learned firsthand of the grave dangers lurking in the great western woods. Yet the Boones and six neighboring families were willing to take a chance and follow Daniel through the Gap. In September, 1773, they set out along the trail for Kentucky. On the way they were joined by the Bryans from Virginia. Women, children, pack horses, and domestic animals were strung out along the trail. In latter years the folk-artist Caleb Bingham was to portray Daniel Boone as an optimistic frontier Moses leading this domestic band through Cumberland Gap, but the promised land was to be denied him and his band. Tragedy struck in the night when lurking Chero- kees killed two youths, one of whom was Daniel's son Nathan.

The stinging attack on the trail frightened the families into fleeing back to the Holston settlements, and Daniel Boone's dream of settle- ment in Kentucky evaporated with the mist of the morning. Kentucky nevertheless was in Boone's blood. At the outbreak of Dunmore's War against the Shawnees in 1774 he and that most doughty of all frontiersmen, Michael Holsteiner, were rushed off to the Falls of the Ohio by Governor Dunmore to warn Thomas Bullitt's survey party to come in until the Indian troubles were ended. On the way the pair came on James Harrod's camp near the headwaters of the Salt River. Harrod was there building a town and robbing Boone of his cherished honor to found the first Kentucky settlement. Undaunted Boone joined Evan Hinton in raising a cabin, a symbol of his hope for the future.

III

Laying the Hearthstone

June in Kentucky is one of the pleasantest months of the year. Meadows are lush and green and mountain ridges come into full leaf on every hand. Birds and animals voice the rising promise of a new season. It was in this month, 1774, that James Harrod led a small party of Pennsylvania traders eight miles south from the Kentucky River to begin the first settlement in the land. Although Harrod was a Pennsylvanian, his settlement quickly became a Virginian stronghold. There were indications that other settlements would soon appear. At the Falls Thomas Bullitt's survey party platted land claims, while in the Bluegrass Hancock Taylor, the McAfee brothers, and others were surveying vast areas.

There was rising tension in white-Indian relationships about the headwaters of the Ohio. In a confused moment barbarities were committed by both whites and Indians, but the source of the trouble arose about as much from land grabbing as from outrageous abuses. Much of the secret of the crises was centered in Governor Dunmore and his associates' land hunger. Before Harrod and his men could build cabins Dunmore's War was under way and they were forced out of Kentucky.

The brief disruption of the war had only limited effect on the settlement of Kentucky. Early in March, 1775, life was resumed at Harrodsburg where it had been halted the previous summer. The three McAfee brothers, David, William, and Adams were searching

for land, this time with far brighter prospects than on their first
starvation-ridden expedition. Everywhere there were signs of rising
interest in Kentucky, and it was only a matter of months before
settlers' cabins would be strung across the land.

Already a part of Kentucky's opening chapter was being written by
a gathering of whites and Indians at the Sycamore Shoals on the
Watauga River deep in the mountains of Tennessee. There a pageant
was in preparation for the negotiating of a treaty with the Cherokee
Indians to surrender their claim to the southern half of Kentucky.
Richard Henderson, in imitation of the French at Sault Sainte Marie,
made a convincing display of argument and goods to the Cherokees.
Judge Henderson had served the court in Hillsboro, North Carolina,
and was involved in the issues of the War of the Alamance. He was
now ready to capitalize on his extended interest in Kentucky lands. In
association with the Hart brothers, James Hogg, John Luttrell, and
others he organized the Transylvania Land Company. His expressed
purpose was the planting of a settlement in Kentucky, but his unex-
pressed ambitions no doubt embraced the formation of a frontier
barony or even the formation of a fourteenth colony.

At Watauga Henderson held court at which were gathered such
frontier notables as James Robertson, John Sevier, William Bailey
Smith, James Hogg, and Nathanial and Thomas Hart. With them
were approximately 1,200 Cherokees including such famous chiefs as
Atta-Kulla-Kulla (Little Carpenter), Oconostata, Dragging Canoe,
and Sononoka (the Raven). Attraction for most of the Indians
was the pile of trade goods which Scotch merchant William Johnson
had brought up from Fayetteville, North Carolina. In the dozen or so
wagonloads of merchandise were coarse woolens, hard liquors, corn,
flour, trinkets, guns, ammunition, shirts, metal brooches, wristbands,
gadgets, salt, bearskins, silver housings, ribbons, and tools. Cherokee
claims on Kentucky might have been tenuous at best, but they had
been recognized in the treaties of Hard Labor and Lochaber in 1768
and 1770. Too, John Donelson had run a diagonal line across Kentucky cutting the eastern section and the area north of the Kentucky
River out of future Cherokee considerations. Nevertheless, Henderson worked away at drafting a treaty, disturbing in the process Governors Dunmore of Virginia and Martin of North Carolina and several Indian chiefs.

Impatient to share the seductive largess before them, the Cherokees signed the treaty of Sycamore Shoals on March 17, 1775. All was not harmony in the Indian ranks, however. The younger chiefs were enraged by the surrender of their lands, and Dragging Canoe and the Raven were eloquent in their protests to keep the white man away from Cherokee hunting grounds, but their words availed nothing. In a burst of temper Dragging Canoe informed members of the Transylvania Company that they had made a noble bargain but their new land would become a dark and bloody ground, thus giving Kentucky one of its earliest nicknames.

So certain were the Transylvanians that a treaty would cede Cherokee lands south of the Kentucky and in northern and middle Tennessee that Daniel Boone and a party of trail blazers hustled off to locate a site for a settlement on the bank of the Kentucky. This time the trail to central Kentucky was to be permanently located and marked. Footlogs were felled across the creeks, and fording places were probed for safety of footing.

Boone and his party advanced toward Kentucky in March, a drab season in which trees were still dormant, but their graying trunks and limbs signaled the burgeoning of spring. Keeping a daily record of the advance of the party of thirty men was Felix Walker of Virginia. He had started west with an exploring party under the leadership of Captain William Twetty, but the party had stopped by the Watauga settlement and learned of the negotiations with the Cherokees. They joined forces with the survey party, and young Walker went forward with an enthusiasm born of inexperience and great expectations. Writing in a highly phonetic style, he gave free rein to his imagination. In later years an unnecessarily sensitive relative corrected his spelling, but retained his wording in describing this advance into paradise. He believed that men

Not since the days of Don Quixote, or before, ever felt so cheerful and elated in prospect; every heart abounded in joy and excitement in anticipating new things we would see, and the romantic scenes through which we would pass . . .

Passing through Cumberland Gap was a moment of great ecstasy. There was game everywhere, wild turkeys were about in flocks, an occasional bear shuffled off for cover, and buffalo tracks pointed northward toward wallows and licks. In the towering forest, as yet untouched by ax, noble trees thrust heavenward as though they were the handiwork of the "Great Architect." Just as the trees cast shadows, so did the land. A discordant note in the journal lamented, "But, Alas! fond man! the vision of a moment made dream of dreams, and shadow of shade! A sad reverse overtook us two days after, on our way to the Kentucky River."

At night Shawnees fell on the trail breakers' camp and killed Captain Twetty and a slave, and wounded Felix Walker. Paradise had unmasked its vicious side, and lying wounded so far from help Walker realized what Dragging Canoe had meant when he predicted that the conquest of Kentucky would be a bloody undertaking. The Kentucky River was near, and serious as were results of the Indian attack, the rule of the wilderness prevailed and Boone pushed on to the mouth of Otter Creek on the south bank to begin the building of Boonesboro. This was a beginning of the fulfillment of his mission and his dream. He had seen men die before in the wilderness and he would see them fall before the tomahawk and rifle again. Symbolically the party had frightened a herd of buffalo and had watched them gallop out of sight. This was the beginning of the end of that animal's grazing sorties below the Ohio.

Boone's selection of the seat of the Transylvania Company was not the happiest one possible. It was crowded by ridges, the valley of the Kentucky was subject to flooding, and the water supply from the two springs, one of which was sulphur, was uncertain. When Richard Henderson arrived at the camp he located the site for the fortress on higher ground.

Henderson had followed Boone's party, making as grand an entry to his domain as trail conditions and company would permit. He also kept a journal and recorded his party's experiences as it followed along Boone's wilderness trail. Obviously his account was literate and fairly complete. Both country and men were subjects of his entries. There was an unspoken fear that the Transylvanians might actually lose their prize before they could come to rest on the bank of the Kentucky.

Where Henderson made rather sophisticated notes, William Calk recorded his small party's ventures on the way to Kentucky with the Transylvanians. His anxieties were those of a simple yeoman moving into a land of uncertainty with all his worldly wealth invested in dogs, horses, and meager packs of domestic goods.

On Wednesday, April 5, the Virginian recorded:

Breaks away fair and we go down the valley and camp on indian Creek
we had this Creek to cross many times and very Bad Banks Abrams/
Hanks saddel turned and the load all fell in we got out this Eavening and
kill two Deer.

On the following Tuesday the party was through Cumberland Gap
and on its way to Boonesboro:

. . . this is a very loury morning and like for Rain But we all agree to Start
Early we cross Cumberland River and travel Down it about 10 miles
through Some turrable Cainbrakes as we went down Abrams /Hanks/
mair Ran into the River with Her load and Swam over he foloed her & got
on her & made her Swim back agin it is avery Raney Eavening we take up
camp near Richland creek they kill a Beef Wm Drake Bakes Bread with
out Washing his hands we Keep Sentry this Night for fear of the indians.

Coming along with Henderson was another pioneer who was to
leave his name on the land. Benjamin Logan traveled as far as the
Rockcastle with the North Carolinians, and there turned westward to
St. Asaph's Creek where John Floyd had already begun a settlement.
Almost before Henderson reached Boone's camp on April 20, Logan
and his party were engaged in building Logan's Fort, a third anchorage of settlement in the Kentucky country.

Boone's activities were purely those of hunter and settler, but Henderson was concerned with the more important issues of an independent proprietary colony. Almost immediately he planned an extensive fortress with an organization within its walls of cabins and
storehouses that would serve both political and military needs. Powder and lead were to be stored in a fire- and dampproof bin. Corner
cabins were reserved as quarters for members of the company, and
common facilities for the care of food and feed were to be provided.
The plan was on a grand scale, and the labor to build it would be
arduous, a thing which Kentucky pioneers were always anxious to
avoid. Only a fear of annihilation was finally to bring about construction of the oblong puncheon fortress with its full complement of
cabins and blockhouses.

Settlers planted corn, turned their herds out to graze, and hunted
for meat. Richard Henderson early got on with political matters.
Delegates were invited from Harrod's, Logan's, and Hinkston's to
attend a legislative assembly at Boonesboro. There the first laws of
Kentucky territory were enacted, the land of Kentucky was delivered

to Henderson in a ceremony of "seizin," and services of the Church of England were read. This was an auspicious, almost medieval, beginning for the fourteenth colony. James Hogg was hustled off to the Continental Congress to present a petition seeking recognition of the new colony. Richard Henderson and several of the other members of the company returned to North Carolina, and affairs at Boonesboro were left in the hands of sweaty pioneers. Henderson was never to return to the seat of his colony, and his petition before Congress failed.

Henderson had started his move to Kentucky too late, if he ever had a chance for success. Political conditions were rapidly changing in the colonial states, and these changes were to bear upon the fate of Boonesboro. Almost before the settlers had unpacked and settled down to plant their corn crops news came through the woods that farmers in Lexington, Massachussetts, had stood their ground against British troops. In Kentucky it was noticeable that Indian raids were becoming more numerous. British officials at Detroit were definitely exerting pressure against the Kentucky pioneers. In another way the hand of the British was revealed. The blundering old windbag, J. F. Dalziel Smythe, the first of a long line of critical British travelers to come out to the western country, was bent on spying against the frontiersmen. Even Governor Dunmore back in Virginia conspired against the west by provoking Indian raids against the settlers.

The story of Boonesboro was mainly one of facing adversity on almost every front. Once Henderson was back east of the mountains, leadership in the new settlement fell largely to Daniel Boone. It was he who ultimately pushed for completion of the fortress, and who helped to negotiate with the Indians, on the one hand, and resisted them, on the other. No man expressed greater faith in the undertaking. In June he went back to Tennessee to escort his wife Rebecca and their daughter Jemima to the new settlement. On September 8 he was proud to know that his womenfolk were the first to come to Kentucky to settle.

The Boone women were not to remain for long the only women in Kentucky. Colonel Richard Callaway brought his family, as did William Pogue and Barney Stagner. Thus life in the fort took on a new tempo. The women not only exerted a certain refining influence in the crude backwoods fortress but they symbolized the arrival of civilization on the banks of the Kentucky. Elsewhere in Kentucky settlements other women arrived and new cabin households multiplied every month. When there were only men settlers they could abandon the camps without too much misgiving as Harrod and his men did in 1774. But with women and children present it was not easy to run for safety to the older settlements. In the first place, it was unseemly for men with families to run. It was not without reason that the Indians were disturbed by the appearance in Cumberland Gap of women and milk cows; this combination meant there soon would be homes, corn patches, and cow pastures.

The opening act of one of Boonesboro's several domestic ordeals occurred on Sunday afternoon, July 14, 1776, when Jemima Boone, and Elizabeth and Frances Callaway set out across the Kentucky to visit a neighbor. The girls paddled a canoe diagonally across the river from the fort, and at the moment its nose rooted into the gravel on the far bank a tawny arm snatched it aground and four Shawnee bucks laid hold of the girls, but not before the spunky Betsey Callaway had bounced an oar off a brave's head. The younger girls were paralyzed with fright, but Betsey kept her wits and was about as much bother to the Shawnees as a gnawing bear would have been. The Shawnees had always shown a fondness for female captives and now they had three young ones in tow. Immediately they headed home by way of the Blue Licks and the buffalo trace to parade their prizes in the Ohio villages.

There was pandemonium in the fort when news spread that the girls were missing. Daniel Boone dashed into the woods with one search party while Colonel Callaway led another. Time was of the essence—in fact, it might already be too late if the Indians could beat their white pursuers to the Ohio River. They might have done so had the unruly girls not created so many delays by complaining and sulking. Never had three Kentucky girls been pursued by such illustrious company. Besides Boone, who had the advantage of having twice been prisoner of the Shawnees and now demonstrated his expert woodsmanship, there were William Bailey Smith, John Holder, Samuel Henderson, John Floyd, Nathanial and David Hart, John Martin, John McMillan, William Bush, John and David Gess, and Flanders Callaway. Three miles below the Blue Licks the Indians stopped for the night, and here they were surprised and shot, and the tattered girls escorted home as Kentucky's first heroines. As their rewards, Samuel Henderson married Betsey Callaway and Flanders Callaway claimed Jemima Boone for his bride.

Life in Boonesboro settled down to a condition of constant vigilance. Some timid settlers gave up and returned to the settlements above the headwater of the Tennessee. In the awesome year of the "three sevens" war parties streamed down from the north to harass the settlers. At Detroit Governor Hamilton egged on the attacks against Kentucky, and the pioneers came to believe the stories that he was paying bounties for scalps. They called him the "hair buyer," one of the most devastating pieces of propaganda that could have been used against an enemy. It was doubtful that the charge was true, but in this case it was what the settlers believed that counted. They were prepared to believe the worst, and to prepare in their lackadaisical way for disaster.

As the frustrating year 1777 drew to a close people at Boonesboro welcomed the arrival of winter. A heavy snow, they believed, would halt the raids. But the salt supply in the fort was short, and in January, 1778, Boone and a party of saltmakers were off to the fatal Blue Licks to boil salt from the rich brines which bubbled up at that place. There was little fear at the moment from the Indians. While diligent saltmakers dipped and boiled brine, Daniel was in the woods hunting for fresh meat. Without warning a band of Shawnees ambushed him. He was forced to go with them to the salt camp, and standing there before his fellows he persuaded the Indians not to go on to Boonesboro. He argued that the settlers were all in the fort during bad weather and that it was too strong to be taken. Summer was the season to attack a fort; at that time all the people were in their cornfields or in the woods with their herds. There at the snow-covered Lower Blue Licks began a series of events which were to have far-reaching effects on the immediate future of the Kentucky settlements, and to a large extent were to sour the remainder of Daniel Boone's stay in Kentucky.

It was tragedy enough for so many men to be captured at once, but to lose the leadership of Daniel Boone was calamitous. Had the Indians gone on to Boonesboro they might have captured the fort, but Daniel Boone outtalked them. Such talk, however, was frightening to some of the naïve whites. Thus Boone became suspect by his own people, a suspicion that was deepened when he was accorded favorable treatment at Detroit and Chillicothe by Chief Black Fish and Governor Henry Hamilton.

Boone's stay with the Shawnees had its moments of comedy. The process of being converted into an Indian required a lot of painful head plucking, sand scrubbing, and dunking in the creek. Too, he may have had to eat more dog meat than he relished. That he was given the Indian name of Sheltowee and a squaw for a wife were facts that Boone did not discuss later in his autobiography, however.

Boone had an opportunity to listen in on Indian and British conversation. Black Fish and Dagnieau De Quindre, a French-Canadian militiaman, plotted a raid against Boonesboro. Black Fish no doubt believed it was safe to discuss such matters before Daniel Boone because he was now a faithful son. This was frightening information. The fort was in no condition for a major defensive effort. The walls were incomplete, manpower was weak, the well had been left unfinished, and the people were improperly alerted of the impending dangers. Now was the time to take the great chance and escape. Black Fish and De Quindre must not be allowed to get there first. Galloping a horse 160 miles to the Ohio, Boone then set out on foot for Boonesboro. Tattered and exhausted by the journey, he arrived before the fortress gate on June 20, 1778. Unhappily news of his statements made at the Blue Licks had been brought home by a returning prisoner. Instead of welcoming him home as a hero, some of the settlers suspected Boone of treachery, and his Indian appearance did nothing to allay their fears.

There was no time to be lost. Black Fish and De Quindre were thought to be on their way. Fortress walls were to be reinforced, powder and bullets readied, food and animals had to be driven into the compound. Again settlers began digging on the well. Happily Boone's escape served to delay the Indian attack; in fact it was so long delayed that some of the settlers were convinced that Daniel had lied. Black Fish knew where his adopted son had gone and why he had hastened away. The element of surprise was not lost. Fortress Boonesboro could only be taken by a crushing blow against it or by soft persuasion, both of which the invaders prepared to use.

The suspense of delay was wearing. Boone himself felt it. He led a spying party back across the Ohio to the Shawnee villages to see what was happening, but not until he had sent a plea to the Holston settlements for help. Beyond the Ohio the Kentuckians found the Indians on the move, and the scouts barely had time to outrun them to Boonesboro. At last the long-awaited attack was on its way.

Approximately 450 braves in war paint and befeathered topknots and twelve Frenchmen advanced on Boonesboro on the first dry hot week in September. Never had Indians come south with so much confidence. They brought with them forty horses on which to mount their female captives. Black Fish was sure that not only Daniel Boone but his entire settlement would want to return to the Ohio with him. Daniel would want to take up life where he had left off as a dutiful son. The Indian force was overwhelming, a fact which was fortunate for the settlers because the Indians were willing to dawdle away precious time. Inside the fortress settlers were desperate. There was a shortage of manpower, of food and water, and of guns and ammunition. Every shot had to count when the attack came, every pair of hands had to serve, and every life lost had to be expended at the greatest possible cost to the enemy.

It may be true that never before in border warfare was such whimsicality associated with an Indian raid. Boone and his companions played for time. Black Fish could wait. Because of this there began a number of leisurely talks followed by extended periods of consideration of terms set forth by Black Fish. These conferences wasted several days, days which the settlers hoped would bring relief from the Holston settlements nearer Boonesboro. In these conversations the settlers perceived that some cheerful Kentucky liar, held captive by the Shawnees, had completely misled Black Fish as to the number of people in the fort. This was a mighty assistance in securing a delay in the attack. But Indian patience was never durable. Eventually the time came, on September 11, to confirm a treaty of surrender, and this would be done by handshakes. For this ceremony young and vigorous braves came to the conference before the fort, and at once the settlers detected duplicity, especially since two warriors were to shake hands with each white man. Hiding in the brush were other warriors who had moved up ready to open fire. This ended the conference, and now it was to be a fight to the finish. Attempts were made by the Indians to pick off riflemen through the porthole openings, but Shawnee riflemen were miserable shots. Other attempts were made to set the fort on fire by shooting flaming arrows onto the rooftops. Inside the fort Squire Boone hit on the ingenious idea of using a hollow log for a cannon. This trick worked once, but on the second firing the log exploded, with disastrous consequences.

Night and day the firing and badinage kept up. Indians taunted Daniel Boone about his good-looking daughter. Settlers shouted

epithets which reflected on Indian ancestry. Wily old Black Fish re-
sorted to strategy. He pretended to lead his warriors away only to
sneak back and renew the attack. Settlers early one morning discovered a pole being worked back and forth down near the water line of
the Kentucky River. Below a point opposite the fort the river ran
muddy. The rascals were attempting to tunnel through the soft loamy
bank of the Kentucky into the fort. Where would they appear inside
the walls? Would warriors undertake to rush the fort from the tunnel?
Or would they attempt to destroy the wall by exploding a charge of
powder under it? There were anxious moments. Vigilance and shrewd
guessing were necessary to head off a surprise attack. Still there was
no help from the Holston settlements, but the water situation was
greatly helped by a heavy rain, and the rooftops of the cabins now
were not nearly so inflammable.

As suddenly as the attack began it stopped. Wednesday morning,
September 16, there were no Indians digging in the tunnel. The
woods were quiet. No rifle fire disturbed the peaceful morning. Was
Black Fish attempting another retreat? Hiding in the woods behind
the enemy, Simon Kenton and Alexander Montgomery had seen them
withdraw and they brought the word to the settlers. Lifting the siege
of the fort and thrusting the gates open again was not only a joyful
moment for the little band of settlers, it was doubtless a moment of
salvation for all of Kentucky. Only two settlers were killed and four
wounded. Daniel Boone claimed thirty-seven Indians were killed, and
he accounted for the death of Pompey who took pot shots at settlers
from the cover of trees. His was the only body left behind by the
retreating Shawnees.

When the siege had lifted at Boonesboro, Daniel had only the
single thought of rushing off to the Yadkin to join Rebecca, who had
fled to North Carolina when word came in January that Daniel had
been captured. Before he left Boonesboro, however, he had to defend
himself before a court-martial at Logan's Fort. He was charged by
Colonel Richard Callaway with indiscretions dating back to the pursuit and rescue of the Callaway and Boone girls. His conversation
with his Indian captors at the Blue Licks in February, 1778, was
charged against him as a bit of duplicity, as were certain actions
which he had taken in the defense of the fort in the siege. These
charges were groundless, and they involved nothing more than the
stupid jealousy of Colonel Callaway. Boone was acquitted and per-

mitted to go to North Carolina. The court-martial charges were unpleasant but not embittering.

The Indian raids were not over with the defense of Boonesboro. No fort or station was free from skulking bands, and tales of horror multiplied quickly in the years before 1780. Captain Henry Bird, a British officer from Detroit, had brought a war party southward in June, 1780, to drive against the rising settlement at the Falls of the Ohio but was diverted inland to the poorly armed Ruddle's and Martin's stations. With small cannon he knocked the walls down and took the settlers prisoners. This was the bloodiest and most horrible of all the British-Indian attacks. Defenseless prisoners were slaughtered in cold blood. For this and other acts against Kentucky the Shawnees needed chastening in their own villages. Colonel George Rogers Clark led a militia attack on the Ohio villages, and with him was Daniel Boone, returning to the scenes of his earlier captivity. Clark's expedition was in part retaliation for the siege of Boonesboro.

The bitterest moment of all for the Kentucky frontiersmen was the Battle of the Blue Licks on August 19, 1782. The Shawnees had attacked several small stations and had besieged Bryan's Station not far from Boone's Station. Boone had gone in pursuit with an attacking party to overtake Captain William Caldwell and the Shawnees before they could cross the Ohio. At the fording place of the Licking River at the Lower Blue Licks Daniel cautioned the settlers to wait for Benjamin Logan and his men to come up, but impulsive settlers ignored his advice and dashed across the stream to attack the Indians in their well-covered position. The ensuing battle was fierce. Many of the settlers, including Daniel Boone's son Israel, were killed. Boone rescued the body of his son and hid it to prevent its being mutilated. This place, the Blue Licks, had been one of horror for the great woodsman. He had come there to rescue his daughter and her companions, there he was taken prisoner in the salt camp, near there he had seen his brother shot from ambush in 1780, and now he was present at the worst slaughter of the Indian raids. Years later old-timers said he told the story of the Battle of the Blue Licks with tears in his eyes.

Though the history of Daniel Boone's activities in Kentucky is concentrated largely in the narrow scope of fifteen years, his fame has endured. There were other frontiersmen as capable as Boone, and many of them had distinguished themselves equally well. Among these were Simon Kenton, Benjamin Logan, Michael Holsteiner, George Rogers Clark, and James Harrod. But with the exception of Clark, none of them had so fluent a biographer as Boone. Although the sketch of Boone's activities which appeared in John Filson's *The Discovery, Settlement and Present State of Kentucke,* 1784, is entitled an autobiography, it was written by Filson and was in fact a highly stilted recitation of Colonel Boone's experiences in Kentucky. John Filson not only wrote Daniel Boone indelibly into Kentucky history, he made him the central figure in the legend of the great westward movement in its advance to the Ohio. Filson wrote in Boone's name:

To conclude, I can now say that I have verified the saying of an old Indian who signed Col. Henderson's deed. Taking me by the hand, at the delivery thereof, Brother, says he, we have given you a fine land, but I believe you will have much trouble in settling it. —My footsteps have often been marked with blood, and therefore I can truly subscribe to its original name. Two darling sons, and a brother, have I lost by savage hands, which have also taken from me forty valuable horses, and abundance of cattle. Many dark and sleepless nights have I been companion for owls, separated from the cheerful society of men, scorched by the summer's sun, and pinched by the Winter's cold, an instrument ordained to settle the wilderness. But now the scene is changed: Peace crowns the sylvan shade.

Peace had come to Kentucky, and with it the competitive struggles of men who sought to possess the land. Daniel Boone was no match for those shrewd claimants who fulfilled the requirements of the law, and because of technicalities the woodsman who had first seen so much of the virgin land in time was to move away from it. Though he had not rescued his land claims, he had implanted his name and his legend inerasably on Kentucky.

For Daniel Boone, however, peace was far off. As years have passed, the legend of Daniel Boone has grown into Gulliverlike proportions in the land where he enjoyed so thoroughly two lonely years of wandering and in which he made such a gallant effort to settle his family. As the Daniel Boone story has evolved from the images created by John Filson, Daniel Bryan the poet, and Lord Byron on through an almost endless number of dime novels, modern pageants, and television series, it would seem the old woodsman wrested Kentucky singlehanded from the woods, the Indians, and the British.

Writers of outdoor pageants have in recent years either defamed or overpraised Daniel Boone. In two outdoor plays presented in Kentucky in the summer of 1966 it was an open question as to whether Daniel Boone or the westward movement in American history was mostly sadly used. None, however, has sinned more deeply than a national broadcasting system. On March 2, 1966, the Kentucky General Assembly paused long enough in its headlong rush for adjournment to single out the National Broadcasting Company and its television series "The Adventures of Daniel Boone" in a righteously critical resolution. Their stand would have been magnificent except for the fact that some of the assemblymen weakened in the end. When the leading actor of the series came to Kentucky to help change the name of "Cumberland National Forest" to "Daniel Boone National Forest" and to open the Kentucky State Fair in September, 1966, they made peace with him. They even signed a treaty forgiving what they had so indignantly called in their resolution "an insult to the intelligence of millions of people, including school children, who know the history of Kentucky and the true story of Daniel Boone."

IV

Shaping a Central Tradition

Mildew had hardly stained the cabins of the earliest Kentucky settlers before restless people turned their attention from Indian fighting to dealing with more troublous and enduring problems. Within a decade after opening Kentucky to settlement, inrushing land claimants had posted claims to more than three times the amount of land available to them in the Kentucky backwoods. Every man who claimed even the most casual and fleeting military service or could extract on other grounds a land warrant from an obliging secretary of state back in Richmond crossed the mountains to blaze boundaries to a plot of wild land for his own. Men like Willis Green, Green Clay, Caleb Wallace, Alexander McConnel, and Matthew Walton laid claims to imperial holdings which enclosed the watersheds of a dozen creeks and long strips along the major waterfronts.

Later, in the Constitutional Convention of 1792, delegates were found to own hundreds of thousands of acres of land. They and their voracious kind imprinted on the face of Kentucky one of the most unsatisfactory land claim and survey systems in North America. Original surveyors' notes read more nearly like botanical inventories of Kentucky's virgin forests than as foundations for legal instruments. Deed books in every county are crammed with legal fantasies called "metes and bounds" descriptions of landholds.

Land-hungry men and their poorly trained surveyors stepped off boundaries of land on courses they sighted through highly imprecise Jacob's staff compasses, and they measured their sightings with ancient sand-worn chains which were inaccurate to begin with and compounded error by being dragged constantly over rocky hillsides. Surveyors' clumsy and involved descriptions of unstable monuments and landmarks constitute some of the most careless rhetoric composed on the American frontier. From a large rock (in an area productive of many large rocks) to a clump of sassafras sprouts, to a large beech tree, quartering a ridge to a stake, down a branch, and back to the beginning by way of a chestnut oak snag—this was the characteristic course of the frontiersmen's boundaries. Markers, identifiable for the present only but gone with the first fire, flood, or storm, were established. This was the kind of whimsical descriptive writing which generated murders, hard feelings, family feuds, and lawsuits by the courthouseful. Seldom if ever could two men agree precisely as to the name of a creek, the variety of trees, or the precise location of the watershed line atop a ridge. Greedy men spied fine trees standing near enough to their boundaries so that by a little manipulation and by browbeating their neighbors into confusion, if not to the commission of murder, they could claim them. Few things historically have stirred the wrath of everyday Kentuckians more than encroachments upon land claims, and this is still true in the state. Modern Kentucky is not without its current stories of fatal shootings over land boundary disputes.

No wonder Henry Clay's mother wrote her son in the early 1790's that he should come out to Kentucky because a young lawyer could earn a good income defending land cases. Already John Breckinridge, Caleb Wallace, George Nicholas, and their colleagues had heard the siren call. The pioneer Kentucky lawyer quickly developed a rich tradition of the law and its powers. The title "judge" became a revered if not always respected one. If not a judge then "colonel" because there was an indiscernible difference between the dignity of a lawyer called "judge" and one called "colonel." It was fitting indeed that the first cases to be appealed to the new Court of Appeals immediately after the formation of the state should involve complicated issues of overlapping boundaries, prior claims, and disputed possessions. Many an old pioneer who had helped to blaze the trails to Kentucky sat in a witness chair in the court recounting as best he could the detailed story of the founding of his community. Oftentimes these ancient chroniclers strayed far afield and recorded for posterity a much better record of historic beginnings than if they had written diaries and memoirs. Daniel Boone, Simon Kenton, Richard Henderson, Michael Stoner, Green Clay, and all of the other famous pioneers had land troubles to recall. Some of these were even put off their claims because they had failed to conform with legal technicalities.

Neither Virginia statutory nor common law was adequate to hold in check violations of land-hungry pioneers. Kentucky even had a brush with the United States Supreme Court in which the state refused to abide by the court's verdict in a land dispute case.

It took more than a land clerk, a justice of the peace, a shaky land title, and a trusty long rifle to adjudicate land issues. And there were other problems, real and imagined, which backwoodsmen wanted settled. When the Indians and British were fairly well subdued, Kentuckians were ready to take up an argument with the Virginia General Assembly looking to independent statehood for the country west of the Appalachians. They proposed to form a new state, but form it free and responsible to western control. Here was a chance to create a political society in an atmosphere of natural freedom. For a decade, and through ten exhausting conventions, delegates argued about the rights of man of nature; some of them argued without ever having heard the name of John Locke. For the more sophisticated Kentuckians it was difficult enough to comprehend the application of the Lockean theories to the realities of their conditions in the raw land below the Ohio; for the unsophisticated it was impossible. Even though men snatched the country from the Indians, some of their leaders did not regard these unlettered pioneers as being capable of self-government.

When delegates finally made up their minds to form the state in constitutional convention in May, 1792, they wrote remarkably little Locke into the document but rather a tremendous amount of Virginia and Maryland commonplace. In fact, there was expressed in this first constitution a genuine fear of the common man—he was denied a direct vote for governor and senators, and he was further handicapped in expressing his strong and impulsive opinions. Fittingly a hard-bitten old hero of the frontier and the American Revolution was chosen first governor. Isaac Shelby, descendant of a Welsh fur-trading father, had proved his mettle against the British at King's Mountain;

now in June, 1792, he assumed the governorship of a new backwoods state. It took almost as much courage for the old hero to make a stand in the Sheaf of Wheat Tavern in Lexington, where Kentucky was organized into a state, as to rush a band of Cherokee Indians. Immediately the capital was moved to Frankfort, which was near the center of population; also it was on the Kentucky River.

Early in its formative years the Commonwealth of Kentucky was victimized by opportunists and self-seekers of all sorts. There were land speculators, border traders, and other schemers. One of the most highhanded of these was James Wilkinson, who appeared in Lexington in 1785 proclaiming his military heroism, boasting a Revolutionary War general's commission, and good mercantile connections back east. Wilkinson, tall, handsome, suave, and a shrewd highbinder, was to stamp his name indelibly in Kentucky history. As salt merchant, adventurer, politician of sorts, and a rascal in general, he was to lay an economic foundation for early Kentucky. He sensed the importance of the western rivers in the state's future development. In 1787 he shipped two flatboatloads of produce down the Kentucky River, the Ohio, and the Mississippi to the port of New Orleans. His first two boatloads were sold for high prices, paid in gold and silver coin. These were readily ascertainable prices. The rewards given Wilkinson by Spanish officials to woo Kentuckians away from Virginia and the Confederation were intangible and may never be fully determined by historians. What secret promises and agreements he made with Governor Miro and Don Gardoqui were kept from public knowledge. Whatever plans the Spanish had for extending their imperial borders up the rivers were never carried out. To contemporary Kentuckians the most important fact was that Wilkinson's boats reached New Orleans. It mattered little to them at the moment that Wilkinson had promised to sell out Kentucky to the Spanish for a handful of coins and empty political promises. What he did was a promise of open treason, a fact that has tarnished his name in American history ever since that date.

In 1788 Wilkinson and his men returned to Kentucky, a part of them by the Natchez Trace, the rest by way of Philadelphia. With cash in their pockets, and slaves and goods to show for their success, and even a fine carriage which was driven overland from Maysville, they produced tangible proof of a prosperous outlet for produce downriver.

Kentucky fields now produced enormously rich returns of grain, cattle, hogs, sheep, fruits, and fiber. The only real obstacle to growing prosperity was the Spanish blockade of the lower Mississippi. Presidents Washington, Adams, and Jefferson were to feel the political pressures exerted by a growing population of western backwoodsmen who wanted the rivers opened freely to their trade. Jefferson most of all felt this pressure during his advance to the Presidency. Not until the purchase of Louisiana in 1803 were Kentucky farmers really certain that the western rivers would be opened to them. If diplomacy and cash had not opened the streams, then the farmers themselves were determined to thrust open the gates of commerce by more direct action.

The first decade of the nineteenth century saw farmers and boatmen haul produce down to the mouths of the Kentucky creeks, and then float it away to New Orleans in great rustic boats built of logs. In this floating company were all sorts of people. Eastern merchants had come to Lexington, Frankfort, Versailles, Georgetown, and other places, and had rented storehouses just long enough to trade their stocks of dry goods, cutlery, guns, hardware, tinware, and shoes for farm products, then they went south to sell their produce and return by way of Philadelphia and Baltimore, thus completing the great circle of trade. Most of the floating company on the western waters, however, was comprised of hardhanded farmers who on land were backwoodsmen scarce out of Indian skirmishes and hunting shirts. On the rivers they turned into wild long-haired ruffians boasting of their bravery, their wealth, and their marksmanship. They promised to stop at nothing, snags and river pirates included. When the Louisiana Purchase Treaty had been consummated and Spaniard and Frenchman were gone from the rivers, there were still pirates, robbers, prostitutes, and every other kind of sharper to be dealt with by wit and fist. The rivers themselves supplied their own natural devils in the forms of high rising, whipping sawyers and planters, sandbars just beneath the muddy current, wild swirling eddies, and unexpected floods. Because of these, men had to be rugged to survive and to convey safely the contents of the rich Kentucky cornucopia away to market. More than this, however, they created an image of Kentuckians which was to survive all across the American frontier.

Kentuckians' boast of being half horse and half alligator became a frontier idiom. They were even more fierce as sons of chained lightning, as the crack shots of creation, insatiable lovers, the bravest militiamen, and even the tallest liars west of the Appalachians. They came from a country so fertile that the topsoil had no known depth; trees grew larger and straighter than anything on the lower Mississippi, and womenfolk were fairer than the seven sisters of the Pleiades on a cloudless night. They were never afraid to fight but, tinctured with the spirits of their grainfields, they even sought a little tooth-busting exercise. They fought rough-and-tumble, claiming eyes for eyes, and noses for noses and ears. Downriver in Natchez-Under-the-Hill and in New Orleans with cash in their pockets and liquor in their bellies they kept the shady quarters in a constant uproar, but even so they were western farmers carrying on the arduous business of their state's commerce. They were the pioneers who opened the rich river trade just as they had opened the trail up from Cumberland Gap to make settlement. It is ironical indeed that this rustic horde with all its battling of current and sharper should actually help to bring a mark of graciousness and refinement to Kentucky society.

In 1811 technology brought a stunning revolution to the turbulent waters of the western rivers. Between that date and 1820 the steamboat became a practical machine which negotiated the rivers in both directions. Where forty men struggled from ninety to a hundred and ten days to force a reluctant keelboat upstream with a load of New Orleans sugar, the first steamboat in the regular trade, the *Enterprise,* made the upriver journey in twenty-five days in 1817, and thirty years later the great side-wheeler *A. L. Shotwell* slashed the time between Louisville and New Orleans to 4 days, 9 hours, and 29 minutes, a record which has never been materially lowered.

By 1820 the great flatboat river village of Louisville, sitting placidly amidst its muddy streets by the Falls of the Ohio, was becoming a bubbling center of commerce, outstripping aristocratic Lexington, belle of the Bluegrass. The best the central Kentucky town could do in this new age to recoup its fame was to proclaim itself even more loudly the "Athens of the West" and a center of "culture and agriculture." That it was a rich center of agriculture was beyond dispute. Bluegrass fields about the town grew abundance of fine hemp, tobacco, corn, and small grains. Pastures were well stocked with cattle, sheep, horses, mules, and hogs. Breeders imported the parental stock of these animals from abroad to improve greatly the bloodlines not only of Kentucky livestock but that of the nation. Men like Lewis

Sanders, Henry Clay, and the Patton brothers brought from England and the Channel Islands fine blooded beef and dairy cattle, and from England and France sheep of splendid fleece and carcass. From Spain Clay and others imported Castilian jacks to rival the Royal Gift which had been sent George Washington.

Livestock and grain growing quickly became synonymous with much of Kentucky. Every year after 1800 the economic influence of the state grew. As the great southern cotton belt bit deeper into the virgin lands toward the Mississippi, the demand for slaves, mules, horses, meat, and fiber increased. Many a bluegrass farmer took the cash he got from hemp, tobacco, and livestock sales and built a pretentious Georgian or Greek Revival house and filled it with handsome furnishings brought from New Orleans and Philadelphia, even France and England.

Local silversmiths—and there were several skilled ones—kept busy hammering out graceful pieces for the adornment of family tables and sideboards. A collection of bright coin silverware bearing the maker's mark of these local craftsmen became a status symbol for the well-to-do. Craftsmen created elegant pitchers, bowls, and julep cups as award pieces to be given livestock breeders at county fairs and exhibitions. The coin silver julep cup was a distinctive regional piece hammered into graceful shape by such craftsmen as Asa Blanchard, Garner and Winchester, and dozens of other smiths who maintained shops in central Kentucky towns. The julep cup was much more precious if it came engraved on the side with descriptions of the merits of a superior cow, sheep, or colt. Even the virtues of a straight-eared mule emblazoned in so elegant a place became a mark of distinction.

While Blanchard, proclaimed the "Paul Revere of the West" by his patrons, and his fellow silversmiths hammered and rolled their pieces, other artists added further distinctions to an affluent society by painting the portraits of wide-eyed patriarchs, their voluptuous wives and daughters, and their sons. Matthew Harris Jouett, Edward West, Joseph Bush, and many others produced the personal likenesses of a generation of Kentuckians grown prosperous enough on the land to afford an artist's fee. These were the ancestors of modern Kentuckians in the making, and no matter what their personal records may have been in deeds of accomplishment, if a modern Kentuckian can show off one of these early paintings he is able to claim distinction for himself by association. If he can produce a Jouett, a West, or a Bush portrait of an ancestor, and an Edward Troye painting of a stallion, a Kentucky shorthorn bull, or a well-fleeced ram, then he has a double claim on the past.

Both the mountain and the Pennyroyal in western Kentucky felt the impact of the new age of economic growth and sophistication. The broad rolling plains were hacked up into plantations of manorial proportions and there was developed in this area a planting society not unlike that of the lower southern cotton belt. Large white frame Carolina-type houses, ample enough to shelter a dozen children, replaced log cabins, and under their roofs a comfortable agrarian society ruled the lands. There were few if any Blanchards to hammer out graceful silver pieces for the sideboards, and Jouett and Troye paintings above the mantles were lacking, but these Kentuckians were just as proud and prosperous agrarians as their brothers in the Bluegrass.

While both Bluegrass and Pennyroyal farmers worked their vast stretches of rolling fertile fields, their neighbors to the east, the mountaineers, hewed meager corn patches out of the steep Appalachian slopes or hacked and burned trees away in narrow creek and river valleys. Corn was planted on stream shoulders almost in the same fashion as ancient Egyptians trailed the floodwaters of the Nile down to low-water mark. It was planted high on the cliff benches a thousand or twelve hundred feet above the chimneytops of mountain cabins to be trundled downhill in the fall. Every foot of good soil was precious and every level place was cherished.

Hill men tussled with the forest and rocky soil as though they were mortal enemies lurking on slopes to pounce on them. It was no wonder that for over a hundred years the image of the mountaineer was that of a rawboned, gangling man with facial features as sharply hewn as the sandstone corners of his native cliffs. It took a lot of muscle and energy to farm the hills of eastern Kentucky. It also took a lot of patience and some complacency to accept the hard challenges of hill life.

Few places in North America produced so genuine a self-sufficient rural society as did nineteenth-century mountainous eastern Kentucky. Isolated from the world, this landlocked society placed a deeper impress upon individuals than did any other part of Kentucky; not even the proud Bluegrass stamped its people so boldly in habit, speech, dress, and philosophy. Folk customs, attitudes toward social relationships, and community mores were indeed distinctive. Superstitions, folkways, and hotheaded sensitivity often set the mountaineer apart from the rest of his fellow Kentuckians. If Pennyroyal and Bluegrass folk aped the society of Richmond, Philadelphia, Cincinnati, and New Orleans, the mountaineer aped no one. He knew nothing of social striving and form, and certainly he did not propose to disturb the tenor of his life with such idiocy. His family home was most often comprised of a roomy hewn-log pen; sometimes it was a double log structure with a wide dogtrot hall between. Overhead were other rooms, and a long shed across the back took care of the overflow of children as they came along. The father was head of the family, and a grizzled old pioneer grandfather was head of the clan.

A mountain boy married a neighbor girl, and they took up housekeeping a short step up the hollow from the old man's place. Every new marriage pushed settlement a corn patch deeper up the cove until the whole area was settled by people, all of whom bore the same name and who lived by the same folk code and ways. These deeply buried pockets of family settlements remained largely untouched by a rising modern America, by education, changing ideas, and technology. The people were wedded to the land, to the hills, and to their ancient ways of life. Courthouses were safe places to record ill-drawn land deeds, to go for marriage licenses, and occasionally to hear lawyers argue land dispute cases. The mountaineer himself, however, felt more secure if he kept outside influences from invading his world. Eloquent proof of this pattern of early mountain life is often contained in testimony over land distribution. It was not at all unusual for an old patriarch with 400 acres of rough mountain land to leave behind him half a hundred claimants, and every one of them deadly determined to get his tiny share of the legacy. Sometimes divisions of such property virtually defied the mathematical capabilities of the courts.

In early Kentucky towns and cities were no more than gathering places for expatriate farmers and a few tradesmen and professional people. They all looked to the countryside rather than within themselves for economic strength. The Bluegrass was one of the few places in this country where farmers were as much or more sophisticated than were their small-town neighbors. It was here that the all-absorbing agrarian tradition of Kentucky was to flourish, and to help shape both the Kentucky personality and the attitude of the people toward the world about them. The story of the great men of Kentucky in the nineteenth century is largely of men with farm backgrounds. Henry Clay was congressman, Secretary of State, and senator. Isaac Shelby, the first governor, came from Travelers Rest to serve as governor on two occasions, and many times he had to be sought in his back fields to make administrative decisions rather than in the confining governor's office back in Frankfort. John Jordan Crittenden, governor and United States senator, was from the farm, Richard Minter Johnson, Vice-President, the judges of the Court of Appeals, other governors and legislators sprang from the soil. Massive reports of the Court of Appeals reveal how intimately the practice of law and the land system were related.

Master farmer of them all was Henry Clay. On his Ashland estate at the edge of Lexington he ran a model farm for his day. There he grew hemp, tobacco, and fine livestock. Had he given full time to his farm operations and maintained a scientific interest in livestock breeding he might well have become a major figure in American agricultural history. With his courageous wife Lucretia he built at Ashland an English gentleman's estate. His house surrounded by a vast park became for the politician a haven of peace and escape. Too, it became a wonderful place from which to launch a political campaign. Many of the etchings of Clay show his Ashland estate in the background, not to emphasize its magnificence but to imply that Clay was a son of the soil.

In an even more intimate and personal way the land has marked the Kentuckian. His folk mores are those of the land, so are his idioms and figures of speech, the tone of his voice, and his mental responses. He feels most comfortable with this heritage. It is the source of his humor, his pathos, and his solace. Even though he has loved the land from the beginning he has committed horrible outrages against it. He has allowed erosion to rob him, he has slashed the forest away, stripped topsoil from coal seams, despoiled mountainsides, and clogged and poisoned streams with chemical-laden debris. Often he has built unsightly shacks in the midst of intoxicating natural beauty, and since World War I he has cluttered the landscape with the corpses of spent automobiles. The native son is now challenged with the problem of reclamation. If his land is to become once again beautiful and inviting, he will have to spend enormous sums of money to undo the misdeeds of his forebears.

The Seeds of Faith

The voice of the evangelist was raised loud in the land in the middle of the eighteenth century. A stubborn and determined group of self-ordained primitive Baptist ministers took the fight of the Lord directly to the people. There was no ritual, no authority, and no give in their actions. British colonial officials were not conditioned to deal with this revolt. The only response they could make was to attempt to foist the established church on the people. Many backwoods communities were without religious ministration, except that provided by the primitive ministers themselves. These had the stirrings of revivalism stemming from the 1730's when Jonathan Edwards and George Whitefield were preaching fervently to the masses. These new voices emphasized the need for deep spiritual experiences and conversion on the part of the individual. It was up to him to reorder his life, and he could do so only by having a deep emotional and psychological experience. Thus it was that the idea was firmly planted that the fate of a man's soul was a personal responsibility.

On June 4, 1768, the streets of Fredericksburg, Virginia, were crowded. People had come from miles around to attend court. Some came for curiosity's sake, but others were there to sympathize with five forlorn prisoners at the bar. Soon the sheriff appeared with the recalcitrant offenders of the King's dignity and breakers of the Crown's colonial laws. These independent colonials, Lewis Craig,

John Waller, James Childs, James Reed, William Marsh, were brought before the court to defend charges of preaching without licenses. This was a source of great aggravation to those officials who attempted to keep order in Virginia, and the royal prosecutor showed his irritation that morning. "May it please your worships," said he, "these men are great disturbers of the peace: they cannot meet a man on the road, but they ram a text of scripture down his throat."

Several times previously the irritated court had listened to charges against these rampant "New Lights." Frontier Virginia was literally on fire with this "infernal" emotional religious zeal. It was not their religion that mattered, but the fact that the preachers were talking independence of man and his soul. This was treason and, frankly, the judges were frightened. They were at a loss to know what steps to take. It was true that the law was clear on the point at issue, and the New Lights were threatening the authority of the established church. Preachers of the new faith were the most determined men in Virginia. They were ready and willing to offer themselves as martyrs to their cause, and this was not at all a pleasant fact for the King's judges to contemplate. There was, they knew full well, only a hairline difference between religious and political independence. One was certain to bring the other.

Before the court in Fredericksburg the five Baptist preachers refused to give security that they would not preach again that year in the county. When they failed to comply with the judgment of the court they were marched away to jail. All this was to the good of the Baptist cause and distinctly to the detriment of the established church. Likewise it helped to spur on the political revolution taking place in America. As the jailer marshaled his stubborn charges down the street, they raised their voices in the rousing Baptist marching song, "Broad Is the Road That Leads to Death."

It was a solemn crowd that followed in the preachers' footsteps or lingered in the street to watch the sorry procession. A story is told that one of those who awaited the jail march of the faithful was "Fighting Joe" Craig, a brother of Lewis. Joe's feelings ran high, and in a commanding voice he shouted, "Arise, ye dead, and come to judgment." This shout of the rambunctious preacher came like a bolt from heaven, and scores of people fell to the ground in a religious stupor as though pierced through the heart.

Lewis Craig, a staunch leader of the frontier faith, continued to preach. Through the grating of the jailhouse he shouted his messages to the crowds that gathered before him. Here was truly a backwoods Joshua trampling down the walls. For the next twelve years Virginia Baptists and established churchmen were in a continuous state of conflict. On every hand, at Dover, at Tuckahoe, at upper King and Queen, and at upper Spotsylvania, Baptist churches were springing up like wild onions in bottom land. The common man was finding great personal satisfaction in the teachings of the new faith. There was none of the lifeless Writ-following sermons in the ceremonies of the informal church meetings which gathered nightly from house to house.

Throughout more than a decade of community bickering between the conflicting religious groups it was seen that the two churches could no longer exist side by side. Some of the Baptists decided to withdraw. For five years Orange and Spotsylvania neighbors had been going west—going west to free Kentucky, where a man could claim a piece of good land and worship God as he pleased. There would be no spying constables to issue abhorrent warrants against "holding conventicles and preaching the gospel contrary to law." There were no puppet judges to order prolonged jail sentences against innocent preachers who refused to conform to the established order of things. News had begun to trickle back over the trails that Kentucky was a rich land and that it needed people badly.

Scouts went out beyond Virginia's mighty frowning wall to the dark and mysterious land of Boone, Clark, and Kenton. In time they brought back the encouraging word that there were rich river valleys where farms could still be claimed almost by right of the hack marks of a tomahawk. The Dick's River valley, all the way from its headwaters to near its junction with the Kentucky, was open to settlement. Here it was, by common assent, that a large company of Spotsylvania Baptists chose to go in a body. The Kentucky Bluegrass country was to become a haven of freedom and future religious promise for peace.

It was a strange congregation that gathered about the old Baptist church on the Catharpin Road, twenty-two miles below Fredericksburg, on September 28, 1781. Virginia crops were ripening for the harvest. Tobacco was already in the curing sheds. Early corn was ripe and waiting to be harvested. Leaves on the trees began to sag and to show growing spots of brown. Grass and weeds had gone to seed. Piedmont Virginia was in the beginning of the delightful season of early Indian summer, when all life was suspended between the ripening influence of late summer and the golden harvest season of autumn. This was not the season when ordinary men planned new undertakings; they were surfeited for the moment with the harvest. This was a time when man felt a close bond between himself and his land. But in the face of all these mellow staying influences, there milled about Lewis Craig's church that September morning as motley an assortment of people and animals as had ever attended a religious service in America.

Farmers had come with their bulging wagons heavily loaded with household plunder and farm tools. Their boys and slaves herded cows, sheep, and droves of pigs behind the teams. Women led small children by the hand or balanced them on pack horses in panniers. Baptist preachers were there by the score. The leader was stern forty-year-old Lewis Craig, but also on hand were Swearing Jack Waller, Elijah Craig, who later was to make the name of Craig famous in Kentucky in an exceedingly unorthodox manner, eccentric Joe Craig, determined Ambrose Dudley, Joseph Bledsoe, who was to sire hot-headed Jesse Bledsoe of the Kentucky Senate, William Cave, and Simeon Walton of Nottaway. Young Captain William Ellis, brave grandson of defiant old rebel Hezekiah Ellis who had openly cried treason in '75 to Governor Dunmore and was imprisoned for his act, was to be chief adviser and spiritual leader.

As the rays of light broke forth in the east on the morning of September 29, Captain Ellis aroused the camp and prepared to start. Morning prayers were held, and then with quiet reverence Lewis Craig closed the lid of the huge pulpit Bible. The clerk gathered up the book, symbol of the church, along with his records. Captain Ellis' bugler sounded the blast which ordered the procession to start. The "traveling church" faced westward and began to move.

Between five and six hundred Virginians were on their way to "New Canaan." Clumsy creaking wagons, loaded to capacity, fell into line. Shouting Negro slaves and excited young boys herded the livestock, and women and children astride pack horses brought up the rear. Many a head was turned back to the old church in a silent, longing farewell. That afternoon, late, the band of immigrants had crossed the Spotsylvania County line, and that night they were in the

neighboring county of Orange. They were traveling southwestward—
southwestward toward the beautiful but mysterious Blue Ridges. The
route led past Gordonsville, to Charlottesville, across the James River
to Lynchburg and to the Blue Ridges. On rolled the wagons, surrounded by restless livestock and followed by a string of pack
horses. In the slow movement of the company many had time to
debate the wisdom of their move, and some, as is always man's story,
wished to turn back. Baptist faith, however, was stubborn and Captain Ellis quickly sensed the current of despondency running through
the company. He commanded the slaves, those lighthearted souls to
whom the journey was high adventure, to sing their lively songs, and
soon there was a happy reversal of feelings.

As the Blue Ridges came nearer the road became narrower, the
woods were closing in, and the villages and stray farmhouses dropped
behind. Then, off in the distance, towered the sentinel Peaks of Otter.
At last the party had arrived at the Blue Ridges. The long blue wall, a
panorama of scenic beauty, was forbidding to weary travelers. Timid
immigrants looked upon it with fear. Far beyond this wall was Kentucky, but likewise there were hostile Indians and a heartless wilderness.

Up the side of the Blue Ridge the company toiled. To most of
the traveling churchmen this was their first experience at mountain
climbing. Back in Spotsylvania scrubby pine flats spread out in gently
rolling slopes, dipping slightly toward the Potomac Valley and the
swampy corner below Richmond. Dragging their weary bodies up the
Blue Ridge behind straining teams and groaning wagons was in reality a process of inching through the great geographical doorway to a
life of grave uncertainties. Parting at the old church had been difficult, but it was not nearly so realistic as the placing of a mountain
wall behind the pilgrim band.

Along the way Lewis Craig's resonant voice was clear and loud in
supplication. There beside the rutted mountain road he stood over the
old pulpit Bible and uttered words full of promise and good cheer.
Brother Craig knew that his stouthearted followers' faith and courage
were to be subjected to sore trial before they reached the land in the
Kentucky valley. Across the Roanoke, then to the New River, and up
the crest of the dividing Allegheny ridges, the traveling church
wound slowly. As they poked along with their burdens, the congregation sang, just as those five stern martyrs had sung back in

the streets of Fredericksburg on that June morning in '68, "Broad Is the Road That Leads to Death." Long "Sunday rests" punctuated the monotonous crawling journey westward. The church was fully organized, and during these weekend lulls church services continued just as they had when there was a settled community and a church-house.

From New River ford to Fort Chiswell was only a short distance. There buried in the first deep fold of the Alleghenies was a frontier militia post where backwoods militiamen guarded the precious lead mines. To Lewis Craig's Baptist company Fort Chiswell was more than an island of safety standing in the way of marauding British and loyalist troops, it was the place where they gave up their wagons. From this place to Kentucky there was no wagon road, and their goods could be carried only on the back of a man or a horse.

When the Baptist pilgrims left their community back in Spotsyl-vania the tug of giving up their homes was somewhat lessened by the fact that there were the wagons. Man in his migrations across Amer-ica's frontier always loved his wagon. To him it was a solid tie with the land of his origin, and a house of sorts. It was a place where he could make down a bed and sleep indoors at night. He could lie in it in a moment of sickness and enjoy in some degree the comforts of civilization. In a moment of Indian attack the wagon made a good fortification behind which he could hide. But man traveling by pack horse severed this last solid bond with civilization and placed himself at the mercy of a fractious horse, the forest, and the elements. When the transfer of goods was made from wagon to pack horse at Chis-well, many a couple stood about a piece of cherished furniture they were leaving behind. A cradle with long rockers which would catch in low-hanging limbs embodied the story of a family; a heavy walnut bed had been a token of home ties for generations. All these things were to be abandoned—abandoned deep in a treacherous wilderness that was brutally oblivious to life's tender sentiments and dreams. This was the place where the frontier began in earnest.

Lewis Craig's congregation now had urgent need for the rifle, pow-der horn, and bullet mold along with their large Bible and crude farming implements. The ax, next to the rifle, became a necessary agent of advancing frontier culture. Women and children struggled on astride wagon horses. Low-hanging limbs and briers crowding the trail raked at their clothing. Hill after hill rolled up and down before them, and at the foot of each rocky descent there was a stream to be forded. Occasionally there were large rivers to be crossed with the use of ferries, or bridges. There were the Holston, the Clinch, and the Powell, each of which spread out wide in its narrow valley. Green water from a thousand mountain streams rushed and eddied about stubborn boulders and over potholes. Fords could be made only where the rocky bottom pushed up toward the stream surface, and where the boulders and suckholes were absent. It was no simple matter to ferry a large company of women, children, and sick people. Nor was it easy to pass rearing and charging pack horses over from one bank to another.

This Appalachian trail had become a land of the skillet. At night the smell of "jerked meat" or fresh venison rose from the campfires. Women rolled tight balls of moistened corn meal into hoecakes for bread. Soon, however, the stock of meal grew scant, and the grim fact faced the fathers that bread would not hold out until the church reached Kentucky. But exhaustion of the supply of meal was not to be the only threat of trouble. Soon there appeared signs of the dreaded Indians and every nightfall brought with it a period of grim fear and horror. It was impossible to tell whether sounds of the night were those of wild animals or of one stealthy warrior communicating with another. Guards were posted well out away from the huge log campfires to maintain a strict watch to see that the company was not surprised or ambushed. More than once the guard fired their rifles into the dark, and the next morning they found signs that their bullets had taken effect in a red-skinned brave.

News came at Abingdon (Wolf Hills) that Washington had cornered his British opponent, Cornwallis, at Yorktown, and the American Revolution was ended. Wolf Hills was the last Virginia post until the pilgrims should reach Logan's Fort at the head of Dick's River in Kentucky. At Wolf Hills, Lewis Craig's congregation overtook another traveling church. A year before, this congregation, under the leadership of Captain Billy Bush, had started for Kentucky. They were caught in the hard, starving winter of '80, a time when game had starved in the woods and many of the Kentucky immigrants had returned east of the mountains. The Indian raids on Kentucky were fierce. Boone and his companions at Boonesboro had just staved off the assault of Black Fish and De Quindre, and Harrod's and Logan's forts were fighting for existence. Leaders of the first congregation had settled down at Wolf Hills to await a time when it would be safe to go on to Kentucky. Until the Spotsylvania church appeared on the scene the Wolf Hills congregation had not organized formally into a church. Lewis Craig proceeded to effect an organization and to prepare it for a future march to the Kentucky country as a church body. This done, Craig headed his congregation toward its goal.

Down the Reedy Creek trail, men of the guard limped ahead with rifles resting in the crooks of their arms. Their feet were masses of sores, and they suffered tortures. "Scald feet," that insidious disease of the western American pioneers wearing porous moccasins, was taking its toll. Men walked days with wet feet, and then suffered deathly agony from galling sores and rheumatism.

Along the flooded Holston River the company traveled with the towering Clinch Mountain above them. For miles the trail spread out on the flat Holston shelf, but where the hills disappeared for a time the mud became deeper. Cutting across from Abingdon the party made its way to the site of the present town of Jonesville in Virginia. Here they came directly under the frowning mountain wall. The last lap of the trail led down under the mountain range, over Clinch Mountain, across the Clinch and Powell rivers to the great Appalachian pass. Clinch Mountain was steep and difficult to cross. It lay like a granite barrier guarding the passage into the Clinch Valley. Where there had been mud and bogs along the Holston there were now rocky ledges covered with a thick slime or eroded soil. Women and children who stood under the dark ledge of the mountain and looked up to points which the party had to pass were ready to give up in despair.

At both Clinch and Powell rivers the Virginia pilgrims were faced with floodtides. Fords were buried deep under swirling currents of green water pouring down from the mountains in a mad race for the great juncture of the Tennessee River system. Brother Craig's church was caught fast in the clutches of beginning winter with the rains and snows falling incessantly upon them. Pack horses were unloaded so that they could cross the rivers, while goods and people were ferried over on clumsy log rafts.

Beyond the rivers the trail was poor, and the going grew worse in each succeeding mile. Kentucky was only thirty miles away, but the most treacherous part of the journey lay within this short distance. For three weeks the band of Virginians fought against the heavy odds of winter and a dim, muddy mountain trail to reach that gateway of promise—Cumberland Gap. Long before they came in sight of the passageway into Kentucky they were under the solid rocky spine of the Appalachians. Alongside of them it reared high and menacing over their path. Farther down the trail the ledge stretched itself higher and higher until it rose in a dizzy pinnacle, and just beyond it dipped into a narrow gateway which opened the way to the wilderness frontier beyond. As the laboring immigrants moved closer and closer to the great depression in the mountainside a feeling of triumph ran through the party. It was with some sense of accomplishment that the Virginians struggled through Cumberland Gap and turned their feet downward into the Cumberland Valley and toward the great Kentucky country.

After the Gap there was the Cumberland River, which rushed its flood southwestward, and then turned about-face in a great sweeping bend and flowed northwestward to the Ohio. It wound like a huge serpent across Boone's Wilderness Road. Several times Lewis Craig's company had to cross its swift, icy current. But deeper into Kentucky the valleys became wider, and many of the smaller streams flowed generally toward the Kentucky. The mountains leveled off and the going became easier. Food was scarce, and the Indian menace somewhat more acute. Through all this the people struggled, singing their Baptist hymns as they plodded forward along the muddy trail. Night and morning the courageous voice of Lewis Craig was raised in earnest prayer. Each morning Captain Ellis' bugler blew the command to move forward, and night after night weary sentinels wandered off into the underbrush to stand anxious guard to intercept any attempted surprise attacks by the Indians.

Along the Rockcastle River a new spirit of hope and cheerfulness was noticeable. Much of the water tumbling down this mountain river was gathered near the land that was to be the company's future home. Across the river was the junction of Skagg's Trace and the Wilderness Trail. The trace led westward toward Crab Orchard and onto the Falls of the Ohio, and the trail went on northward to the Kentucky River and Boonesboro. Soon the traveling church reached the Hazel Patch, a meeting place of the frontier for return trips eastward, then they were at Crab Orchard, and within a short time they reached Logan's Fort. At last they were in central Kentucky, and they were glad to see once again a haven of safety for the white man. But the restless Baptists were too anxious to locate their land, to build a church and homes, to remain long at Logan's.

Scouts were sent to Gilbert's Creek, a small tributary of Dick's River. A central point was located, and quickly the woods were cut back, and as the axes rang out in battle against the virgin wilderness, Craig's Station rose log by log to turn back both the elements and the Indians. It was a simple matter, where strong hands were so willing, to build a frontier post. Within a short time packs of household goods were moved in, the livestock penned, and the traveling churchmen were transformed into frontiersmen ready to assist in creating a new America.

Here buried deep in the forest that securely hid the creeks which were combined to make Dick's River an important lateral of the Kentucky, pioneering Baptists were at home. Brother Craig deposited the revered old Spotsylvania Bible on its new pedestal, the clerk unpacked his records, and the church began in its new home. On the second Sunday in December, 1781, the Baptists who had fled persecution from the established church in Virginia worshiped God freely and according to the dictates of their consciences in this new land of freedom. Here was a formal beginning of the church in the Kentucky valley. It was the first churchhouse built in Kentucky.

Gilbert's Creek became a closely organized community. Homes were built near the fortress, and plans were made to take up domestic economy where it had been interrupted back in Virginia. By spring other immigrants were trudging overland or drifting down the Ohio River to boost the Baptist cause. Kentucky, said one denominational observer, quickly became a "vortex of Baptist preachers." Restless immigrants soon left Craig's Fort on Gilbert's Creek and crossed the Kentucky River to the rich Bluegrass Plateau which lay along the northern bank. Here they founded, under the leadership of Lewis Craig, South Elkhorn in Fayette County, the mother church of Kentucky Baptists. Brother Billy Bush's band, which had lingered on the Holston at Wolf Hills, came on to Kentucky and stopped for a short time at Gilbert's Creek. They then moved on to the Kentucky River near Boonesboro at Howard Creek. There they founded Providence Church.

These traveling churches constitute an important web of American frontier history. A list of early churchmen would constitute a roll call of important pioneers. No more famous name can be found among

them than that of Craig. Besides Lewis Craig, whose services to his
traveling parishioners have almost become Kentucky legends, there
were two other Craig brothers. Old Joe Craig, in his eccentricities,
almost rivaled that forthright servant of the Lord, Peter Cartwright,
who later rode the frontier roads on farther west in behalf of Methodism and salvation. Along the trail from Virginia when the traveling
church faced hardship and adversity it was Joe who showed courage
to move on, and to the rousing tune of a Baptist hymn he urged the
company forward. There was little formality about the practical Joe.
Back in Virginia the constables had hunted him with bloodhounds,
and on one occasion the officers shook him out of a tree as if he were
an opossum. They arrested Joe and attempted to march him off to
jail, but the stubborn Baptist proceeded to lie down in the road,
saying, "A good man ought not to be put in prison, I won't have a
hand in it."

Brother Elijah Craig distinguished himself during the early years
of Baptist persecution in Virginia. Later he came to Kentucky and
settled on the banks of the Elkhorn in Scott County. He laid out the
village of Georgetown, and soon his thousand acres of rich bluegrass
land were yielding an abundant return in worldly goods. Once a poor
and fervent disciple of the unpopular New Light cause back in state-
church ridden Virginia, he now became a wealthy man of affairs
along the Kentucky River. A Baptist historian, bewailing the worldly
demoralization of so fervent a disciple, wrote that "he erected a saw
and grist mill, then the first fulling mill, the first rope works, and the
first paper mill in Kentucky." The Craig-Parker paper mill produced
the stock paper on which many issues of the pioneer newspaper, the
Kentucky Gazette, were printed. The church historian failed to mention another service which Brother Elijah Craig and his Parker partners rendered the Kentucky farmers. They used charred hardwood
kegs to produce bourbon whiskey. There is still a question of whether
or not they discovered the process of making this type of whiskey, but
nevertheless their distillery was well known.

It was a long and difficult road to travel in 1781 from Spotsylvania
County to Kentucky, but the route, with all its hardships, was more
than a trudging journey from one point on the map of the country to
another. It was a journey for freedom. It was the same stern and
discouraging journey which American colonials took in flight from
religious persecution abroad. Washington spoke of these New Lights

with prophetic foresight as "firm friends of civil liberty and the promoters of our glorious revolution."

An attorney for the Crown knew that the preaching of these rebellious and determined Baptists through the gratings of the King's jailhouses was the beginning of the end of English government in the colonies. He had warned the court that "The Baptist are like a bed of camomile; the more they are trodden the more they spread."

As Baptist flocks, like the ancient Israelites, wandered across the mountains in search of a haven of freedom, individual preachers and families came to settle on the Kentucky frontier. Almost overnight after 1780 new churches came into existence, and the faithful were active on every hand. They were not, however, to have the field to themselves. Presbyterians were almost as hardy pioneers, and their leaven was to raise a mighty loaf of religious leadership. Father of the faith beyond the mountains was logical and unemotional David Rice. He came from the east with a missionary's zeal and a Scotsman's sense of stern religious order. He preached an unadulterated Calvinism which found its mark in the hearts of men who daily faced the inevitable choice of submitting to the will of a power greater than themselves. Father Rice's preaching extended beyond the pulpit, and in those years of political turmoil when Kentucky sought to free itself from Virginia his calm but authoritarian voice was raised above the ceaseless noise of debate by men who were ignorant of the fundamentals of government, on the one hand, and quailed before the power of the masses, on the other. He also lifted a voice against slavery in Kentucky, and even published the first locally written attack upon the institution.

Crossing back and forth over the Appalachians in tireless crusades, Bishop Francis Asbury spread the gospel of brotherly love under the cloak of Methodism. From one cabin door to the next he smote the devil and rival faiths with mighty spiritual fists. He instructed the backwoodsmen in the elemental joys of total emotional release and gave them hope for more pleasant and enduring joys on another frontier. No part of the westward movement was to be accomplished by greater religious energy, with the exception of Mormon expansion in Utah, than was the founding of Kentucky.

In his wanderings Bishop Asbury recorded an enlightening story of social life on his circuit. On Tuesday, May 11, 1790, the bishop wrote that he had crossed Kentucky River. I was strangely outdone for want of sleep, having been greatly deprived of it in my journey through the wilderness; which is like being at sea, in some respects, and in others worse. Our way is over mountains, steep hills, deep rivers, and muddy creeks; a thick growth of reeds for miles together; and no inhabitants but wild beast and savage men. Sometimes, before I am aware, my ideas would be leading me to be looking out ahead for a fence; and I would, without reflection, try to recollect the houses I should have lodged at in the wilderness. I slept about an hour the first night, and about two the last; we ate no regular meal; our bread grew short, and I was much spent.

I saw the graves of the slain—twenty-four in one camp. I learn that they had set no guard, and that they were up late playing cards. A poor woman of the company had dreamed three times that the Indians had surprised and killed them all; she urged her husband to entreat the people to set a guard, but they only abused him, and cursed him for his pains.

The old preacher was pained to see the destruction wrought by Indians on people who did not heed the warnings of a dreaming female, but not all the evilly inclined people were Indians. The white rowdies caused equally as much trouble. In 1793, a year after Kentucky had been admitted to the Union and most of the people felt politically secure in their new independence, Bishop Asbury was again on the trail to Cumberland Gap. This time he traveled with a "troop of poor, very poor sinners" to whom he "gave dreadful offence by a prayer." At the famous gathering place, the Crab Orchard, he found

company rough enough, some of whom were very wild: we had a company of our own, and refused to go with them. Some of them gave us very abusive language; and one man went upon a hill above us, and fired a pistol towards our company. We resolved to travel in our order, and bound ourselves by honor and conscience to support and defend each other, and to see every man through the wilderness. But we could not depend upon wicked and unprincipled men, who would leave and neglect us, and even curse us to our faces. Nor were we at liberty to mix with swearers, liars, drunkards; and for aught we know, this may not be the worst with some. We were about fourteen or fifteen in company; and had twelve guns and pistols.

This was taking the word to Kentucky with a vengeance.

The militant Wesleyan viewed Kentucky pioneering from the perspective of the cabin door. He was, however, so bent on his spiritual mission that like Quaker John Wool in the east, he felt too little of his deep human experiences worthy of recording. It remained for other preachers to tell of the human side of their flocks. To the ardent circuit riders Kentuckians were children of God, untutored and untamed, who were equally ready to take a scalp or a drink of hard liquor. They were just as quick to break up a religious meeting as to offer shelter and sustenance to the preacher and his horse. For many the itinerate preacher was a link between them and the past, and he was a symbol of promise.

Early American revivalism was to have one phase of its beginning in Kentucky. At the turn of the nineteenth century three uninhibited men, William and John Magee and William McCready, provoked an emotional orgy on the Mud River in Logan County. Here they began a second great awakening which was to have far-reaching effects on American life. From a Mud River brush arbor revivalism spread to Cane Ridge in Bourbon County and to an explosion which made 1801 a landmark year in American religious history. Here Baptists, Presbyterians, Methodists, and even the uncommitted were drawn into one mighty vortex of hysteria. Like a raging storm the roar of the converted was heard from a distance. Men preached, shouted, danced, and fell speechless as though hit by heavy blows. Some screamed agonizingly that they were caught in the jaws of death itself, while others climbed trees, stood atop stumps and logs to confess sins real and imagined. They pleaded with the unsaved to seek forgiveness and with the converted to remain steadfast. The gathering at Cane Ridge was the largest one to come together on the frontier. Twenty thousand persons flocked to this place in 1,143 vehicles, and over three thousand persons fell victims to their emotions.

A frontier population let go its restraints at Cane Ridge. Here was begun the camp meeting which was to combine a strong sociality with annual religious refreshment. All across America in years to come the repentant cried out in seasonal outpourings of agony while zealous revivalists described with Miltonian imaginativeness the horrors awaiting the wayward and the sinful. For backwoodsmen listening to these horrendous admonitions life took on a sinister meaning. The individual's mind was thrust into a new dimensional concept of the awfulness of eternity itself. For them sin was undefined and all-involving. Every human act was after some fashion an involvement of the spiritually saved, and those backwoods Jeremiahs who thundered their grim warnings saw in the upturned faces of their congregations the graven images of carnal man.

For Kentucky these early years of religious pioneering were to harden a social pattern for the future. Where partisan political hands were laid heavily on the land, the hand of narrow if not bigoted evangelical religion clamped its mind tightly in a rigid pattern of intolerance. No institution, not even the state, was to be spared. The measure of a maturing Kentucky culture was to be gauged in terms of the ever-growing strength of religious denominationalism. In the same manner the worth of an individual was that of his religious denominational association. Even his social status was cast first in this mold. Though persecuted pilgrims moved away from Spotsylvania County, Virginia, while the American Revolution was still in process, and faced the hard road to Kentucky, they brought with them less sense of fundamental religious freedom than of a desire to worship God according to their own restricted views.

Kentucky pioneers shaped religious concepts and behavior which have lasted. Scriptural literalists themselves, they bound future generations to live by their inflexible concepts. They allowed few opportunities for the intellectually adventurous in their society. The religious skeptic was as welcome as a smallpox epidemic, and even the orthodox found themselves involved in bitter clashes over matters of literal interpretations not only of the Scriptures but of religious procedures.

For sixteen days in 1843 Alexander Campbell, of the Disciples faith, and Nathan Rice, Presbyterian, debated doctrinal issues relating to baptism, especially that of infants. Like two antediluvian turtles locked in mortal combat they dragged up voluminous opinion and comment to sustain their contentions. In this conflict neither the Scriptures nor the sacrament of baptism was dignified, but the public mind was tightened further in bigotry and religious conflict. In the 1920's the literalists were still tugging at straw-man issues. Many pulpits in the state thundered with tirades against evolution, scientists, Charles Darwin, monkeys, and any local brother who happened to stand in line of fire. So vigorous did this debate become that it spilled over into the chamber of the state legislature, where it became mixed with internal politics, regulation of railroad facilities, the science of evolution, the contents of school textbooks, and even the academic classroom. The dramatic moment was reached in 1925 when a spiritual descendant of the pioneer Hardshells threw a science textbook on the floor of the House of Representatives and jumped up and down on it invoking the wrath of God.

VI

Athens of the West

Hunters from Harrodsburg were encamped about a spring in the heart of the rolling Bluegrass Plateau in early summer, 1775, when news of the Battle of Lexington reached them. Thus, say the traditionalists, the spot was named Lexington. The founding of the town, however, had to await a more propitious moment in the future. Early in the 1780's backwoodsmen slashed a hole in the canebrake smothering the banks of the tiny lateral of the Elkhorn. There they built a circular fortress and bared their teeth at marauding Shawnees. This was the beginning of the new West's first important town.

Lexington from the beginning was destined to be a flourishing farmers' town. Too, it would be one to which itinerant merchants and peddlers would bring their merchandise for sale and where academy masters would come to organize schools. Travelers on their way around the great "western circuit" headed for Lexington. Adventurers like Benjamin Sebastian, Robert D. Short, and James Wilkinson came this way looking for the "main chance." Wilkinson brought the town a certain amount of questionable glamour. Most important of all, John Bradford came to Lexington and in 1787 began publication of his seminal *Kentucky Gazette*.

Once they had argued every possible question down to the most thoroughly bolted essentials, the founding fathers of the commonwealth came to the Sheaf of Wheat Tavern on Broadway to organize the commonwealth's government in June, 1792. People have not yet quit asking why Lexington was not made the permanent capital of Kentucky. The town was one of several places which made the bid for the state capital, but Frankfort was chosen because it was centrally located on the Kentucky River and the old Midland Trail. Citizens of that rising village were generous in providing funds and materials for building a statehouse. Thus the "Athens of the West" lost its opportunity to center the Kentucky political focus in its borders.

Lexington was the chief commercial town of the old frontier. Its merchants grew heady on the strong economic surge of the opening decade of the nineteenth century. The flow of farm products from the bluegrass farmlands primed the inflow of cash from the outside markets. High Street towering above the Town Branch was lined with the new homes of merchants growing rich from the trade of the country. Near the seat of Transylvania Seminary Benjamin Gratz and John Hunt built magnificent mansions as monuments to their successes.

The nineteenth century roared into being in Lexington in a burst of prosperity. John Bradford's *Kentucky Gazette* sparkled with news of the changes which were coming for the town and for Kentucky. In the closing of the old century in which Kentucky was founded, and in which its people had struggled so hard against Indian and elements to plant themselves on the land, Lexington's people could take pride in their advancement. Their town had grown from a tottering puncheon blockhouse raised in the middle of a cane-brake into a respectable commercial and agricultural town. Lexington's founding fathers had planned with unusual wisdom in laying out the order of the streets and in the distribution of "in" and "out" lots, the last time this was to happen in the town's history.

Changes in leadership in the Lexington political and social community came with the opening of the new century. Venerable George Nicholas had been dead two months; guardian father of the constitution making process in Kentucky in two conventions, his passing left open the position of political leadership to John Breckinridge and Henry Clay. On January 27, 1800, the *Gazette* announced the end of another era. A procession, it said, would form in front of the Masonic Hall and march to the Presbyterian church where orators would eulogize the late George Washington.

By no means was the spirit of the new century a funereal one.

Lexington's citizens could take deep satisfaction in the fact that the town's population numbered 1,806 persons, of whom 439 were slaves. Every week new families came up the Wilderness Road or down from Maysville to swell the population total. Fayette County's rolling bluegrass fields and meadows were now nearly all in full cultivation and use. Hemp was grown in great abundance as were corn, wheat, and tobacco. Roads leading out of town were named for enterprising millmasters who had trapped the waters of neighboring streams to turn their stones. At last Transylvania Seminary had put down its roots permanently north of Main Street in a delightful park, and among wealthy neighbors and their handsome new brick houses. Its Board of Trustees had procured from the state a charter making it a university, and its friends predicted a brilliant future for higher education in Lexington.

Most Lexington people, however, took more pride perhaps in the growing prominence of the Fayette bar. They looked upon the first courthouse as the crown of their Mars Hill. To them it symbolized the rise of the new West. Lewis Collins, the famous early historian, wrote: "The courthouse at Lexington is a relic of the early civilization of the interior of Kentucky. It was up with the times when it was built. In 1806, it was a noticeable fingerboard of advancing architecture. In 1814, it indicated another advance. The outlook bespoke pride, intelligence, and comfort. Within it resounded with eloquence, such as the old world never heard, and to which the new world, except Virginia, was stranger."

Land issues arising out of the conflicting titles and irregular registry were open sesame for ambitious lawyers. Clustered about the courthouse square were the offices of John Breckinridge, Henry Clay, Joseph Hamilton Daviess, Fielding L. Turner, John Pope, Jesse Bledsoe, Adam Beatty, Isham Talbert, William T. Barry, and John Allen. These were men of superior legal talents. John Breckinridge and Henry Clay had just dealt the Federalists a heavy blow in their contentions over the Alien and Sedition Laws. Breckinridge in 1797 brought back from Virginia Jefferson's draft of the Kentucky Resolutions, and Clay had joined George Nicholas in an oratorical stoning of the Federalists and their iniquitous laws at a political rally gathered at Maxwell Spring.

Everywhere men were excited by land speculation, especially about the large tracts now available in the opening areas beyond the Ohio.

Too, the British and Indian menace in the Northwest still created a bit of uneasiness and was more than a casual topic of conversation. Advertisements appearing in the *Kentucky Gazette* reflected the prevalence of land fever which beset the speculators.

When François A. Michaux, the French botanist, viewed Lexington in 1802 he found it a thriving place located on 300 acres of cleared land surrounded by woods. Its streets were laid out in an established pattern of "in" and "out" lots, and its streets ran at right angles to each other. On every hand permanent brick-type houses were being constructed to replace the old log structures. Like ancient Athens, Lexington was dominated by two hills, the one along which High Street ran and the gentler rise on which Transylvania University stood. Lexington's immediate flood-ridden plain fell far short of the broad sweep of Attica. The surrounding farm country, however, put to shame anything ancient Greece could offer. The Town Branch of the Elkhorn split the place in two, and periodically its raging waters brought disaster in direct damage and lingering disease.

This was the town which at the turn of the century was the trans-Appalachian frontier's commercial, legal, and cultural center. Michaux found there two printing houses, two ropewalks, a nail-cutting machine, two powder mills, and other factories. Two or three inns served travelers and local customers alike. For $2 a week a boarder ate and drank off the fat of the land. Hunters, farmers, and even housewives brought to market an almost inexhaustible variety of meats, vegetables, and produce, but as Thomas Ashe complained, no fish. What the country failed to supply, itinerant merchants from Philadelphia and Baltimore brought to their temporary stands on Main Street. Lists of merchandise published in the *Gazette* and the *Reporter* read like mercantile inventories from a more sophisticated age. For instance, there must have appeared in local stores almost every variety of textile woven in Britain. There were cutlery, china-ware, spices, and drugs; most all of which had been hauled across Pennsylvania in freight wagons, drifted down the Ohio aboard flat-boats, and lugged inland to Lexington.

A third mail route was opened in 1800 to connect Lexington directly with the new national capital at Washington; this one went by way of the Kanawha Valley across western Virginia, and up the Shenandoah Valley to the Potomac. Even so the town still remained landlocked for unreasonably long periods when the delivery of mail was uncertain or ceased altogether. In winter ice jammed the Ohio and in summer shoal water delayed boat traffic. John Bradford and his colleagues complained bitterly about these insufferable delays, but they had no nearby Piraeus to which they could turn with sailing ships.

In spite of its primitive pioneer conditions, Lexington attracted a number of people who appreciated the significance of schools, libraries, and colleges. Already by the turn of the century a distinguished list of academy masters had served the community. Among these were "Wildcat" John McKinney, John Filson, William Scott, Isaac Wilson, James More, and others. These men taught the "3 R's" to reluctant frontier youth, and some of them even introduced Greek and Latin to the banks of the Elkhorn. Nevertheless, there were those of the town who were denied the privileges of the classroom because of their poverty or lack of schools. It was not until after the middle of the century that universal education could be accomplished. More important was the fact that cultural and intellectual fermentation stirred the leadership of the town during the first quarter of the century. There were men who had at least a glimmer of what it meant to build a university.

Before Transylvania was finally located and organized into a university, the Trustees of Lexington chartered the "Transylvania Library" on January 1, 1795. This was the beginning of the present Lexington Public Library, and its founders had great ambition for this tiny spark of culture in the West. Funds were solicited from donors both at home and abroad. George Washington gave $100, John Adams $100, and Aaron Burr, $40. The remaining funds were raised locally. The committee did remarkably well with the funds it raised from this first subscription drive. Among their initial purchases were Rapin's *History of England,* an ancient parchment deed to the property on which the Apostles Peter and Paul stood in London, and a London street directory of the sixteenth century. Later they purchased Diderot's *Encyclopédie* along with many other European rarities. One can only wonder what motivated the Kentucky backwoodsmen to buy such esoteric items for their new library. When the first order of 400 books arrived in January, 1796, the collection was opened to public use. For a time the library was maintained in connection with an academy, but in 1803 it was established as an independent institution. Aside from its functions as a dispenser of books to a literature-deprived public, the Public Library became a depository for Lexington newspapers, pamphlets, and locally published books. Thus it was that the precious file of the *Kentucky Gazette* was preserved.

Within the first decades of the nineteenth century the number of both newspapers and locally published periodicals was to be increased. There were the *Gazette,* the *American Statesman,* and the *Kentucky Reporter.* Thomas Curry began the publication of the *Western Monitor,* which later became William Gibbs Hunt's *Western Review.* A half dozen publishers were producing books of good quality in Lexington. Among these were John and Daniel Bradford, Joseph Charless, Maxwell and Gooch, Thomas T. Skillman, Worsly and Smith, and Downing and Phillips. In the decades before 1830 these publishers and booksellers made available in the western country a fairly extensive number of titles. Beginning with John Bradford's *Voyages and Adventures and Literature of the French Emigrants from the Year 1789-1799* (1800) to Robert H. Bishop's severely narrow *Outline of the History of the Church in Kentucky* (1821) an interesting list of books flowed from Lexington presses. None was more unusual than the memoirs of John Robert Shaw, a well digger (1807), whose drinking habits and the highly volatile nature of black powder made this a hazardous calling for so careless a man. David Barlow's *Defense of the Trinity* (1804) and his *Infernal Conference,* or *Dialogue of the Devils,* were to stir the fundamentalists into a rage, especially those rigid Calvinists who would have subjected the whole mind of Kentucky to their views.

John Bradford produced on his rickety old press a three-volume compilation of the *Laws of Kentucky* which not only supplemented the original printing of the Acts of the Kentucky General Assembly but made a distinctive contribution to the early graphic arts of the West. The same publisher produced David Ramsey's *The History of the American Revolution* (1815), a contemporary book which has had a surprising durability. It is one of the early titles of its kind which bibliographers still list for its continuing usefulness as a contemporary view of the war years. Equally valid was Robert B. McAfee's *History of the Late War in the Western Country* published by Worsly and Smith in 1816. With excitement still fresh in the minds of the Westerners, McAfee's narrative helped to shape Kentuckians' views as to their heroic role in the border fight against Indian and

British forces. Five years later Samuel L. Metcalfe published *A Collection of Some of the Most Interesting Narratives of Indian Warfare in the West,* a documentary history of a good part of Kentucky's struggle during its earlier years of settlement.

Lexington publishers undertook to capture the western school textbook market by producing such titles as Harrison's *English Grammar, The Union Primer, The Schoolmaster's Assistant, The American Orator, The Western Lecturer, The Monitor, The Kentucky English Grammar,* and the *Kentucky Preceptor.* The last-named book was published in 1811 by MacCoun and Tilford, and had a fairly extensive sale across the frontier. It was an eclectic reader, a forerunner of McGuffey's readers. Besides this rather extensive collection of textbooks, one or two ambitious local publishers even printed Bibles, and some of them pirated European and English novels.

There was ever a literary stirring on the frontier. Both poet and narrative writer sought to express something of the spirit of the times and of the country in their writings. Throughout the first decades of the nineteenth century editors undertook to establish literary periodicals in which they hoped to present local literary offerings, and no doubt to pirate much material from abroad. In 1803 Daniel Bradford published the *Medley or Monthly Miscellany,* the West's first literary magazine, but it died a sudden death for lack of worthy contributors and subscribers. William Gibbs Hunt struggled for two years, 1819-1821, to sustain the *Western Review and Miscellaneous Magazine.* In his last issue Hunt had the good fortune to publish William O. Butler's "Boatman's Horn," a nostalgic poem which has endured. In 1824 the *Western Luminary* budded brightly only to wither and shrivel quickly on the stem of public indifference. Somewhat more successful was the *Transylvania Literary Journal,* edited by Thomas J. Matthews. Frankly the frontier town of Lexington, no matter how gracious its way of life, was not intellectually mature enough in the early years to be properly hospitable to a literary journal. This even in the face of the fact that Timothy Flint observed, "It [Lexington] is not so large and flourishing as Cincinnati, but has an air of leisure and opulence, that distinguishes it from the busy bustle and occupation of the town. In the circles where I visited, literature was most commonly the topic of conversation. The window seats presented the blank covers of the new and most interesting publications. The modern works had been most generously read." To this he could have added that local booksellers advertised for sale titles which would have shocked the bigots into unconsciousness with rage had they ever read them.

In 1806 Lexington enjoyed the doubtful distinction of being visited by the notorious Irishman, Captain Thomas Ashe. Recording his observations a year or so later in England he paid eloquent tribute to the fair Kentucky countryside, but he libeled its principal city with a free hand. He said, "The inhabitants shew demonstrations of civilization; but at particular times, on Sundays and market days, they give loose to their dispositions, and exhibit many traits that should exclusively belong to unnatural savages. Their churches have never been finished, and they have all the glass struck out by boys in the day time, and the insides torn up by rogues and prostitutes who frequent them at night." Otherwise Ashe gave the town a friendly tribute, but he had already wounded its people. Prostitutes in the churchhouses struck the town's protectors as an inexcusable libel. In those weeks when the mails failed to arrive from the east, local editors could always raise copy by attacking the captain.

Since Lexington was the leading town of the old frontier situated on a main crossroads, all sorts of visitors appeared on Main Street and in Mr. Satterwhite's tavern. In 1805 the town trustees granted a permit to Thomas Ardon to "shew his lyon." Three years later an elephant was driven overland to be shown in the town, and the editor of the *Reporter* urged people to go see it because they might never in that generation see another one. Of almost as great a curiosity was the arrival of the first merino sheep from Spain on the neighboring bluegrass farms. They offered such great promise to the local livestock industry that Samuel Trotter was able to contract with a builder to construct an elegant high-columned mansion in exchange for three of the animals. In time a great many blooded animals were to be shipped from abroad to Lexington. Among these were the many thoroughbred horses brought from England, and the shorthorn cattle gathered from Scotch, Irish, Welsh and English pastures. The Kentucky Agricultural Society was organized in 1814, and in time it awarded a fancy assortment of locally hammered silver cups, ladles, bowls, and pitchers as prizes. Reflective of the importance of the horse in local society and economy was the fact that almost from the beginning of settlement there were race paths and tracks in the town. Too, it was said that there were twice as many carriages in Lexington as in any other town in the West.

Economically Lexington reached a peak of development in 1810. Fortesque Cuming said he saw there nearly every type of industry then operating in America. There were nail factories, copper- and tinsmiths, jewelers and silversmiths, saddlers' shops, cabinetmakers, umbrella makers, hatters, dye masters, bootmakers, brewers, textile mills, ropewalks, hemp mills, tobacco factories, Venetian blind makers, brickyards, and printing plants. He said, "Lexington is expected to become the largest inland town of the United States. Perhaps there is no manufactory in this country which is not known here."

In the reorganization and redirection of Transylvania University, Lexington people began to think of their town as bearing a resemblance to classical Athens. Here the arts, the sciences, the classics, and the practical would be taught. Dr. Samuel Brown was a prime mover in the foundation of an early medical tradition in the Bluegrass. He had studied medicine in the University of Edinburgh and with several leading doctors on the east coast. He was credited with bringing the virus of cowpox across the mountains on a woolen cord with which to inoculate individuals against the dread smallpox. Dr. Benjamin W. Dudley became a highly successful surgeon and professor of surgery in the Transylvania Medical School. During his career he performed 225 bladder and kidney stone operations. His patients came from many places to have him operate on them, all without benefit of anesthetics or antiseptics. In fact there were few operations that Dr. Dudley did not undertake, even to opening the cranium to release pressure on the brain.

The Transylvania Medical School was to bring to its staff some of the great medical pioneers of the West. Among these were James Blythe, chemistry; William H. Richardson, obstetrics; Daniel Drake, materia medica; James Overton, theory and practice; Charles Caldwell, Frederick Ridgely, materia medica, midwifery, and the practice of physics; Charles W. Short, John Esten Cooke, and L. P. Yandell in general medicine. These men comprised an excellent early American medical staff. With proper institutional support and leadership they could well have matured into one of the best teaching and practicing faculties in North America.

Not all professional talent was concentrated in the Medical School. Henry Clay was for a time professor of law. He was succeeded in this position by Judge Jesse Bledsoe and William T. Barry. Perhaps no university ever had a more eccentric man on its staff than Constantine

Rafinesque. This erratic man of Turkish birth but of mixed international origins was naïve, self-centered, impetuous, a dreamer, and an insatiable seeker after knowledge. The American backwoods fired him with a zeal unequaled in his time. When he appeared at Transylvania in 1819 Rafinesque had not focused his attention and energies on main scientific objectives. He was at once botanist, paleontologist, ecologist, ichthyologist, and archaeologist. He gathered materials with a passion, planned a botanical garden, a museum display of artifacts, and irritated everybody around him. He prepared for publication the first section of his ambitious *Tellus, or the History of the Earth and Mankind, chiefly in America.* This was published under the title "Ancient History or Annals of Kentucky" as a part of Humphrey Marshall's *History of Kentucky* (1824). President Horace Holley curbed many of Rafinesque's multifarious activities, once removing some of his collections from much-needed rooms in the college building. Partly because of this the irascible scientist, after a seven-year stay, left Transylvania in a fit of anger and went to live in Philadelphia.

Hardly so erratic or omnivorous in his intellectual pursuits was Joseph Buchanan, medical scientist, philosopher, mathematician, inventor, and pedagogue. In 1812 he published a study on the *Philosophy of Human Nature.* Abandoning medicine, Dr. Buchanan turned to education and was the first Kentuckian to adopt the Pestalozzian system of instruction. Perhaps his most unusual scientific contribution was his attempt to invent a musical instrument constructed with a series of glass tubes filled with water at different levels to produce a variety of sounds when struck with a soft hammer. He was also the father of the famous Dr. John Buchanan who lectured throughout the Ohio Valley on the subject of phrenology.

The Pestalozzian method of teaching caught the imagination of many Midwesterners. One of these was the young Scots minister Benjamin O. Peers, who experimented with the method at Transylvania until he ceased to be president of that institution. He headed a general survey committe entrusted with the responsibility of bringing in a report with farsighted recommendations for the organization of a system of public schools in Kentucky. In the 1820's and early 1830's Kentuckians, then as now, undertook to survey their way out of an educational dilemma. In 1822 William T. Barry had produced a committee report which was in fact an excellent blueprint for public education, but it was filed away by a lethargic legislature. At the end of the decade Benjamin O. Peers and Alva Woods, president of Transylvania, made an even more extensive and significantly pioneering report only to have it ignored.

The man who gave Kentucky education, and Transylvania University in particular, great personal leadership was Horace Holley. A Yale graduate and a Unitarian minister from Boston, he kindled in Lexington in 1817 a vigorous spark of intellectualism. It was he who drew together the university's good faculty and had conceived of Transylvania as serving a broad regional purpose. No doubt the New Englander was dreamy-eyed and a bit impulsive in promoting his ideas. As a minister of the gospel he was too blunt and critical of many of the old literalists' dogmatic tenets. He dared offer higher criticism of the Scriptures in his classes, and to discuss sensitive points of interpretation with young ministerial candidates who were as impervious to learning as were many Kentucky ministers. Nevertheless, the Holley period, 1817-1827, formed the golden years of promise of real intellectual maturity for both Lexington and the Ohio Valley.

By 1820 the experimental testing of the steamboat on the Ohio as a practical vehicle of commerce was ended. Lexington rapidly lost its western leadership position to Cincinnati and Louisville. Desperately it attempted to promote and build a railroad to connect the town with the Ohio in the 1830's, but this venture was too costly and so long in the building that most of the former glory of the town was fading. An even greater determinant was the loss of cultural leadership. The insidious serpent of bigotry and narrow denominational dogmatism had sullied the garden of the angels. Quibbling little men had struck fatal blows at the thriving university by criticizing every move and remark of President Horace Holley. They had gone to the ridiculous extent of raising issues about pictures and statuary in his home. In later years Dr. Robert Peter commented that Lexington society was so priggish in this age that it draped piano legs in pantalettes.

Holley was persecuted at Transylvania not so much because he was a Yankee as for the fact that he was smarter than his critics. Robert H. Bishop and Robert Davidson were stubborn illiberal ministers given to dishonest and ignorant tirades against Holley and his management of the university. It was they who set the dogs of dissension against the New Englander. The bigots won and Holley was forced to retire. By March, 1827, he had left the office of president, and with his departure went the great spark which had helped make Lexington a promising intellectual center.

Transylvania's Board of Trustees tried valiantly to maintain the institution, but the forces of reaction were too strong. The medical faculty, comprised of willful men of the most fragile sensitivities and jealousies, became divided by internal quarrels and began the move to Louisville and Cincinnati to associate themselves with medical schools in those places. They showered the public with attacks on their colleagues, filling the press with professorial bickerings in this messy quarrel. By 1837 the professors had left behind the shattered remains of what had promised to be a brilliant school of medicine. It had much of the library and scientific equipment necessary to mature into a good school, but the human spirit was bitter and self-destructive.

Commerce on Main Street was as brisk as ever. Slave dealers brazenly exhibited their wares on the auction block at the corner of Cheapside. County court days brought in multitudes of country people to dispose of farm produce and implements. Droves of young cotton mules, hogs, sheep, and cattle passed through this market bound for the rapidly expanding cotton belt. Pastures and paddocks throughout the Bluegrass contained some of the finest blooded sporting horses in the country. From its earliest settlement horse racing had been a part of life in Lexington. Advertising columns of the newspapers indicated how important famous stallions and good bloodlines were in this horsy community. Bluegrass squires were sportsmen in every sense; many of them were not averse to whooping it up about the local cockpits.

Rich merchants like John Hunt, Benjamin Gratz, and David Sayre adorned the town with their fine houses, and their tables with crisp napery and elegant pieces of silver. Gideon Shryock designed the stately temple of Athena in the midst of the Transylvania campus to commemorate the generosity of Colonel James Morrison, one of Kentucky's few philanthropists.

The agora still thrived as a source of supply for Bluegrass farmers, while the mount shriveled and was all but consumed by bigotry and narrow sectarianism. Merchants still came from Philadelphia, Baltimore, New York, and New Orleans to offer a wide assortment of merchandise. Hemp planters, tobacco growers, producers of fine livestock, and corn and wheat millers enjoyed profitable markets for their goods. There were, however, fewer ingenious men like Edward West, Asa Blanchard, Thomas Harris Barlow, E. S. Noble, Joseph Buchanan, Nathan Burrowes, and George Norton. These inventors and skilled artisans had moved on to the river towns and the more thriving centers.

There was still the bar with its brilliant coterie of lawyers. Henry Clay had brought national prominence to the community, and in the 1830's Lexington citizens hoped he would be elected President of the United States. A constant stream of visitors came this way, but the center of interest had shifted from the university to Ashland and its master. The university, true enough, had gained materially in enrollment, but ignorant and penurious state officials had sustained the hands of its enemies and were starving it to death. The temple of Athena stood on the banks of Town Branch, but like its classical counterpart it stood intellectually vacant and hollow. The muse had fled. What once promised to be a seminal center of culture and intellectual refinement for the whole western country was now submerged in the provincial affairs of the Attica Plain and its narrowing world of agrarian aspirations.

Cincinnati, St. Louis, and Louisville had flirted with and won the affections of the goddess. The "Corinth" beyond the mouth of the Licking now had the printers and publishers, the merchants, founders, professors, bankers, and most important of all, the river and the steamboats. In Lexington what had once been regional newspapers were now reduced to local journals, forced into this position by vigorous new competitors on the river.

The die was cast, Louisville would become Kentucky's major city. After 1820 the steamboat brought the trade and the travelers to the Falls of the Ohio. Never, however, could the rowdy city on the river really be so arrogant as to call itself an "Athens." Though its fate was clearly sealed, Lexington refused to surrender without a fight, and for more than a century the rivalry between the two Kentucky towns has been noticeable, if not heated, at times.

Louisville was rollicking and commercial. Its river brought not only commerce but a decided flavor to its history. Its businessmen, newspaper editors, and steamboat captains looked southward and to the west for customers. With foundries, breweries, distilleries, packing houses, and brokers of all sorts of goods the people soon had the money in hand to build libraries, schools, theatres, and universities. Nearly every actor who appeared in America visited the Louisville theatres, and every traveler who reached the Ohio Valley stopped there to visit, to criticize, and to make copious notes of what he saw. Louisville quickly became a part of the heart throb of material America. It left the lavish rural hospitality, the traditions, and the nostalgia to Lexington while it eyed the future.

VII

The Stranger Within

Thomas Walker and Christopher Gist were travelers representing land companies, who came to Kentucky in the middle of the eighteenth century to locate baronial tracts and to write seductive descriptions of their adventures. These visitors opened both ends of the "grand tour," a route which in later years was traveled by almost every foreigner who came to see what Americans were up to. They plodded up and down the Wilderness Road or drifted down the Ohio from Pittsburgh or came by keelboat up the Mississippi from New Orleans. In time a motley procession of visitors passed through Kentucky. In its ranks were land and emigrant agents, wandering scientists, quacks and mountebanks, companies of actors, social and political reformers, speculators, dollar-inspired lecturers, soldiers, preachers, peddlers, lawyers, and gamblers. To the first wave of visitors Kentucky was back country where the great American democratic experiment was being tested in primitive surroundings. Almost every newcomer noted that he could have done a better job than the Kentuckians, but he was willing to leave to them the grubby task of getting on.

Many in this swarm of journal-writing visitors came frankly to prepare prospectuses to attract emigrants. In recent years some historians have read into these accounts implications that Kentuckians themselves believed they lived in a natural paradise, or in a river- and mountain-bound Eden. Land salesmen have always sought to create idyllic images, and in Kentucky they worked at their jobs. Setting out downstream from Pittsburgh, or climbing through the eastern highland rim, early emigrant and transient alike sensed they were cutting themselves off from the civilized world. Inside this landlocked empire they could turn savage or revolt against established authority as they chose. Here was a crucible for the eighteenth-century American concept of personal freedom. Would the bond of states expand to include the western fringe, or would the Union be stifled in space? For a long time Kentucky was the West, and its struggle to survive guided other territories. This was the core of political interest on the Kentucky frontier. How would a primitive community respond to established political ideas?

Socially Kentucky was a vast spawning ground for new forms of society and new human types. The frontier rowdy and the land-enriched patrician both reacted in kind to the promise of the land. Some appeared no better, if not worse, than wild Indians, while others adapted quickly to new conditions and in time bent conditions to their wills. The harshness of frontier environment was quickly softened, and a rising local aristocracy, founded largely on fertile acres, appeared which had no specific anchorage east of the mountains. Many a penniless emigrant who fled the economic slavery imposed by exhausted soils in Virginia soon found himself a man of substance in Kentucky. In quick order he was able to make pretensions to ways of a good life.

Transfers of basic institutions were made from the East. Moved intact were home, church, school, and community. The very figure of frontier advance was that of a trail-weary family lugging the makings of a home across the mountains on pack horse or drifting them downstream aboard a flatboat. With them they brought spinning wheels, carpenter tools, plantings of field and garden seeds, trail herds of milk cows, sheep, hogs, and fowls. There was no such thing as an unyielding nature in the face of such group determination. A young yeoman and his plucky bride comprised a mighty striking force which ensured perseverance of the home. Annual family increases encouraged the organization of churches, schools, and even counties.

Both visitor and native often mistook the forms of society for the basic implications of democracy itself. There was less false modesty in relationships among the sexes than in the older settled parts where more spacious and commodious homes encouraged more formal social intercourse. Men and women were often described as undressing and dressing in the presence of each other in cramped cabin common rooms without doing violence to rugged modesty or resorting to promiscuity. Acceptance of the stranger at the door was an expression of genuine hospitality without offering assurances of either sophistication or refinement. The stranger was crowded in at the table to partake of whatever came from the pot, and he was bedded down on the floor amidst a host of tossing children. This kind of hospitality was from its beginning a Kentucky pride. Kentuckians have often extended themselves to take in company when there was scarcely enough food or floor space to go around.

For some the hard years of pioneering were relatively short, while others endured hardship for generations. By the harvest time of the third crop of corn some people were able to provide comforts and refinements. As families became more secure, their thoughts turned to their places of origin. Revolutionary veterans flocked to Kentucky in droves to claim Virginia's land bounty in lieu of devaluated scrip or of no pay at all. These patriots constituted a kind of aristocracy. Behind them was a Maryland, Virginia, or Carolina background. Men left native hearthstones and ancestral graves behind to be overrun by undergrowth. In time their descendants retraced their steps to hunt for ancestors. They mauled paths through weeds and briers to locate moss-covered stones, not out of filial reverence but to gather fragments of self-glorifying genealogical data. For a Kentuckian ancestral origin in Virginia is linkage with nobility.

Before the end of the Virginia period social distinctions were visible in that knobby democratic Eden west of the mountains. That so many Kentucky immigrants came from Virginia was indicative of the social transfer made by pioneers. Virginia possessed a proud background even if many plodding immigrants did not. Mountain, Bluegrass, Pennyroyal, and Purchase, all alike cherished an Old Dominion heritage. Seldom if ever did a rising Kentucky gentry bid for social distinction on its own accomplishments or on its Kentucky background alone. However proud the people were of Kentucky, there was more distinction to one's having originated in an older state.

Kentucky quickly became more than a struggling frontier community striving to achieve social maturity, or the first tier of American backwoods hastening the process of independent statehood and economic security. Here early the foundation was laid for one of the most intensely rural societies in America. The Kentucky dream was not particularly made of growing urban communities and the rise of a commercially minded population. It was of a prospering agrarian condition of life which would make changes, if any, within the restrictive confines of farm-country land. This was a condition of life which impressed most visitors to the state. Life went at an everyday pace—with the joyful and sorrowful events of localities filling the thoughts of the people.

Because of its backwoods origin, its rising flood of immigrants, intense rurality, and proximity to the arterial river system, Kentucky developed a variegated public character. Simple landbound yeomen whose sources of information about the outside world were severely limited questioned travelers on every subject that came to mind. They frequently bored them with their incessant questioning, but the persistence of their queries was equaled by a desire to garner information. In return they willingly answered visitors' questions which often were as numerous and ridiculous as those asked by natives. But not all Kentuckians were quizzing bores. There were merchants, prosperous farmers, professional men, and ministers who were more sophisticated but less colorful in manner. Almost the first literate visitor to Kentucky detected the differences in personalities. He spotted the braggart and bully in every crowd, many of them rivermen who tugged at oar and tiller on long journeys and who drank bad liquor and fought one another for relaxation. Wherever a traveler stopped at a river landing he was surrounded by these characters. For many the first Kentuckians they saw and the ones they remembered longest were rowdies. They were the "Kentucks" of many a travel journal and the butt of humorous backwoods stories. They were natural men who found freedom not in the great forests and on cheap lands but on the rivers aboard produce-laden flatboats and later about steamboat woodyards and landings.

Kentucky was a natural wonderland. Nature was prodigal everywhere in Kentucky. Its mountains alone grew large varieties of trees and shrubs. The swamps of the Purchase and the hills of the Pennyroyal and Bluegrass were covered with trees and plants in profusion. Naturalists came to view woods, barrens, and savannas. Botanists listed plants and took measurements of giant trees which had stood for a century or more. Even so unscientific an observer as Madam Stuart-Wortley listed trees and plants she spotted between Louisville and the Mammoth Cave. Scientists described botanical specimens ranging from the lowly and ill-smelling Jamestown or hog-lot jimson weed to the rare cove-grown ginseng.

Woods and streams abounded with game and fish. Settlers drove away the buffalo almost at the raising of the first cabins, but there were still enough animals to make up for its disappearance. F. A. Michaux, John James Audubon, Constantine Rafinesque, Alexander Wilson, all left notes which documented many boastful accounts of hunters and speculators. Audubon traveled widely in Kentucky, and his *Delineations of American Life* and other writings contain rich accounts of social life there. Not only did Audubon recount his own activities, he noted those of other scientists and pioneers. Daniel Boone appeared in more convincing human terms in Audubon's notes than in Filson's "autobiography." Audubon was ever more naturalist than merchant and miller. It was almost a century before the people of Henderson recognized that the indolent miller and storekeeper who had lived briefly in their community was indeed an artist.

From the sophisticated East came Philadelphian Alexander Wilson to look down his nose on his more natural brethren beyond the mountains and to open a feud with Audubon. His visit to Kentucky was made ostensibly to study birds, but much of what he recorded in his journal dealt with the foibles of backwoods society. He provoked an argument which endured for several years. Every time an editor wanted to get mad he read anew the Philadelphian's descriptions of Kentucky. He was whimsical in describing Lexington and its people, but his deepest cut was a claim that he saw squirrels slashed into quarters and offered for sale in the market house. In the ensuing angry outbursts he offered to retract this libel on the land of plenty by raising his ante to half squirrels.

Naturalists wrote vivid descriptions of the flights of passenger pigeons. These gregarious birds flocked to roosting grounds by hundreds of thousands. Tree limbs cracked under their weight, and guano accumulated in mounds under the roosts. When flocks flew out to feed in the mornings they left behind hundreds of birds that had been crushed to death in nightly scramble for roosting purchase.

John Filson was essentially a visitor despite the fact that he came west to organize an academy and to locate land. In New Jersey he had caught the western fever, and his *Kentucke* is little more than a prospectus offering the wonders of an Eden in the still-unclaimed portions of the Kentucky domain. Where Filson left off in the roistering years of pioneering, Gilbert Imlay, another Jerseyman, took up. Imlay, rascal and adventurer, came to Kentucky in those years when its people were agitated over separating their district from Virginia and forming an independent state. To Europeans, if they thought on the subject at all, the creation of a political state in the wild western country was preposterous, but even more so was the fact that sweaty backwoodsmen would undertake the organization of a traditional Anglo-type government.

In March, 1788, Imlay embarked upon a five-day journey down-river from Pittsburgh. The upper Ohio was still in the unrelenting clutches of winter. The woods were barren and there was little promise that trees would ever bud again. Five hundred miles southward advancing spring wrought its recurring miracle of life. He wrote an English friend (maybe his letters were actually written in England instead of Kentucky) that "Everything assumes a dignity and splendor I have never seen in any part of the world." At that moment he claimed to be drifting beneath the rolling slopes which confined the impulsive Ohio within its course. Here boatmen did not clear one leaf-shrouded point until another shouldered its way down to the water's edge. From a canoe the woods seemed to pile up in vast slanting troughs which magnified in full focus even the slightest show of color. The surface of the cold green river reflected the first burst of buds in such a way as to provoke Imlay to exclaim:

You ascend a considerable distance from the shore of the Ohio, when you suppose you had arrived at the summit of a mountain, you find yourself upon an extensive level. Here an eternal verdure reigns, and the azure heavens, produces, in this prolific soil, an early maturity which is truly astonishing. Flowers full and perfect, as if they had been cultivated by the hand of a florist, and with all the variegated charms which colour and nature can produce, here in the lap of elegance and beauty, decorate the smiling groves. Soft zephyrs gently breathe on sweets, and the inhaled air gives a voluptuous glow of health and vigour, that seems to ravish the intoxicated senses. The sweet songsters of the forests appear to feel the influence of this gentle clime, and, in more soft and modulated tones, warble their tender notes in unison with love and nature. Everything here gives delight; and, in that mild effulgence which beams around us, we feel a glow of gratitude for the revelation which our all bountiful creator has bestowed upon us in the creation; but which has been contaminated by the base alloy of meanness, the concomitant of European education, and what is more lamentable is, that is the consequence of your very laws and government.

This was not the first oration delivered on the beauties of virginal Kentucky, but it did credit to the orator and inspired other outpourings on the subject. Imlay's outburst must have caused Englishmen to believe that the land along the Ohio was a subtropical paradise where government and education would indeed be unnecessary. There were nevertheless practical considerations in Imlay's descriptions. He knew that men went west to possess the land, and this they could do at minimum investment. It is not difficult to imagine an Englishman unbridling his imagination when he read that the land would produce 75 bushels of corn an acre the first year, half of which could be shipped downriver to market as net profit. The second year he could expect 100 bushels, and from the third crop he harvested 125 bushels. In the meantime the farmer would have paid for his land, horses, cattle, lived well, and had money in his pocket. Even more cheerful was the fact that taxes on property did not exceed five shillings.

If the reader was not swept off his feet by Imlay's unreliable ode to the yeoman landholder, his mouth no doubt watered when he read the nominal prices of hams, bacon, beef, dried tongue, buffalo meat, chickens, ducks, geese, turkeys, butter, and cheese. Perch in the local streams ranged from five to twelve pounds, trout eight to thirty pounds, and soft-shell turtles could be caught in every creek.

These were vivid descriptions of the bounties of the land, but Imlay was inhibited by neither fact nor direct association with Kentucky when he wrote. He was vague in his descriptions of people. Movements of immigrants down the Ohio or coming overland through Cumberland Gap were blurred. He was interested in feeding this population stream but he knew that realistic descriptions of hard labor and the perseverance necessary to claim corn patch and cabin would not be attractive. He failed to discuss the loud wails of protest which arose in Richmond in settlers' petitions asking for everything from the right to build a milldam across a navigable stream to that of taking the fight to Shawnee Indian villages along the Miami.

Imlay admittedly was a romanticist, and to his critics he was faker and bounder. After him came less eloquent visitors, among whom was Harry Toulmin, a London bookseller and apostle of Joseph

Priestley. This philosophical Englishman followed Priestley to America partly to converse with Thomas Jefferson, James Madison, and other leaders of the new republicanism. Once here he moved on to the frontier to enjoy idyllic eighteenth-century liberty and personal freedom. Here in the wilderness, unspoiled by time and tradition, men were creating a new state and helping to lay the foundations for an empire. Toulmin was highly perceptive of social and political institutions, and he was immediately aware of the fermentation taking place on the trans-Appalachian frontier. A rising flow of immigrants not only enlarged Kentucky's population but brought social fusion of national groups from which a basic Kentucky type sprang. In a population doubling every fifteen years and where youthful marriages were commonplace it was only natural that older social barriers would be destroyed. Here democratization occurred at marriage altar and cabin hearthside. Some years 10,000 new people arrived in Kentucky, and before 1792 there were never fewer than 4,000 newcomers.

Like his predecessors, J. P. Brissot de Warville and William Bartram, Harry Toulmin hoped to see the Kentucky "Eden" converted into a land overflowing with English yeomen. Here they would establish happy families and accumulate fortunes from selling half their annual corn crops at a profit. Think of the dietary fare mutton-eating Englishmen could enjoy in a country where meat was 2 pence a pound, and fowls were 4, 6 and 8 apiece. All a downtrodden Britisher had to do in Toulmin's eyes was to transport his family out to Kentucky and fetch along enough coffee and tea to satisfy his appetite.

Missing from these accounts, if the authors even knew it, was a sense of what it meant to swing an ax all day in heavy timber, to chop, notch, and "snake" up enough logs to build a cabin, or to scratch a crop of corn out of a root-bound new ground. Their observations were purely academic when it came to these arduous matters. Too often people were treated in terms of statistics extracted from Jedediah Morse's *Geography* or as political abstractions gathered from Thomas Jefferson's *Notes on Virginia*.

Occasionally a native son took a look at life around him. Major Erkuries Beatty, paymaster for the western army of the United States, viewed Kentucky society from the perspective of a soldier. In a brief tour of duty at the Falls of the Ohio he had an opporunity to savor the stirring life of the frontier in its most natural forms. Monotony of backwoods drudgery was broken with barbecues, dances, and fights. An officer in Harmar's command became involved with a Virginia gouger who had a reputation for mayhem. He was forced to fight this bully barehanded and no holds barred, knowing that he might be maimed. These ruffians lived in Imlay and Toulmin's western paradise but they took no notice of them.

In the upheaval of the French Revolution an agent of Republican France, F. A. Michaux, came west to catalogue botanical specimens, but more precisely to seek support for his political cause. A decade later his son François retraced his father's steps. He came down the Ohio from Pittsburgh, but he viewed the scenery more as scientist than romanticist. His was not a mission of writing a real-estate tract or spinning a seductive web to ensnare gullible emigrants. Unlike his fellow French travelers, Michaux described both country and people without dwelling endlessly on history and geography. He arrived at the mouth of Limestone Creek on April 1, 1802, and instead of describing the long bluffs with their great rolls of vegetation and forest just then coming into leaf and bloom, he noted the lowly mullein and vile-smelling Jamestown weed. The weather was hot and a thousand miles lay between him and Charleston, South Carolina, his destination.

Along the Kentucky shore Michaux saw the backwoodsmen who reaped greater reward from the chase than from cornfield and meadow. Their cabins had breath-taking views of the river, but their mode of living was no better than that of the Shawnees to the north. Doors were opened hospitably to travelers, but visitors competed with numerous children and dogs for corn bread and smoked bacon, and for pallet space at night. The simplicity of rivermen and migrating families appealed to the republican Frenchman. The people he saw moved westward with great expectancy. Somewhere ahead of them was a fresh chance and hope for a better fortune. They asked no odds of the country and proposed to give no quarter to hardship. This was the raw moving frontier. By 1802 life about Lexington had settled into the firmer pattern of a fixed society. There people were aping those of Baltimore, Philadelphia, and St. Louis where Bluegrass merchants did business.

Where Michaux was gentle with backwoodsmen, Thomas Ashe, Irishman, was critical. He regarded the Kentuckians as "fallen people living atop an older Indian civilization over which they had made little improvement." He came west in search of anthropological and archaeological materials. Some said he came on a grand thieving mission. He was accused of filching mastodon bones dug at the Big Bone Lick from the famous Dr. William Goforth in Cincinnati, and appeared to be ready to do the same thing in Kentucky. He informed his readers at the outset that he intended to correct errors committed by former travelers, and in some ways he did. He, however, made greater blunders, and travelers for the next three decades were correcting Ashe.

Whatever the indiscretions of Thomas Ashe, his descriptions of the land are little short of being poetic. No Kentuckian could have found fault with him on this score. Too, no known traveler left so gripping an account of a descent into the maelstrom of the Ohio Falls. Edgar Allan Poe improved little on this adventurer's journey through the furiously churning water of the great breaks opposite Louisville. Fortunately there are many contemporary travel accounts against which to check the "great libeler of Kentucky."

Thomas Ashe had hardly blotted the ink on his last written observation before Christian Schultz, a New Yorker (*Travels on an Inland Voyage,* 1810), and Fortesque Cuming (*Sketches of a Tour to the Western Country,* 1810) appeared in the West. Schultz heard two Kentucky boatmen near Natchez excoriate each other in boisterous language. One called himself a half-horse and half-alligator, while the other boasted he was a snapping turtle born to stir up a fuss. This was perhaps the earliest recorded note of this wild boast which Kentuckians were never allowed to forget.

Where Schultz was impressed with the Kentuckians' loud boasts, their humor captivated the hurrying Captain Thomas Hamilton. Landing momentarily in Louisville, this pompous visitor proclaimed:

The Kentuckians may be called the Irish of America. They have all the levity of character, that subjection of the moral to the convivial, that buoyance of spirit, that jocular ferocity, that ardour, both of attachment and of hatred, which distinguish the natives of the Emerald Isle. The Kentuckians are the only Americans who can understand a joke. There is a kind of native humor about them which is very pleasant; and, I must say, that several Kentucky gentlemen were among the most agreeable companions, with whom I had the good fortune to become acquainted during my tour.

In his haste Captain Hamilton did not spend as much time with the Kentuckians as did that dour emigrant agent Henry Bradshaw Fearon. Fearon took on faith their warmth of character and learned that "they drink a great deal, and gamble a great deal." They were restless people, walking the floors of tavern common rooms at all hours of the day smoking strong cigars and mumbling to themselves. Their eating habits were enough to startle anybody born beyond the Atlantic. "At half past seven," he wrote, "the first bell rings; breakfast is then set, the dining room is unlocked, a general rush commences, and some activity, as well as dexterity, is essentially necessary to obtain a seat at table. A boy, as clerk, attends to take down the names in order that when bills are settled no improper deduction should be made. The breakfast consists of a profuse supply of fish, flesh, and fowl, which is consumed with a rapidity truly extraordinary; often before I had finished my first cup of tea, the room which when I had commenced was crowded to suffocation, had become nearly empty."

Fearon thought Kentucky land was good, but like most of his countrymen he abhorred slavery. To him it would be almost impossible for emigrants to compete with such a system of involuntary labor. Across the river in Indiana and Illinois the frontier was still in a raw stage, but even so there were no slaves.

With regularity other visitors came to Kentucky. Among them were Englishmen, Scotsmen, Frenchmen, Irishmen, and occasionally a New Englander. They all came this way with ready notebook and fixed opinions. Sitting in Buckingham Palace on a humid June day in 1839, one of this throng, the Honorable Charles Augustus Murray, a Scotsman, inscribed the text of his American travels to young Queen Victoria. In veiled language he all but confirmed the Queen's belief that the American states were the outskirts of the British Empire. One of his objectives was to describe for her what went on deep in her tenuous province south of the Ohio. In Cincinnati, Murray was certain he sensed a sharp contrast between Kentucky and Ohio. Ohio, a free state, was populated largely by New Englanders and Germans, both of whom had brought with them to the frontier pronounced culture patterns. Below the river Kentucky was slave territory and was "settled chiefly by the western Virginians, a wild high spirited, and somewhat rough tribe of hunters." There were sharp differences between the soils of the two states. Kentucky soils varied sharply, and large areas were still forest-bound so no one knew for certain the quality of the lands.

Ohio society was stolid in its plain republicanism. The people were quiet in demeanor and industrious in habit. Kentucky republicanism was expressed vigorously in news story and editorial. Often the authors of these published pieces involved themselves in controversies and threats of physical retaliation. Kentuckians seemed to Her Majesty's observer to have greater faults and greater merits than their neighbors. Their moral features were distinctive, they were frank, hospitable, rough, overbearing, and inclined to bragging. They had a strange affinity for gambling and horse racing, caused partly, Murray believed, by close association with the river.

The Scotsman was startled to see men carrying "dirk knives," and he said he saw well-dressed citizens picking their teeth with these murderous blades. In conversation Kentuckians were constantly opening and closing their knives or whetting them on their boots. He questioned the chivalry of these men, especially after he had witnessed rough-and-tumble fighting in which he said eyes were gouged and ears were bitten off. Even worse, spectators stood by and encouraged the antagonists to disfigure each other.

Louisville was a bustling city where the Falls and the Canal halted river traffic. Down steamboat gangplanks came gaunt Southerners fleeing miasmatic vapors of fever-ridden swamps, long-fingered gamblers, rowdy boatmen, countrymen, merchants, and politicans. A polyglot throng roamed the streets. At the race course (a predecessor of Churchill Downs) a boisterous crowd whooped and shouted, placed bets, and kicked up a general commotion. Their conduct provoked Murray to write that "indeed, the swearing of some of the lower orders in the West, especially among the horsetraders and gamblers, would shock ears accustomed to the language of Billingsgate or a London gin shop, so full is it of blasphemy."

Queen Victoria's subject nevertheless found Louisville a lively place, but like its neighbors it was miserably lighted and paved "at present." More to his taste was the open farming country between Louisville and Lexington. In the latter city the visitor was transported back to England by farmers Henry Clay, his son-in-law James Erwin, and General Isaac Shelby. They showed him livestock and pastures which were reminiscent of Suffolk and Scotland.

Later Charles Dickens interrupted a steamboat journey to spend a night at the Galt House in Louisville. He said the hotel was good, and there were two pigs in the street—hardly an impressive report. Harriet Martineau was a guest at Ashland for an extended period and was in Louisville, where she too saw pigs in the streets. All foreigners were startled by the violence they either claimed to witness or read about in the papers. They compared unfavorably a state of backwoods and slave origin with the free states across the Ohio stocked by sturdy New Englanders and freedom-loving Germans. They saw two cultures developing alongside each other in which one was threatened with moral decay, rowdiness, and violence. Slavery would in time, said the visitors, disrupt the democratic institutions of the land.

Travelers imagined many things they could not have known about Kentucky. From the moment most of them sighted the shore of the state along the Ohio they began contrasting conditions north and south of the river. Perhaps one of the most serious-minded of the slave sleuths to come along was the Scotsman James Stirling. He arrived in 1856 to see firsthand what life in the slave states was like. His remarks, while far less dramatic than Mrs. Stowe's of a few years before, were equally pointed. He not only viewed slavery adversely, he sized up the people. Because Kentucky was settled in a semimilitary fashion, he said, and by a militant people they were a "taller, larger race of men than any other in America. . . . I found this corroborated by my own observation. The men are not only of a larger size, but have a franker, jollier, freer old English look, than most Americans." He erroneously believed this resulted because only men of great physical endurance came to Kentucky. "Here," he said, "only men of vigorous constitution and hardy frame could find a continuing city; the weak, if by chance, they came, must soon be cut off: a powerful winnowing would leave only the strong. And it is the descendants of these strong bold men whom we now find in the fields of Kentucky, six feet upwards, with broad athletic frames, and full, broad, open faces; as different as can be from the sharp, lean, furrowed physiognomy of the eastern states." The traveler found society backward, however. "The moment you cross the Ohio you are painfully struck with the contrast, and as you advance into the interior things get worse and worse. You miss entirely that progress which is the charm of the East and the wonder of the West." The presence of slavery no doubt made the difference. Most travelers agreed with this point of view. They believed Kentucky was caught in a bind from which it could escape only by freeing its slaves and patterning its mode of life after that in the free states.

These visitors arrived at a solution of Kentucky's social problems without truly understanding the history and temperament of the people whom they visited. Some of their observations revealed clearly the Kentuckian's genius for covering up his real situation to strangers. To make Kentucky in the images of Ohio and Indiana was a spiritual impossibility, yet this is what the later travelers thought should be done.

VIII

On the Face of the Land

Early Kentucky pioneers came into the state over game trails or mashed down luscious undergrowth and made trails of their own. They knew nothing of improved roads, and cared even less. So long as a horse could stand up under a pack of goods, why should a man in search of land stop to bother about roads? When New Orleans silver became available for buying wheeled vehicles there would be time to think about roads. But what of the roads? A farmer had his farming to do, and he had no time to build roads! Let the legislature do that, but let it build roads without spending much of the peoples' money!

Early Kentucky legislatures were composed for the most part of frugal shortsighted human beings. No official possessed the magic power to decree the building of a road and have it done. An early general assembly did commission hardy old Daniel Boone to see what he could do once again with the ancient Wilderness Trail. But Boone, who blazed the trail originally, was little better at the magic art of road building than was the legislature. There were two hundred miles or more of main road and laterals which could be called public roads, and the general assembly provided no more than enough money to cut the low-hanging limbs and to locate the shallowest fording places across the river.

To appropriate enough money from the state treasury would displease the taxpayers, and politically sensitive legislators disliked displeasing voting taxpayers. Kentucky needed roads, as everyone could see, but how to get them painlessly was an unanswerable question. Older states had organized toll companies when they could not answer this same question. Possibly this was an answer to Kentucky's transportation riddle. A public wagon road was provided in 1792 along a part of the old wilderness route which was known as Shelby's Wagon Road. It ran from Mount Vernon to Richmond. This was a fine official gesture, but the road itself was never more than a rocky and muddy nightmare. The need for bridges and grades was great, but the cost was too high. No one was experienced in road building. There were no engineers, and no machines, not even the most primitive plows and scrapes. No one had built a bridge in Kentucky despite the fact that an abundance of broken stone from which to build pilasters and arches lay in easy reach of every stream crossing. The traveler still had to cross at fording places and to be constantly on guard that he did not drive off into deep water and drown.

Legislators, glad to get around the necessity of injuring the sensitive feelings of their highly respected constituents, shifted the burden of highway construction onto private shoulders. Turnpike rights were awarded local capitalists with the instruction that they build roads for the people. This seemed to be an equitable way to build roads. Let the man who wanted to travel on good roads pay for the right. Let him pay for this privilege in the same way he bought the shirt on his back or the saddle on his horse.

For several decades it seemed that in accepting the toll-road plan the legislators were more nearly right than is customary with assemblymen who spend much of their time escaping their responsibilities. Toll roads, in a highly limited way, were successful.

Every session of the legislature received requests for the organization of new roads and the extension of old ones. A massive amount of legislation was passed in time, but new laws did no more than perpetuate the stultifying effects of the old ones. No ingenious citizen or legislator proposed a revolutionary piece of legislation which would lift Kentucky out of the mud. Drovers going to market with livestock paid one quarter cent per head for pigs, sheep, goats, mules, and cattle at each gate. Ministers of the gospel astride bony nags, widows sending their corn to mill, funerals, and sometimes devout church-goers had the pikes lifted gratis. Freight wagons, farmers' rigs, fine carriages, horsemen, and stage coaches paid to go under the pike poles, and only in some cases were the rates reasonable and the roads passable in the same bargain. Where exorbitant charges were made on poor roads, cries were loud against the "grasping" toll companies. Toll company officials argued that the people could haul their products to the river, they could get to church, attend an election or a neighbor's funeral without too much bother. After all, the toll roads were in a large degree community assets.

Statistically Kentucky in 1860 was shown to have had a relatively extensive mileage of roads. In the Bluegrass there was a short length of Macadam highway, one of the first in America. Some of the more heavily used toll roads were of fair construction. But between 1862 and 1865 a condition was to arise which caused deep consternation for both public and toll-road management. In the movement of Civil War troops over the roads both Confederate and Union armies mauled the surface to pieces. Bragg brought his army up from Tennessee, and his endless wagon train destroyed roads wherever it went, to say nothing of its rolling roughshod through toll gates causing an appreciable financial loss to toll companies. Union forces did the same thing, except that they were in the state almost three years and in this time they all but obliterated roads in sections without paying for the damage. There was no way by which offended road proprietors could collect tolls due them from either the Confederate or the United States government. Certainly neither the United States Congress nor the Kentucky legislature was willing to make appropriations to restore the roads.

There were many drawbacks to the private toll system: toll companies took over only profitable roads. The sparsely settled backcountry had to get highways as best it could. Ordinarily legislators refused to listen to the wailings of badly scattered and isolated constituents. Community cooperative roads were built. Men along the route subscribed for shares of stock and gave their indifferent labor to support the plan in order to open the way to town and to market. In years to come, however, stockholders in the community cooperatives died and at public sales of estates large blocks of highway shares were bought for a song by scheming speculators. Many community roads fell under the control of one or two owners. Rates of toll were increased while roadbeds went to pieces. This became a matter of grave public concern. Gaunt farmers began to rebel at the prospect of jolting to market with half-loaded wagons and at having to pay exorbitant privilege fees in doing so.

In Anderson and Washington counties, patrons of worn-out roads were angry. Roads were poor, and users felt they could scarcely get their wagons and teams from Glensborough to Lawrenceburg, for instance, without being robbed by the tollkeepers. Money was scarce, so scarce in fact that in 1890 a farmer often debated whether to buy a nickel orange from the scanty stock of the country store at Glensborough or wait until he could get to Lawrenceburg where a range of choices was greater, and possibly where he could get a bigger one for the same money. To pay more than fifteen cents for a meal was to indulge in an outrageous and sinful extravagance.

There was an old custom, which was really a bit of common law, that a man going to mill in some communities could pass the "gates" free. Anderson County farmers began riding to Lawrenceburg astride bags of bran. But even this was no answer to the oppression of grasping companies. Too, it did something to Kentucky pride to sit astride a bag of bran and know that it was a lie done up in cotton twill. Why not tear down the gates and be done with hypocrisy? What was the matter with the legislature? The days of Jacksonian frowning upon public internal improvement were past. The people needed and were going to have free roads. They wanted to drive out the annoying gates and gatekeepers and go to market like decent free men. Tollkeepers themselves aroused animosity, for many of them had come into their jobs because of their earlier connection with the roads. For the most part they were rock pounding "turnpike" Irish who had been elevated to the position of toll collectors.

One example is enough to indicate how public opinion was aroused in the 1890's to overthrow the toll-road system in several Kentucky counties. At Glensborough, Tom and Ezra Gillis were young community leaders and schoolteachers. These boys were public-spirited citizens, and, as the Glensborough wisemen said, they had "long heads." Tom and Ezra appreciated the significance of the transportation problem which confronted their neighbors. All their lives they had lived in Anderson County, and some of their forebears were members of the famous Salt River Tigers who fought so courageously in the Mexican War. They had definite ideas about starting a move to abolish the gates. Why not have their pupils debate the question, and the idea might eventually spread to the whole state? The Gillis boys were honest, frugal men and they did not wish to teach a doctrine of force, nor did they think they would have to if public opinion was aroused.

The brothers set their neighbors' children to work on the question of free versus toll roads. It was easy to find arguments for free roads but difficult to answer the negative's questions as to how the roads could be built and maintained. Roads, said the affirmative, were state governmental responsibilities. Affirmative speakers made the idea of free roads sound so attractive that plans were made to abolish the toll gates one way or another.

Kentuckians had always been independent, proud people and if they were stimulated to action they generally got what they wanted. Farmers of Washington and Anderson counties were no exception to the rule. They had made up their minds that the gates were coming down, and the best way to bring them down permanently was to intimidate the gatekeepers.

Armed and masked men rode out of Washington County early in April, 1897, and forced frightened gatekeepers to chop their pikes (poles) into pieces. Keepers were warned not to bar the roads again, and if the pikes were restored there would be urgent need for buggy whips tapered off with rawhide crackers, warm buckets of tar, and goose-feather pillows.

Vigorous resistance to the toll roads spread like wildfire. While enraged Washington County yeomen destroyed gates and issued dire warnings to shivering Irish tollkeepers, Anderson County raiders stormed against the lordly keepers of the pikes. They masked their faces, mounted themselves on their best horses, and galloped up to gatehouses cursing the attendants. They forced shivering Irishmen to crawl out of bed, come out on brisk April nights, and to destroy the gates under the drawn guns of their tormentors. County officials were as badly frightened as were the benighted toll collectors. When men rode with their faces masked, sheriffs and constables were at a loss to know how to stop the marauders. A stern circuit judge in Anderson commanded the sheriff to fetch the raiders into his court. Since the circuit judge is lord of all he surveys in Kentucky county affairs, the sheriff had to capture somebody. When court convened in December he had on hand a hundred witnesses, who militantly favored the idea of free roads. One of these was old Uncle Hiram Bucy, an ex-slave, who could identify the raiders, but Uncle Hiram had no fundamental objection to the even tenor of his present life. He had no desire to become involved with ghostly tollgate raiders and their infernal mixture of tar, pistols, buggy whips, and feathers. When a juryman asked him if he knew any of the raiders, the old man became hysterical and shouted, "No, sir, I don't know nothing," and bending low for emphasis he rasped, *"My God, I don't know nothing!"*

Bench warrants were issued for six suspects, and Sheriff Oliver brought before the court John Walker, William Bond, Cabell McKee, Alonzo Casey, Buckner McKee, and Burt Casey. Two of these men were wealthy and they could go bond for the other four. They were charged with destruction of property and masking for purposes of intimidation; but after all, most of the people in the courtroom hoped they would go free. They wished this even after Judge Carroll, in his charge to the jury, had called upon them in stirring terms to deal with the culprits with sternness. The judge had likewise appealed to the press and the pulpit to help him wage war against mask-wearing yeomen who were driving the toll companies out of business.

The Anderson County court failed to convict the raiders. Farmers needed free roads and they were going to have them if they had to resort to the use of fire and brimstone. After all, farmers were voters and could head off Judge Carroll and his preachers and newspapermen who opposed direct action.

Once the raids had begun, gates were destroyed over a wide area. In Mercer County people were likewise agitated over the shameless profiteering of the road companies. They were served poor roads in return for high tolls. Now was the time to strike! On the night of April 4, 1897, night riders raided the Cornishville gatehouse. The gatekeeper was the grizzled Irishman Cal Atkinson, who attempted to defend his besieged family with his shotgun. The raiders were too numerous for the stubborn Cal, and within a few moments his house was surrounded. There were raiders hammering away at both front and back doors, and when they met with resistance the mob became excited. Cries for drastic action were loud, and one trigger-happy raider emptied his shotgun into the Irishman's face. The gang rushed on and left their victim, with sight in one eye destroyed, to suffer the agony of death in the arms of a frantic wife.

News of the Cornishville raid traveled fast. Gatekeepers all over central and northern Kentucky grew panicky lest they should be the next victims. One tollkeeper's wife said that she couldn't go to sleep at night for fear the raiders would come and burn the house over their heads and shoot her husband. This same wife cried out in her anguish that "lawless men seem desirous of overturning all law and order. We do not know what minute our property will be destroyed and we live in dread every hour of the day and night. I do not know what can be done, for our relief, but it seems to me the legislature at Frankfort ought to take some action whereby the governor could legally investigate the outrages against the citizens of the commonwealth and bring them to just punishment." The assembly in 1898 did pass an anti-tollgate raider law, but the raiders had to be caught first, and on this point the law was silent. Every morning newspapers published stories of new raids; at Maysville, Georgetown, and Owingsville the raiders were busy. Near Harrodsburg, gatekeeper Ericson was forced at the point of drawn pistols held by masked raiders to stand in the door of his burning house with his screaming children huddled about his knees until the structure was ready to fall in. Six other gates were leveled to the ground that night, and each succeeding night brought stories of other gates having been destroyed.

Owners of the roads and gates swore they would keep them open at all costs. This was an idle boast, however, for ninety-one raiders galloped across the Kentucky River and, just beyond the famous old Wernwag Bridge at Camp Nelson, made keeper Whitaker fetch out his ax and slash his pole into the customary pile of "stovewood." That same night other raiders made half-naked gatekeepers hack down several gates on the Elkhorn Creek in Scott County. Two widows were deprived of their means of livelihood, and several prominent neighbors were accused of the crime, but the court took no action. A hundred men stormed into Lancaster on the night of May 29 and destroyed four gates. They left instructions that no more toll was to be collected, and they were positive in their note scribbled on dirty, cheap school tablet paper that "they meant what they said."

Other gatekeepers were warned by letters and bunches of switches thrown on their porches that tollgates would no longer be tolerated. One ingenious agitator notified the "Toll Gate Keepers of Garrard County, Kentucky" that their days were numbered. A local detective named Welch was advised to make his estate over to an undertaker. Officials of the road were threatened with whippings, and a raid over the whole county was promised. Positive and picturesque notes asserted:

NOTICE TO GATEKEEPER
We ast you not to collect no more tole, you must
Not collect one cent if you do we are Going to Destroy

> your House with fire are Denamite So you must Not
> collect No more tole at all. We don't want to do this but
> we want a Free Road are agoing to have it, if we have
> to kill and burn up everything. Collect no more tole
> we mean what we say, so Fair warning to you.

A distraught people was on the warpath, and frequent raids seemed
to indicate that the irate authors of the threatening notes did mean
what they said. A fellow raider wrote the hard-boiled workhouse
supervisor, Thomas Durr, of Mercer County, a pointed note:

> Thomas Durr and William Schuman; We don't want no more
> toll collected. If you collect anymore will hang you
> we will wait on you in ten days. If you do not quit
> collecting toll, then hang.
>
> TOLLGATE RAIDERS

Durr, however, was a stubborn Irishman and refused to surrender
his lucrative post to the raiders, thus making a second warning necessary. This time the appeal was even more direct and specific:

> To the Honorable Thomas Durr: We don't want no more toll
> collected here. If you do (sic) look out for your neck,
> the board must take heed to this warning.
>
> MERCER COUNTY REGULATORS

These were ominous warnings, warnings that even Thomas Durr
could understand. He was reasonably certain that he would be killed
if he didn't give up his job as toll collector. Directors of the road were
less frightened than Thomas Durr and they hired two tramp printers,
Dick White and Jim Saunders, of Lexington to keep watch over the
gate. Raiders had destroyed the gatehouse, so a whiskey barrel was
planted on each side of the road and a pole rested across the heads.
The bold printers consented only to collect toll in the daylight.

At Harrodsburg the grand jury failed to make headway in its indictments. Prospective witnesses fled the county and the state, and
refused to be brought back. No one would admit that he knew who
the raiders were; in fact, members of the grand jury might have been
raiders for all the court knew. Crafty county officials refused to pay
guards for their services at the gates, and men were unwilling to stand
guard and take chances of being injured without pay. Courts became
useless instruments of protection; even some lawyers and judges be-

lieved the anti-tollgate raiders' law, passed by a frantic legislature, might be declared unconstitutional.

Active leadership in Kentucky faltered in those drab years 1880-1908. It failed largely because a baggy-pants political control throttled everything that even smelled of progress, and because this was the age in which the lost generation born in the Civil War came to maturity. A wave of conservatism and fear swept the state. Kentuckians shied away from taxation, on the one hand, and were ignorant of the advantages of good roads, on the other. Nevertheless, a faint impulse of progress stirred, and some people responded blindly to demands for better roads.

A better way to serve the people and to restore peace would be for the state to buy the tollgates and make the roads free. Permit a man to go to town with his wagonload of corn, or drive his buggy courting, or ride his horse where he pleased. Snatch the Kentucky highways free from the shrewd, scheming rascals who held the people in slavery to the pike poll and gatehouse. The county should buy the roads from the private companies, and where they could not buy them, build competing roads that would break the oppressors. For instance, the county could buy, at a reasonable price, the roads of old Billy Baldwin, "the turnpike king," from Maysville, or build "shun-pikes" and bankrupt him. County officials, like legislators, were slow to see the point, but before another year of raiding passed the roads in much of Kentucky were freed.

Like most militant and highhanded direct reforms, the misguided messengers of progress before the tollgates never stopped to think through their demands for free and better roads. This would mean new taxes and new political manipulations and self-seeking. A public roads authority functioning under the domination of courthouse rings produced luscious political plums, but slender results on the roads themselves. Thus it was, in a moment of violence, that Kentucky was directed along a new path of progress clogged by the usual political shackles.

Never before had such a boon of political favoritism been dropped into the hands of the courthouse rings as was the oversight of public roads. Voters could now not only be bought in larger numbers, they could be kept bought. It is doubtful that publicly maintained roads in this era were any better than they had been under private management. However, they bore the magic label of "free" at the moment of usage. Many "deserving" people shared in the fruits of road building and maintenance, or in the favorable location of new routes, and in other public favors.

A responsible Kentuckian penetrating the fog of political vaporings in 1900 would have realized that poor economic and social conditions were intimately associated with the fact that much of the state was hopelessly landbound. The rural fastness of western Kentucky or of the Appalachian Plateau was still unscored by public roads worthy of the name. Few Pennyroyal and Purchase farmers could go long distances to market. A few mountaineers could visit the "outside" by pitching downstream on the annual freshets aboard unruly log rafts. Everywhere about them were indelible signs of primitiveness and backwardness. Schools were few in number and unbelievably poor. Communities were terrorized by blood feuds, and human bodies were racked by parasites and disease.

All across Kentucky hundreds of streams wound back and forth across roads. Every river crossing promised a major tragedy to travelers. The Cumberland, Tennessee, Green, Barren, Kentucky, Licking, and Big Sandy remained unbridged in most places. Leaky manpowered ferries inched across these streams with great uncertainty of making a safe landing on the other side. A century and a quarter of human occupation of the country had brought few improvements in the roads, so few in fact that in many places travelers might well have believed the Indians still controlled the land.

Though tollgate raiders had stormed the countryside in the 1890's it was not until 1912 that something like a new day dawned in Kentucky. It was hard to detect the throb of change, but it beat nevertheless. At Frankfort a fumbling general assembly, that bastion of the *status quo,* was stirred as much by foggy memory of the tollgate raiders as by the vibrations of change. Public agitation in Kentucky, as well as in the whole South, had forced a desire for improved roads into the public consciousness. So little was known about organizing an acceptable public roads authority that there were no native sons with enough technical training or experience to make an effective beginning. Though automobiles were becoming more numerous on the roads, they were still curiosities. Perhaps no one in Kentucky realized that this mechanical toy would force a revolution in highway building and management in the state.

World War I swept Kentucky into the maelstrom of the roaring twentieth century. Never before had Kentuckians been called upon to transport heavy goods so far and so fast. Soaring tonnages of coal were gouged out of pits and thrust into hillsides, mounting piles of farm produce waited to be hustled off to feed armies of soldiers and workers. Even the people themselves scurried about Kentucky on defense errands. In all this frantic movement of goods and people it became clearer than ever that the state's highways were more adaptable to the use of George Washington's shivering troops before Valley Forge than to those of a modern nation engaged in a mechanized war in the twentieth century.

Four years of war wrought changes in isolated Kentucky. In 1918 no rational person doubted that the automobile had come to stay. Again legislators concerned themselves with public roads. This time progress was thrust upon them, and they thought in terms of connecting county seats and even of interstate roads. Fortunately gasoline could be measured and taxed. Automobiles could be licensed, and much of the cost for highways could be hidden in the forms of sales and privilege levies. For the first time the legislators found themselves levying a tax which would not pinch the poor, the halt, the lame, and the farmer. If a man was rich enough to buy a car he was adjudged rich enough to buy a road to drive it on.

In Kentucky there was deep irony in the changing times. While legislators debated the public road issue in Frankfort, the mails covered the South with tons of colorful advertising brochures proclaiming the sturdy qualities of Kentucky-made wagons and carriages. Made from the virgin hickories and oaks of the hills, these vehicles came from the shops in Harrodsburg, Lawrenceburg, Louisville, Owensboro, Paducah, and Maysville, their makers too busily engaged in serving the past to see their day was closing. Individualistic manufacturers were without appreciable political influence. They plodded on, bragging up the qualities of their vehicles, built strong enough to withstand the hammerings of rough roads and mudholes. They spent no time campaigning for better roads or even looking to the future. Their whole philosophy of production and salesmanship was conditioned to a state of primitivism in transportation. The poor roads philosophy of the ancient Jacksonian period still served them. But by the second decade of the twentieth century the rising influence of the automobile manufacturer and his demanding customers forced reconsideration of highway needs.

Detroit was too far away from Kentucky, and the rising automobile industry was too impersonal for backwoods legislators either to engage in debate or to silence with the stock retort of "Where is the money coming from?" Too, there was intimately associated with the coming of the automobile that sacred American subtlety—"progress." The new machine was dazzling in its confirmation of American pride in the imaginative and the new of this age.

From Lexington to Whitesburg and from Louisville to Hickman land barriers were lowered. By 1921 the rocky and rutty trail from Winchester to Hazard was under survey and construction. Where at the turn of the century a traveler from the Bluegrass driving down the muddy main street of Hazard in a buggy created a bigger sensation than a circus parade, the automobile appeared later with much less acclaim. The new road wound along the shoulders of streams, inched up the slopes of hills through wind gaps, making little more indentation than a fresh gash in the earth, but it was a road, and in time it was given a hard surface.

Southward from the Ohio and along the old Wilderness Road, where once the United States Post Office Department withdrew mail contracts because of the impassability of the road, the automobile floundered in and out of mudholes and dust pockets. Across the waist of Kentucky interstate roads led down from the northwest, across from the Chesapeake Bay, and southward to the cotton belt. A federal law in 1921 gave these routes new dignity by assigning numbers to them but, of more importance, the Federal Highway Act had made the national government a partner in road building and management.

New all-season roads wrought social and economic revolution in Kentucky. In the highlands the last of the major blood feuds was ended. The old-time mountaineer of quaint colonial backwoods American speech and even more quaint folk traditions began to disappear, as did his blood brother the green country hick from the rest of the state. The last of the virgin timber was slashed to pieces and hauled away, leaving the land impoverished. Coal mines of all sorts were opened and exhausted. In good times and in bad, hundreds and thousands of migrant workers fled to the "outside" to seek employment and a livelihood.

So long as roads were either nonexistent or usable only during dry seasons education in Kentucky was pegged to the trifling standard of the one-room school, the ineffectively trained teacher, and the illiterate school board member. Consolidation of schools was out of the question, as was compulsory attendance. Idealists campaigned in Louisville, Paducah, Frankfort, Bowling Green, and Lexington, but their pleas could be heeded only in favored towns and counties. There was no more certain gauge to Kentuckians' attitude toward the necessity for better educational standards than the progress they made in building roads and bridges.

Organization of a state highway department in Kentucky created the finest political instrument ever wielded by those masterful technicians south of the Ohio. Old-timers had only the petty little jobs in the penitentiary, the insane asylums, and a few other piddling public sinecures in which to lodge the faithful, but here in the new highway age was a veritable patronage cornucopia whose bountiful largess could be spread locally for all to see and enjoy. Everybody from self-seeking governor to precinct lackey appreciated the superb opportunities of the new day. They could now spin and weave a fine gossamer of political control over the state in the name of progress. The more roads they promised the more funds the politically oriented highway departments could spend, and the more jobs they could create with which to reward the deserving and even to make new converts. This was political patronage of refined vintage—not even the old Jacksonian spoilsmen could have dreamed of such a heartening windfall.

Before the days of the mechanized weed cutter, and the more obscured partisan hand in highway management, it was wonderful to observe the seasonal anxiety of governors, county judges, highway commissioners, foremen, and almost everybody else with weed-grown roadsides. It was safe to argue that weeds gave Kentucky a shaggy appearance in the eyes of tourists who visited the state, but this civic consciousness always asserted itself strongest just before elections. "Six-week pre-election scythe swingers" squatted along the roads like the famous Kentucky ground hogs. Bold yellow signs proclaimed "Men Working," but the rounding of bends in the road more often than not belied the signs. Indolent political favorites had to take time off to discuss the virtues of their benefactors.

Though the construction and maintenance of highways may well be considered a highly technical job, some Kentucky highway commissioners have been more distinguished as masters of political finesse and instinct than as masters of the T square, drafting board, and transit. In a state where a public job may make a monstrous difference in an individual's standard of living, the commissioners have often been more active in the field of social welfare than as highway managers. Kentuckians themselves have forced their officials to accept this fact. Kentucky would be eminently better off if the people of the state had spent their time in more productive pursuits than that of sitting interminably in anterooms of governors and highway commissioners, waiting to wheedle favors from those officials.

The great depression of the 1930's was not wholly without virtues in Kentucky. The Civilian Conservation Corps and the armies of laborers in the ranks of the New Deal alphabetical agencies cut roads, built bridges, and made a start at digging sections of Kentucky out of stifling isolation. While these roads hardly measured up to standards of "good" or even "improved," they did trace faintly the outlines of highways in sections which had been without them. In many respects this period of economic stringency gave birth to a new Kentucky, if for no other reason than that of allowing thousands of migrant workers to flee the state dragging behind them tilting trailerloads of pitiful household goods. They headed across the Ohio to those spreading industrial havens between Cincinnati and Detroit.

With his whimsical sense of humor, on the one hand, and his everlasting cynicism, on the other, the Kentuckian watched pre-election activities. Engineers in uncommitted counties hacked out base lines, made mysterious figures on portable drafting boards, and otherwise made it appear that a main road was going to be built past almost every voter's door. A loafer in a country store beside a long-neglected dirt road answered an inquiry as to what surveyors were doing by saying, "We ain't sure yet. We're waiting until after the election to see ourselves." A country editor with longer memory, in a county seat town landlocked behind a treacherous mountain grade, proposed that pre-election survey parties drive down varicolored stakes so that local citizens could review occasionally the promises made by succeeding governors and highway officials.

Lucky was the community that got a native son elected governor. It was assured an improved road to Frankfort. Unfortunately the terms of the governors are too long to hasten the process of highway building all over the state. If enough governors could be elected from enough faraway places, maybe Kentucky would eventually have modern highways from Mills Point to the Breaks of Sandy. Many of the "political" roads which have been built in parts of Kentucky have had far more meaningful effects on public welfare than did the administrations of the governors who had built them.

Despite the late start in highway construction and the intricacies of partisan politics, there was in 1967 a tangled skein of more than 63,000 miles of roads of all kinds in Kentucky. Some of these only grazed the landscape, some wound like clinging vines about mountain domes, while others bored deep tunnels into river swamps and bogs. Bulldozers and motor graders slashed at ridge and creek bottom alike. These voracious machines laid bare the entrails of mountain and slough to make way for trucks and automobiles.

It was a long step in time from that day in 1769 when Daniel Boone, John Finley, and their companions huddled atop Pilot Knob to spy out the virginal countryside and that moment in the twentieth century when mechanical monsters roared into their valley to crush mountain ridge and creek bed under wheel. They had come to literally bore a passageway into the very bowels of the Appalachian Plateau. To the south along the historic Wilderness Road, ancient landmarks were either bypassed or gnawed to pieces by machines. The cost of a single mile of these two-hundred-yard-wide roads would have sent Isaac Shelby and his pennypinching eighteenth-century legislatures into a permanent state of shock, and Kentucky would have been financially out of business for a decade. Even the poor old weed cutters of two decades ago and their solicitous patrons would be confounded by the hundreds of acres of sloping banks. A slip of a foot on one of these plantation-sized roads where traffic goes with the speed and fury of Hermes, and a pliant voter would be lost forever.

Speed of the modern automobile in Kentucky is a fierce thing. Never was the Indian menace along the Wilderness Trail so deadly or so lingering as is the threat of the heedless driver and his high-powered machine. Annual statistics of today's Kentucky traffic deaths make pioneer Kentucky seem in comparison like a haven of safety. A single major holiday weekend offers a more ominous certainty of death to Kentuckians than did all the Shawnee Indian raids of the eighteenth century put together. Almost as startling is the fact that those semiliterate rowdies who whipped tollgate keepers, slashed their pike poles to pieces, and left behind their illegible notes were among Kentucky's most accomplished revolutionaries.

IX

Mother of the West

By 1815, like a mighty sink, Kentucky had received a westward flowing tide of settlers and had swallowed them. Hardly had the Congressional gavel been rapped in 1792 in granting statehood before 73,000 souls had come to live in the state. Three decades later a half million people called themselves Kentuckians. They were more than Kentuckians—most of them had become a distinct American type, called for lack of a better name "backwoodsmen." This horde was land hungry, adventurous, and above all restless. Somewhere in the sprawling western littoral there was possible fame if not fortune lurking in the vast wilderness solitude. Thousands of these people thrust themselves across the Ohio long before the struggling Confederation had reached an agreement about this country, or with its Indian neighbors.

The civilization which they packed along was more often than not stripped of both polish and subtleties. It was at once rowdy, adaptable, fatalistic, humorous, and at best semiliterate. Seventeenth-century English speech was further corrupted and modified by isolation and carelessness. A realistic folklore had supplanted sophistication, if such a condition had ever prevailed. A nasal drawl was deepened with successive moves away from the older rim of American beginnings. Old English speech forms were twisted into backwoods colloquialisms. An old folk culture was rejuvenated by fresh and raw experiences, born of the stark realities of an uncurbed nature. The primitive cultural and social resources of a new country supplanted the refinements of an old world. In all this Kentucky was a conditioning ground for the great West. To move on west was a simple thing. A vast number of Kentuckians were already backwoodsmen before they laid eyes on Cumberland Gap, and they settled comfortably in new homes beyond the Appalachian rim.

Like the narrow mouth of a rock-choked cove, Kentucky received a swirling, roily mass of humanity and settled it down for a generation before it poised itself for another leap westward. From Cumberland Gap the arrow of destiny pointed to the Ohio—westward to the Bluegrass, to the great river, to the rich lands beyond, and on and on with the rim of settlement widening across Indiana, Illinois, and Missouri territories, and on beyond to the limitless far West.

The people who lingered in Kentucky long enough to brood a new generation often moved on themselves. Whether they sought "elbow room," a fresh and free Eden of unclaimed and unspoiled land, the wisp of fresh opportunity or adventure, it little mattered. Old-timers whose very names had become synonymous with the Kentucky frontier deserted the scenes of their first lingerings. Daniel Boone followed a son across the Mississippi to Missouri. Don Zenon Trudeau, Spanish lieutenant governor of the territory, held out promise of free land to the old pioneer. Back in Kentucky and, later, in West Virginia the lawyers had made such deep inroads on Boone's carelessly surveyed and recorded land claims that he was left almost propertyless. In 1798 he left for Missouri with family and plunder crammed into a poplar dugout canoe.

While the Boones paddled westward to Missouri, their old pioneering friend Simon Kenton suffered losses at the hands of the courts and land lawyers, and crossed to the north of the Ohio to spend the rest of his life in territory where he had survived both the running of an Indian gantlet and a mazeppa ride. The old man brought fame to the new frontier of his choice, and his name was imprinted on this land, as it had been back in Kentucky.

In a year when politicians in Frankfort and Washington orated, legislated, and soon resolved the nation into a war against British highhandedness, and the pulse of expansion beat fiercely in the western country, Abraham Lincoln was born. Thomas Lincoln's family had followed the immigrant trail westward through Cumberland Gap to the Green River country, haven of hundreds of Revolutionary War veterans. Abraham, the grandfather, had left Virginia and a captaincy in the militia in the middle of the Revolution. Fetching with him land warrants under terms of the Virginia land law of 1779, he claimed 800 acres of Green River lands bought from Jacob Gum and Oliver Dever and settled on it to plant a patch of corn and build a cabin.

From Green River Tom Lincoln moved to Elizabethtown, and later with his young wife Nancy Hanks to the Sinking Spring farm on the waters of the Nolin River. Thomas had been a cabinetmaker and carpenter, but now he had turned farmer. It was in their crude one-room cabin that their son Abraham was born on February 12, 1809.

Whether or not the true cabin of Lincoln's birth is the one now enshrined in a marble palace is perhaps not too fundamentally important in the long span of the Lincoln saga. His political success was enormously heightened by the fact of his log cabin birth, already both a symbol and a myth in American history. For seven years young Abraham lived at the Sinking Spring, and beyond the encircling Muldraugh's Hill in the Knob Creek Valley. Then in late spring of 1816 the Lincolns grew restless under the expansionist excitement following the War of 1812 and picked up body-and-baggage and wandered across the Ohio to seek fortune afresh in the Indiana wilderness.

A small army of Kentuckians moved westward to Indiana and then on to Illinois with the Lincolns. There were among them the Hankses, Sparrows, Bushes, Edwardses, Stuarts, Brownings, Elkinses, Johnstons, and scores of others. Many of these were simple backwoodsmen who slashed meager clearings in virgin forests and duplicated cabins they had built back in Kentucky. They dammed the streams to catch water to turn their mill wheels, they organized loose-jointed villages, threw a political blanket about an area and called it a county; thus they planted a pattern of civilization which was to be stamped a thousand times upon the face of the land as the wash of settlement move westward.

The Lincolns, like fallen leaves on the babbling waters of Knob Creek, had been swept westward with the onrush of settlers. Not far south of them in a fertile vale of the Pennyroyal, Samuel Davis, emigrant from Georgia, located a post-Revolutionary War land claim. Here he built a modest house near present Fairview. But like the Lincolns, the Davis family heard the call of fortune to move elsewhere, and they left the Kentucky backwoods to move downriver to the rich cotton lands of Mississippi in 1815. Samuel's youngest son and tenth child, Jefferson, was only two years of age, and he carried away with him no personal recollections of Kentucky. He came back to his native state, however, as a youth to attend St. Thomas Academy in Washington County, and Transylvania University in Lexington.

Two frontier families had come to rest in Kentucky before moving on. Two sons were born there and were then swept on to expanding territory. One went south down the Ohio and Mississippi and the other crossed the river. This fortuitous parting of the ways of two backwoods families was no doubt one of the most exciting ever to occur in restless, transitory Kentucky. By mere accident young Lincoln and Davis found themselves thrust into two different sectional settings which in time would force them into political and military rivalry in which the fate of the Union itself would be involved.

Crossing the Ohio to settle in Illinois went a considerable tribe of speculators, lawyers, and fledgling politicians. Among these John T. Stuart, two years Lincoln's senior, a native of Lexington who took west with him a stern Scotch Presbyterian faith and a pride of Bluegrass origin. His father had taught languages in Transylvania University and his mother was a daughter of General Levi Todd. In 1828, as a freshly licensed attorney, John Stuart rode away from Lexington on his way to Illinois. In the backwoods circuit court district of Sangamon, Stuart combined practice of law with politics. For four years, 1837-1841, Lincoln and Stuart were partners, during which time, and even in succeeding years, the handsome meticulous Stuart brought some order and discipline to Lincoln's law business. More important than this, he expanded his partner's legal horizons. Earlier he had helped initiate the raw country bumpkin into the mysteries of lawmaking in the legislature at Vandalia.

Another Kentuckian had already given the backwoodsman both a sense of business conduct and a peep at the world outside. Denton Offutt, like Stuart, had come from Fayette County. He was an expert with horses, able to handle even the most recalcitrant animal. Early in 1831 he appeared in Illinois seeking flatboatmen to help him float a cargo of country produce downriver to New Orleans. He employed Abraham Lincoln and John Hanks as his crew and set out down the river to undergo numerous adventures. In May of that year the weatherbeaten crew drifted their boat into the New Orleans port where they sold their produce and lingered a short time to take in the sights of the city.

Back in Illinois Offutt opened a store and employed Abraham

Lincoln and "Slicky" Bill Green as clerks. A clerkship in a slabsided frontier store was unremunerative so far as income was concerned, but this was an important formative period in Lincoln's life.

By the opening decade of 1830 there were Kentuckians everywhere in Illinois. As captain of the 31st Illinois Militia in the Black Hawk War, Lincoln was to be associated almost wholly with boys from south of the Ohio. The *Sangamon Journal* of Springfield took note of this fact in a bit of doggerel:

> Brave Sangamon both arm'd
> All to defend her right.
> Arouse ye old Kentucky boys,
> The foremost in the fight.
> Away! Away! Away!

The brave old Kentucky boys did little to distinguish themselves in their search for Black Hawk. Before the 31st returned home, Captain Lincoln had become Private Lincoln because of the misbehavior of his "troops"; but even at that the Sangamon army achieved a more distinguished record than an unnamed Kentuckian who had fled the onslaught at Stillman's defeat, leaving behind his precious copy of *Chitty on Pleading* and his courage, if he had any.

Lincoln and Davis became famous as Kentucky expatriates because of extraordinary political circumstance. There were, however, hundreds of others who left their marks largely because they were professional frontiersmen. One of these was that shadowy figure whose life story has become so intertwined in fact and legend that facts are hard to identify. Philip Nolan was apparently born in Frankfort, where he became a ward of General James Wilkinson. He was, said his guardian, "a child of my own raising." In New Orleans the young man served his mentor as agent, a responsibility which matured him rapidly for future adventures in the troubled territory beyond the Sabine. He traded with the east Texas Indians, and bought horses from Spanish borderers. For a time he was with Andrew Ellicott on his famous survey of the line between the United States and Spain in Mississippi and Alabama territories. He was also with Governor Gayoso on his north Texas survey.

Nolan lost his life on a horse drive in 1801, the victim of a military party led by Lieutenant M. Musquiz. On both sides of the border the Kentuckian had the reputation of being a mysterious man engaged no doubt in spying in that vague zone between the Red and Rio Grande rivers. In later years he was erroneously called the prototype of Edward Everett Hale's character, *The Man Without a Country*.

While great mystery shrouded the life of Philip Nolan, there was no lack of central facts relating to the four Sublette brothers. They were grandsons of the hoary old Indian fighter William Whitley who had built a handsome brick house beside a wilderness trail between Stanford and Crab Orchard. He fell in the Battle of the Thames in 1813 and thereby created a lingering argument as to whether he or Richard M. Johnson shot Tecumseh. The restless Sublettes left the Dick's River Valley to move out to St. Charles, Missouri, in 1818. William associated himself with Captain William Henry Ashley, the rising fur baron of the upper Missouri. Ashley and Sublette fought Arikaras in their journey up the Missouri in 1823, and in time they fought and traded their way deep into the upper Missouri country. The four brothers, Solomon R., Andrew, Milton G., and William L. became mountain men. In 1826 William entered into a partnership with Jedediah S. Smith and David E. Jackson to form the Rocky Mountain Fur Company. Milton associated himself with Jim Bridger and Thomas Fitzpatrick in another company.

The Sublettes, like their old grandfather back in Lincoln County, were trail breakers. Wherever beaver streams in the West yielded pelts they were known. On the grounds of the annual rendezvous, along the trails leading westward from St. Louis, with the trader trains, and in St. Louis itself the Sublette influence was strong. They were important agents in the business of thrusting open the great gates of the far western empire.

While Sublettes garnered fame and fortune in the Rockies, there were other Kentuckians on the border. One of the most famous of these was Christopher (Kit) Carson from Madison County. His family moved to that famous focal point for Kentuckians in Missouri, Boone's Lick, where a fallen tree limb killed the elder Carson. Kit was apprenticed to a saddler, but the saddler's shop was entirely too tame a place for a boy who already had the "West" in his blood. He ran away from the bench and saddletree to serve as "cavvy" boy on a Santa Fe trading expedition. From Santa Fe he went on west to California was the Tennessean Ewing Young. Like the Sublettes, he took a postgraduate course in pioneering under the tutelage of Thomas Fitzpatrick and Jim Bridger.

Kit Carson began his rise to frontier fame as a scout and guide for John C. Frémont's western expedition. Later he distinguished himself in the Mexican War as a scout in California, even going as far away as Washington, D.C., on one occasion to carry dispatches. The sprawling basin and mountain West became familiar grounds to the Bluegrass Kentuckian. Whether trapping for beaver in the Rockies, guiding Frémont's expedition, bearing dispatches, fighting Indians, or herding sheep from New Mexico, the lean, mustachioed, and soft-spoken frontiersman proved himself a highly dependable scout.

Behind the Carsons and Sublettes came a redheaded lawyer following the public land frontier in search of clients and former neighbors. In Missouri ex-patriate Kentuckians had already embroiled themselves in the disputes which made the practice of law in the West such a masculine profession. Alexander William Doniphan was born in Mason County, graduated from Augusta College, and was "finished off" in the law office of Martin Marshall. In Lexington, Missouri, he hung up his newly won shingle and pitched in to savor life about him. Quick-witted and highly self-assured, he soon mastered the art of getting clients "off" in court and getting the other fellow's clients deeper into trouble. A highly profitable case for the young barrister was that of Orrin P. Rockwell, a Mormon who was charged with conspiracy to murder Governor McNair of Missouri. Later Doniphan was to lead militiamen against the Mormons, and refused to have Joseph Smith shot, an act which the Mormons did not forget.

Part lawyer and part soldier, the redheaded Kentuckian was active in border militia affairs. His big moment came when he led his famous 1st Missouri Mounted Volunteers in the long march from Fort Leavenworth by way of Bent's Fort and across the Arkansas to Santa Fe, Chihuahua, and on to Matamoros, 3,600 miles overland and 2,000 miles by water. Between Independence and Matamoros he fought Mexican forces at Santa Fe, Brazito, and Sacramento, and returned to Lexington, where he was a western hero.

Doniphan was to play out his hand with vigor. When the nation was faced with secession, he like many Kentuckians of his old home-land advocated neutrality of his state, if not loyalty to the Union. In convention and in private conversation his was a powerful voice in shaping the course of events in Missouri during the Civil War.

Three names of Kentuckians were imprinted on the sandy distances of the Southwest and middle basin regions. The first of these was William Becknell who, like Daniel Boone, helped open a western trail. In 1821 he set out with a pack train from Independence for Santa Fe. He was successful, and in 1822 he introduced the wagon to the trail, discovered the Cimarron-Canadian short cut, and greatly shortened the distance to be traveled to Santa Fe.

Before the last rail was laid on the Union Pacific and Central Pacific railroads, Alexander Majors and Ben Holloday had distinguished themselves as transportation pioneers. Majors was born in Simpson County, Kentucky, and was swept westward as a youth by the great Missouri migration following the War of 1812. As farm boy and miller Majors learned the meaning of hard labor and the serious limitations of farming on the frontier. After the Mexican War he discovered that there was more profit in driving oxen and mules hitched to freight wagons headed for Santa Fe than to plows. Majors was a most unusual wagon master in that he believed freight could be moved across the sandy wastes of the trail in a Sunday-school atmosphere. Normally muleskinners considered beating mules, getting drunk, and swearing to high heaven attributes of their trade. He bound his employees by strict blue-law pledges which kept them free of all the sins of the Southwest, including the desecration of the Sabbath.

Associating himself with William Hepburn Russell and William B. Waddell, Majors helped organize the historic overland freighting firm of Russell, Waddell, and Majors. The inventory of draft animals and equipment sounded more like that of an invading army than a company dispatching crawling caravans across the hundreds of miles of arid plains. At one time the company owned 40,000 oxen to say nothing of droves of mules and horses. Spectacular as lugging freight over vast distances was, however, it did not possess the romance and excitement of the far less significant pony express. Failing to take full notice of what was happening in the nation and the West, Russell, Waddell, and Majors organized this colorful adventure just on the eve of the completion of the transcontinental telegraph line. The pony express did not fail, however, until Alexander Majors had also bound his pony riders hard and fast with his famous puritanical pledge.

Somewhat more successful in the long run than Majors of the Simpson County backwoods was Ben Holloday, born in Carlisle County, Kentucky, in the year of the great depression of 1819. He too matured into early manhood along with hundreds of Kentuckians in frontier Missouri. He was a frontier trader, military supplier, and storekeeper, all trades which taught an imaginative young man the art of getting along on the outskirts of civilization. The freighting and cattle business appealed to young Holloday. He drove one of his earliest herds across Utah to California to reap a rich return from the gold rush. He was able to cross the Mormon territory because he carried a letter to Brigham Young from Alexander W. Doniphan.

In the fierce competitive years 1850–1860 Ben Holloday, like Russell, Waddell, and Majors, struggled with distance, weather, sagging profits, and rising intensity of Indian resistance to operate his Pike's Peak and Overland express lines. His Concord coaches and freight wagons became tremendously important attributes in the settlement of the West. The memory of these picturesque vehicles is kept alive even now in modern western movies.

At almost the moment that farmer Alexander Majors was anticipating profits from his first venture on the Santa Fe Trail, the Coleman brothers of Cynthiana, Kentucky, were pushing west toward the golden riches of the Sacramento. William Tell Coleman used his good Kentucky eye and native judgment when he arrived at Sutter's Mill. There might be gold in the veins of the hills, but young Coleman was more familiar with riches which came from lush pastures back in Harrison County. He went into the cattle-raising and mercantile businesses. At Placerville he had his first success before pushing on to the bayside and San Francisco to establish the mercantile house of William T. Coleman and Company. Following a practice of shrewd merchandising and fierce honesty he became a major figure in that city. In later years when his house was bankrupted he promised to pay off his creditors in full, a promise he fulfilled before he died.

Coleman took west with him both an impulse for direct action and a sense of the forms at least of the orderly administration of justice, western style. As presiding officer over a vigilante committee he held in check the extremists who were led by the powerful Mormon Sam Brannan, on the one hand, and the lawless rowdies, on the other. Justice of a direct and unappealable sort was rendered quickly to public offenders. Charles Cora and James Casey, charged with the murder of James King of William, editor of the San Francisco *Call*, were tried, convicted, and hanged in what amounted to one continuous action by the vigilantes. In 1877 Coleman again helped to deal directly with a public disturbance which arose from anti-Chinese activities.

Thus it was that many individual Kentuckians stood out from the crowd in the opening of the West. Since the third quarter of the eighteenth century they had been charged with the excitement of pioneering. As Timothy Flint said in 1825:

They seem to feel that they have an hereditary claim to command, place, and observance. This perfect repose of self-confidence is in fact their good star. I have often seen one of these young men, in the new states farther west, with no more qualifications than the ease and perfect command of all they knew, which result from self-satisfaction, step down into the "mourning waters" before the tardy, bashful and self-criticizing young man from the North had made up his mind to attempt to avail himself of the opportunity.

There were plenty of self-confident young Kentuckians who stepped down into the "mourning waters" of western office. The creation of new territories and states was open sesame for the politically ambitious. Presidents of the United States had in the rising territories political plums in the form of governorships, secretariats, judgeships, and marshals' badges which they could pass out to the faithful. The boys from the Bluegrass managed to keep someone in power in Washington who could always make way for them to reach the trough of political preferment.

Three characteristics seemed to have given young expatriate Kentuckians a lead against those from many other states. They were motivated toward if not trained for the law. When they were Whigs, they were most likely to be "Henry Clay Whigs." They had both love and experience for politics and were brassy enough to use their experience to good advantage. In nearly every case where a Kentuckian succeeded in either the law or politics there are accounts of his use of persuasive voice and manner. His oratory was good if not superb, and often a more cultivated accent gave him an aura of culture and aristocracy which he seldom possessed.

Of the many Kentuckians who moved on to greener pastures and gained sufficient reputations to be mentioned in almost all standard histories of the United States were Ninian Edwards, Ninian Wirt Edwards, Lillburn Boggs, David R. Atchison, Richard Oglesby, Thomas Corwin, Orville Browning, William H. Herndon, Samuel Freeman Miller, Adlai Stevenson, Richard B. Bland, John M. Palmer, John M. Harlan, Oscar W. Underwood, and Walker D. Hines.

Ninian Edwards was not a native son, but he left his mark in

Kentucky. He came to the state when he was twenty years of age to take up a tract of land for his father. Quickly he developed a law practice, and by the time he had been in the state a dozen years he became a member of the Court of Appeals, and then its chief justice. President James Madison sent young Judge Edwards west to Illinois during troubled years just prior to the War of 1812 to be territorial governor. He was governor until the state was created.

Judge Edwards' son Ninian Wirt was born in Frankfort the year his father went out to the Illinois Territory. A socially conscious lad, he went back to Lexington and Transylvania University to study law. There he married Elizabeth P. Todd and took her to Illinois, where she became a matron of influence in the rising new state capital at Springfield. Elizabeth Edwards' sister Mary went to visit her. There she met and married Abraham Lincoln. Edwards was influential in establishing a system of public schools and in making the people of Illinois conscious of the need for education.

From Lexington went Lillburn Boggs to engage in the fur trade centered about St. Louis. He established a reputation as a frontier trader, and in time he turned from the hazardous business of buying and selling skins and furs to the even more hazardous one of banking. As with his fellow Kentuckians, the politics of Missouri proved irresistible and he got himself elected governor of that state. A strong-willed man who dared venture out into fields which a more timid man would have shunned, he built an expensive state capitol, founded a university, and improved an orderless state banking system. His name was even more indelibly stamped in Missouri history because of his involvement with the Mormons. He was credited with driving the Saints across the Mississippi to Illinois. In 1846 Boggs grew restive under the criticism and bickering of this state and he moved his family to California. On the way he became for a time captain of the wagon train which included the ill-fated Donner party. With him, too, was Edwin Bryant, the Louisville editor, who later described the journey west in *What I Saw in California.* West of the Sierras, Boggs became alcalde of northern California, and in this office he proved as forthright and powerful as he had been in Missouri.

Thus Mother Kentucky distributed her brood, some to become leaders in the ever-expanding West, while others were scapegraces and rascals. But wherever they went they never forgot their background in the land south of the Ohio.

Uncle Tom, Good Night

On a rolling bluegrass knoll just south of Richmond in an early spring night in 1775 Shawnee Indians raided the camp of Daniel Boone's trail-blazing party. They killed three persons and seriously wounded another. Two of those killed were Negro slaves, the first to be brought to Kentucky. In time hundreds of others came over the Wilderness Road or were drifted down the Ohio with families fleeing the leached soils of Maryland and Virginia.

Pioneering in the backwoods offered a new challenge to slavery, and the Negro proved himself an excellent frontiersman. Many a vast cleared area in central Kentucky still documents this fact. Slaves chopped down the heavy timber, helped build the cabins, planted crops, and performed a thousand and one laborious tasks which had to do with settling people on the western waters.

If slaves, as tradition has it, lifted in fact all the slabs of limestone which went into the building of rock fences up and down bluegrass slopes, then they performed Herculean tasks of drudgery. Many a Kentuckian likes to point to these rapidly disappearing walls and explain that they were constructed by slaves as if in some way this fact gives an extra dimension to the land. Some slaves became expert at laying these sturdy walls which have defied the ravages of elements and time. Some of these structures are among the finest examples of primitive handicraft and creativeness to be found in Kentucky.

Slavery nevertheless early became a heavy social stone about Ken-

109

tucky's neck. From the beginning of settlement there were those who suffered aching consciences because of the anachronism of the system in a land where men placed such great store by individual liberty and institutional freedom. Among early conscientious objectors were the Presbyterian missionaries who came across the mountains to assure the church a role in pioneering. David Rice, a native of Hanover County, Virginia, who had followed his neighbors to their new lands, was ardent in his efforts to plant Presbyterianism in the fresh country and equally so in contending that slavery should not be allowed to flourish. So loudly was his voice raised in protest that he frightened members of the first constitutional convention into writing a rigid clause which guaranteed that slavery would exist until it was struck down by amendment to the United States Constitution.

Father Rice was not alone in his views. Other liberal Virginians came west to add their protests against slavery, among them young Henry Clay, who raised the issue in his first Kentucky speech before a Lexington debating society. This, however, was an inept mistake which the young politician never repeated.

Useful as slaves were in opening the new country to settlement, the day came early when they were not nearly so necessary. By 1820 and the time of the opening of the great southern cotton belt Kentucky slaves came to have less economic significance as laborers in the production of hemp, tobacco, and livestock. In the South cotton barons were in need of armies of labor to clear their black lands and to grow their staple. This was a profitable market for Kentucky's surplus slaves. In fact many Kentuckians moved away to become cotton farmers, took their slaves with them, and sent home for more. Between 1830 and 1860 the sale of slaves southward became as commonplace as the sale of mules, hogs, and cattle. This era of Kentucky social history was sullied by accusations of slave breeding to supply the southern trade.

Again the Kentucky conscience was guilt-burdened. Nothing seemed more repulsive to the religious Kentuckian than separation of members of families: fathers were taken from children and children from parents. London Farrell, the famous slave preacher of Lexington, acknowledged the precariousness of social relationships for his parishioners when he concluded the marriage ceremony by saying, "until death or distance do thee part." A constant threat to unruly slaves was "Behave or be sold south!"

Slaveholders undertook to make their peace with God. They left behind them wills which specified that their slaves should not be sold into the interstate slave trade. However, once the ownership of slaves was transferred, the former master no longer had legal control over where they could be sold in the future. Slave dealers owned farms as way stations on which they employed their chattels, bought in estate sales, long enough for the memories of people to grow dim and then moved them to the slave pens of New Orleans, Natchez, Memphis, and Mobile.

Lexington and Louisville newspapers were spiced with the advertisements of slave dealers in the Kentucky market for "wares." Some names, like those of William A. Pullum, Lewis Robards, and William F. Talbott came to represent the inhumanity of the slave trade. Public slave auctions in Louisville and Lexington were often repulsive enough to turn the heart and stomach of even the most rabid slaveholder. Bestial slave auctioneers like Jerry Delph exhibited female stock with shameless disregard for modesty and decency. So deeply etched on the Kentucky mind were some of these sales that until the present day Cheapside in Lexington is still tainted by the indignities committed there against humanity.

So bitter was much of public opinion against the interstate slave trade that in 1833 the legislature passed a nonimportation law which forbade dealers to bring slaves from Maryland and Virginia for resale to the South. Perhaps no other legislative act in the history of Kentucky stirred more bitter emotions for so extended a time as did this one. It became a central issue in many political campaigns and was the source of debate in a constitutional convention. Special slave interests fought for its repeal, and moralists were equally determined to retain it. Until the adoption of the Thirteenth Amendment in 1866 the Nonimportation Law remained a bloody bone of political contention and many a Kentucky politician was defeated because of his attitude toward it.

From the outset of the abolition crusade Kentucky slaveholders bore the brunt of criticism. Because they lived along the sprawling river frontier between freedom and slavery, every traveler who came down the Ohio made insidious comparisons between people living in the fresh air of freedom of the Northwest Territory and those withering in that of slavery. Every unfortunate incident was magnified and publicized. By the time the organized abolitionists had reached the peak of their crusade against the "peculiar institution" Kentuckians knew well the sting of their opposition.

Some Kentucky and southern slaveholders undertook to free their land of its social troubles. They organized the American Colonization Society, and for several years Henry Clay was its president. They proposed to abolish slavery by sending their Negroes back to Africa. Some did go to Liberia, but colonization was no answer to Kentucky slavery. The price of slaves was too high for any significant number of slaveholders to suffer so heavy a property loss as freedom involved.

By the mid-1840's the hand of fate wrote boldly a traumatic end to slavery. Every abolitionist in the land had his eye on the Kentuckians. Theodore Weld gathered information about hundreds of incidents in Kentucky slavery to fill the columns of his source book *American Slavery As It Is; Testimony of a Thousand Witnesses.* He described the horrors wrought by the Lewis brothers, nephews of Thomas Jefferson, who hacked a slave boy to pieces and burned his flesh before the rest of their slaves as a lesson in discipline. He reproduced slave dealer advertisements and described the plight of slave families separated by sales. Generally Weld made the treatment of slaves appear in an unfavorable if not horrible light, and quickly his book became a rich mother lode for abolitionist thunder.

No criticism of slavery in Kentucky was more dramatic, however, than that of Cassius M. Clay of Lexington. Clay, son of a large land- and slaveholder and descended of rugged pioneer stock, attended Yale University, and in New Haven he fell under the influence of William Lloyd Garrison and his cohorts. When the young student returned to Lexington, the heart of the slave system, he established a weekly emancipationist newspaper, *The True American.* For an editor to publish a mildly antislavery paper in the town was bad enough, but to have it edited and published by the son of so prominent a slaveholder as General Green Clay made it doubly offensive.

Cassius M. Clay was never a man to do things by halves or to exercise tact. Instead of gently persuading his neighbors to reconsider the issue of slavery, he girded himself as if he were a Roman soldier setting off to war and openly defied the proslavery mob. His newspaper office was turned into an arsenal armed with small cannon, rifles, a stand of lances, and black powder bombs and other explosives. If he had been publishing a Sunday-school paper behind such a formidable barrier he would no doubt have incurred anger. A slave-holding mob caught the militant editor while he was ill, and packed up his press and type and sent them off to Cincinnati. Later Clay was to collect damages from the mob, but the effectiveness of *The True American* was ended. Never a consistent man, editor Clay in 1847 rushed off to the Mexican War at the head of troops to fight in the "Slaveholders' War."

The *True American* incident in the summer of 1845 was truly the beginning of much greater troubles for the Kentucky slaveholders. Kidnapers and underground railroad operators proved both a nuisance and a threat. No one knew when a slave might be lured away to the freedom stations beyond the Ohio. For instance, Delia Anne Webster and Calvin Fairbank, Yankee schoolteachers serving a school in Lexington, smuggled three Phoenix Hotel slaves away to the Rankin House station on the underground railroad across the Ohio from Maysville. Runaway slaves brought serious property losses. Columns of newspaper advertisements described these fugitives, often damning the institution of slavery itself by giving peculiar physical marks on the bodies of the slaves, placed there by whip and cudgel.

Theodore Weld and Cassius M. Clay's blows were indeed mild as compared with that rendered by Harriet Beecher Stowe. Wife of a professor at Lane Seminary in Cincinnati and member of the famous Beecher family, this lady put Kentucky slavery on exhibit before the world. So much local legend and myth has grown up about *Uncle Tom's Cabin* that it is now difficult to separate fact from fancy. Mrs. Stowe documented the fact that she did visit the Kennedy family in Garrard County, and on their farm she had her first intimate view of slavery. Whether or not she attended a slave sale in Washington in Mason County is uncertain. She sought a story in Kentucky and she found it. Uncle Tom personified all the faithful slaves sold south, Liza represented mother love to the fullest—no matter the status of the mother—and Colonel Shelby spoke for the Kentucky aristocracy and slaveholders. The sensuous slave dealer who held Colonel Shelby in debt might well have been Jerry Delph, Lewis Robards, or William A. Pullum.

Harriet Beecher Stowe knew about the Nonimportation Law of 1833, and living in Cincinnati she no doubt had read some of the emotional attacks upon it. She knew little fundamentally about Kentucky slavery, but she drew on what little she knew to create the opening scenes of her book. In time Liza and Uncle Tom became as real as was the Kentucky River itself, and the abuses of the interstate slave trade which she described became household knowledge throughout the English-speaking world.

An irony of American social history is the fact that two of the bitterest terms of racial discrimination became intimately associated with Kentucky. These were "Uncle Tomism" and "Jim Crow." The latter term originated in Louisville when the actor Thomas Dartmouth Rice heard an aged Negro in 1828 singing a jingle, "Every time I wheel about, I jump Jim Crow." Rice introduced this jingle and phrase into the black-face minstrel shows which grew in popularity during the antebellum years. It became popular first as referring to black-face entertainment, but in the 1890's it became a malodorous term of racial discrimination.

In a tremendously interesting reversal of sentiment Kentuckians accepted Stephen Collins Foster's "My Old Kentucky Home" as their state song. Wherever this song is played or sung it stirs Kentuckians' hearts. No matter what strange key it may be played in, or on what strange instrument, the Kentuckian quickly recognizes the melody. At home Kentuckians open many of their public meetings and sports events by singing and playing this song. Crowds at the Kentucky Derby, at football games, at political gatherings stand with bared heads in reverence when the band strikes up the melody of this gripping human story set to music. Only an infinitesimal number recognize in it the basic theme of *Uncle Tom's Cabin*. Foster gave it the original title "Den Poor Uncle Tom, Good Night," but across the foot of the manuscript in a scrawling hand he changed the title to "My Old Kentucky Home, Good Night."

Quickly this slave lament took its place along with other songs such as "Carry Me Back to Ol' Virginny" and "My Darling Nellie Gray." Foster was a song writer and not an abolitionist crusader, which accounted in part for his change of titles, and the fact that his music became popular below the Ohio where Mrs. Stowe's book was anathema. His song had the advantage of a rich melody which was lacking in the plodding novelist's book.

Kentuckians never reconciled the fact that slavery on their soil was so bitterly attacked with their conviction that they were humane masters. They were convinced there was a difference between their attitudes toward their slaves and those of the cotton barons. To them Kentucky slaves were well off because they were often considered members of family circles rather than as chattel property.

It was the destruction of this myth by the abolitionists that created so much anger. The publicizing of the evils of the interstate slave trade and of slave treatment was as shocking as if the institution of the family itself had been brought under adverse scrutiny. Kentucky humanity stood charged with acts as monstrous as those of ancient Egypt. The very foundation of their way of life seemed threatened because they tolerated the social sin of slavery. Kentuckians regarded themselves as generous and humanitarian. The haunting spirits of Liza and Uncle Tom became destroyers of the myth of humaneness. The major reason why abolitionists were regarded as such threats was the fact that they wiped away the last shred of illusion that slavery in Kentucky was truly a domestic institution in which the Negro was better off than if he were given his freedom.

The Civil War completed the destruction of slavery. Even before the Thirteenth Amendment was ratified large numbers of slaves had taken the short journey to freedom across the Ohio. The end of the war brought more than mere freedom to the Kentucky slaves, it introduced a new phase of history in which Negroes had to be fitted into a free society. They had to find new moorings in both economics and education.

In the long postwar crusade in which many self-sacrificing souls battled to establish public education as a fundamental part of Kentucky life, the education of the newly freed Negroes became both a cause and an issue. There were those of limited vision and spiteful memory who believed the Negro should be educated to the extent that he contributed directly to the support of schools with his taxes. More farsighted leaders saw in the Negro a potential contributor to the economic and cultural life of Kentucky. There was discrimination against the Negro, and even bitter resentment toward him. In a state where the educational effort was so meager, however, discrimination in the schools was almost imperceptible. Everybody suffered from lack of educational opportunity.

At Berea College, an institution founded in the 1850's as an opportunity school for enslaved Negroes and poor whites alike, there was difficulty and even intimidation. John G. Fee, the founder, was driven from Kentucky but, stouthearted man that he was, he persisted and Berea was reopened at the end of the war as a biracial institution, and so it remained until 1904. Mounting racial prejudice took a curious tack at the turn of the century. A mountain man introduced and succeeded in getting passed a law to bar Negroes from Berea. Both state and federal courts upheld the constitutionality of the law, and it was necessary to divide Berea along racial lines. The parent college served white students from Appalachia while the new Lincoln Institute at Simpsonville served Negroes. A second piece of legislation was so vicious in intent that the courts nullified it immediately. It forbade the location of Negro schools closer than twenty-five miles to white schools.

In the years between the end of the Civil War and 1954 Kentucky struggled with the staggering problem of providing adequate schooling for its people. The publication of perennial tables of comparative statistics deepened the state's humiliation. The tables seemed permanently tilted against it. Surveys habitually showed it near the bottom of the heap. The people were unwilling to provide enough tax base to restore their pride and to educate their children. The legislators were no more willing to assume the responsibility for the state.

The cause of education was a central theme of continuous crusading. Many a public-spirited Kentuckian elevated himself to heroic stature in his efforts to lift the people of his state out of the bogs of illiteracy and ignorance. A part of the state's history is set off by these landmarks in social and cultural history, and it is personified by the manful efforts of individuals who sacrificed energy and time to awaken a sluggish public. Two such persons were John Grant Crabbe and Cora Wilson Stewart. Crabbe literally butted Kentucky lawmakers into the assumption of responsibility for public education. Cora Wilson Stewart dramatized the stigma of illiteracy by organizing the "Moonlight Schools." In these she undertook to aid a part of the adult Kentucky population to overcome the failures of the past by teaching them to read and write.

Historically the Negro profited from the great crusades. A state college was established for him in Frankfort in the 1880's but, like the land-grant college in Lexington, it was kept a starveling for decades. It struggled just to survive, to say nothing of employing and maintaining an adequate faculty, a decent library, and a mature educational program.

Negro public schools in Kentucky operated on a kindred basis with those in the lower South. They were given leftover support. A sparse Negro population in many parts of the state made it practically impossible to maintain separate schools for Negroes within reach of all the families, yet the discriminatory Berea Law barred co-racial education.

The first real crack in the racially segregated educational wall came in 1948 when the district federal court in Lexington ordered, in *Johnson v. the University of Kentucky,* that the university open its doors to qualified Negro students. This decision came after Negroes had sought for several years to gain admission to the university and at a time when public sentiment had mellowed on this issue. For instance, professors in the university's Law School had refused to go to Frankfort to teach segregated classes for the benefit of a single Negro student who sought a law degree from his state university. They were, however, quite willing to teach him in their regular classes in the university. They made their refusal to engage in hypocrisy stick, and the university's administration was made to appear ridiculous in court because of its floundering attempts to continue classes in Frankfort with local attorneys for professors.

There has always been a marked difference between Kentucky attitudes in the face of cold realities and those of many of its southern neighbors. Truly a border state and people, Kentuckians have been able to recognize the fundamentals of a social situation. They have also been able to accept change somewhat more gracefully.

The university's Board of Trustees refused to appeal the Johnson case. In time all of the university was opened to all qualified Kentuckians. The last bastion of discrimination was the athletic teams. The university is a member of the Southeastern Athletic Conference where racial discrimination has been rampant. Thus the issue of desegregation hung on the question of whether it would withdraw its membership from that body or attempt to desegregate the Kentucky teams and let nature take its course. By 1968, no Negro had played on a Kentucky team and the issue of conference contests remained untested.

When the monumental *Brown v. Board of Education of Topeka* decision was rendered by the United States Supreme Court in May, 1954, Kentucky was partially conditioned to accept the stern realities of the decision. In sharp contrast to the attitudes of many of the southern governors, Governor Lawrence Wetherby told newspaper reporters that Kentucky would obey the law of the land. A decision by the Supreme Court on so vital a social issue and the actual accomplishment of its objectives, however, were altogether different matters. Kentucky had a long way to go to accomplish the integration of its classrooms and to improve the quality of public education.

Governor Wetherby's initial statement went far toward setting the stage.

Basic planning and action took place in the two big centers of Negro population, Louisville and Lexington. Fortunately Louisville had Omer Carmichael as its superintendent of schools. A Lower Southerner from Alabama with an extremely liberal and generous outlook, he was able to make an intelligent approach to desegregating the schools. He and his school board began making careful plans for the admission of Negroes to mixed classes. Because of this planning Louisville presented a marked contrast to the experiences of Nashville and Little Rock. In fact the Louisville plan set a constructive pattern for other American communities faced with the same court mandate.

Lexington made fewer plans and embarked upon desegregation of its schools on a less extensive scale, but perhaps with no less success than Louisville. In 1966, however, the United States Office of Education was critical of what had been accomplished in the Lexington area in the light of the new mandates of the Civil Rights Law of 1965.

Elsewhere in Kentucky desegregation was accomplished in varying degrees of reluctance to conform with the law. In some communities, where the Negro population was small, people were glad to throw off the burden of maintaining small Negro schools. In others there was hesitancy and foot-dragging. Happily Kentuckians are even more passionately fond of basketball than of horse racing, and the Negro youth has proved himself a good basketball player. In many communities basketball teams are comprised of a generous mixture of white and black players, and some of the really good Negro players have been as actively sought after by colleges and universities as have first-rate professors of chemistry and physics. Perhaps they have been offered almost as many emoluments. In May, 1954, a chairman of a school board in a southern Kentucky town observed that his community would have no difficulty in complying with the Supreme Court decision if it could find two or three good Negro basketball stars. The will to win in Kentucky outweighs even racial prejudices.

The break with the past was widened mightily in 1966 when the Kentucky General Assembly enacted a far-reaching civil rights law. In many respects this law went beyond provisions of the federal law passed the year before. In principle, however, the most pronounced criticism of the law was in the field of the practicality of its application. This, however, was largely a legalistic criticism which could only be answered by the courts and in the enforcement and acceptance of the law.

Some Negro leaders, influenced by long years of discrimination in many areas of Kentucky life, no doubt look with doubt and suspicion on how far the new era ushered in by court decisions and civil rights legislation will go in erasing old hurts and injuries. They think of all the changes at local and personal levels which have to come before the past can be erased. They still eye the state institutions of higher learning with a generous amount of suspicion. It is hard for them to accept the fact that the old barriers have been lowered or that they themselves have new responsibilities for making this an everyday acceptable fact in Kentucky life. First of all they have the enormous challenge of overcoming the evils of past discriminations in order to accept the full challenge of the new freedoms in Kentucky. Liza, Uncle Tom, Jerry Delph, Lewis Robards, and all the others belong to the dead past.

Spiritually Kentuckians are proud people. Their pride exceeds their prejudices, and a good majority of them take deep satisfaction in the fact that their state has the courage to set so bold an example for its southern neighbors. Kentucky's liberal civil rights law was a huge stone plucked out of the wall of resistance of the Old South. No doubt this challenge is one which its border neighbors can scarcely ignore—even "Mother" Virginia must notice it.

For Negro and white alike in Kentucky social change has come at breath-taking speed. Indeed a revolution of deep implications has already occurred.

The educational crusade no longer has a biracial complexity; it now confronts the much greater problem of attaining adequate qualitative standards to enable Kentuckians to survive economically. This fact has little or no profound racial implication, and certainly less so in the face of two powerful pieces of civil rights legislation.

Negro leadership is sensitive about many things, some of them highly superficial. For instance, it has objected to the phraseology of "My Old Kentucky Home." This is indeed trivial. In a more positive vein Negroes might look with some reverence upon this song as a touching recitation of their historic plight. It is to be doubted that any Kentuckian ever acquitted himself more nobly in the face of adversity than did the fictitious Uncle Tom. It is almost tragic that his name came to be associated with the modern Negro's bitter disapproval of the subservient attitudes of some members of his race. "Uncle Tomism" is dead in Kentucky even though there are still many hard adjustments to be made between the races in so many areas of Kentucky life. Kentucky has indeed embarked upon a new era in human relations which promises to have nothing much in common with the past.

A Bolt Unloosed

When national political storms thundered through the nation in the 1850's Kentuckians struggled to maintain at least the figure of peace for their state. At the opening of that decade Kentucky's great compromiser, the aging Henry Clay, worked to preserve unity by means of the Compromise of 1850. He spoke both for his people and for his colleagues in Congress. Clay had known many political successes and almost as many disappointments, but none more frustrating than the willfulness of Congress in those searing early summer months of mid-century. The heat and nervous strain were too much for this enfeebled member of the great senatorial triumvirate and he went away to Newport, Rhode Island, to recuperate while younger colleagues, led by Stephen A. Douglas, carried on the fight to accomplish compromise. Back in Kentucky informed persons were happy that at least a promise of national peace had been restored. Kentucky slaveholders were especially relieved that runaway slaves who crossed the Ohio could be recovered under protection of federal law. Governors of bordering Tennessee, Kentucky, Indiana, and Ohio met in conferences during later years in efforts to resolve this thickening problem.

In Kentucky in 1848, Irishmen still fleeing famine and lack of opportunity in their native island, and political refugees from Germany had flocked to the Ohio Valley. Louisville had filled up with Germans who proved themselves thrifty, clever people and they with their Irish neighbors threatened native political control of the city. Too, the influx of Catholics nibbled away at this stronghold of native Protestantism. Native sons reacted with extraordinary vigor. They resented the encroachment of both foreigners and Catholics. A spirit of nativism ran as strong in politics as in religion. Like a rumbling volcano, every contest between native and immigrant brought the issue nearer eruption. On Monday, August 6, 1855, the hotly contested local election in Louisville and Jefferson County brought political matters to a head between the growing nativistic Know-Nothings and the immigrants. This election day resulted in open battle between the two forces in which lives were lost and property worth thousands of dollars was destroyed. "Bloody Monday" symbolized fear, on the one hand, and an ugly stain of shame and prejudice, on the other. The orderly democratic process was dragged in the bloody gutters of Main and Eleventh streets in Louisville. Thoughtful Kentuckians were sobered by this fact. This sort of provincialism and bigotry could only bring social shame and economic ruin to their state.

The deeper conflict in Kentucky was a three-cornered one. Slaveholders were not actually wholly dependent upon their slaves for labor. As the population of towns and cities increased and as the eastern and more isolated rural counties of western Kentucky grew in population, slavery became less significant to the state's economy. Slavery was inefficient, on the one hand, and an economic liability, on the other. Every nightfall threatened loss when a slave might make his way to an underground railway station to be spirited away across the Ohio, a fact which was publicized by almost every critic of slavery who came near the Ohio Valley.

Whatever Kentucky was in 1860 it could hardly have been called a southern state comparable to Mississippi, Alabama, and South Carolina. It was definitely a borderland. A sprawling riverfront of approximately 450 miles made it almost as much a part of the Old Northwest as were Ohio, Indiana, and Illinois. The bonds among this cluster were strong. It is an irony of history that Kentucky allowed itself to be grouped with the lower southern states, even in the categories of the United States Census.

It has been noted already that emigrants from Kentucky went in both directions in their movement away from the state. Scores of them moved families and property to delta and black lowlands of the new cotton states, and quickly sent back to Kentucky for more slaves.

During hot steamy summers when malaria was rampant the cotton barons moved northward to the fashionable summering spas of Kentucky. Their extended visits often resulted in marriages, economic liaisons, and exchanges of political ideas, and even in stirring sectional prejudices. Characteristic of these seasonal gatherings was the fact that only well-to-do and socially prominent individuals came to the springs. Yeoman Kentuckians remained uninfluenced by such intercourse.

Where social loyalties were strong, economic interests were even more binding. From the moment the first frontiersman drifted southward to sell fur and skin packs, and later to peddle hemp, tobacco, liquor, and cured meats, Kentucky's big market lay downstream, but not necessarily with Southerners. Millions of bushels of grain, hogsheads of tobacco, and mounting bales of hemp fiber went this way to market. Both flatboats and steamboats hauled away enormous quantities of processed and manufactured goods to be sold to middlemen. Merchandise was brought from eastern manufacturers and sold to southern and western customers. An observant contemporary said, "Right here, in the very center of the Mississippi Valley, lying like a crouching lion, stretched east and west, is Kentucky, the thoroughbred of the continent." It had direct connections with almost 17,000 miles of navigable water, beginning across its upper border, in its mountain fastness, and leading out to the great arterial Mississippi Valley system. This connected the state with a market serving 12 million people. Kentucky's source of prosperity in the 1850's was this trade. The streets of Louisville were thronged with commercial activity. The riverfront was crowded with steamboats shoving their blunt noses into position to load and unload freight. Stores and warehouses bulged with goods, and merchants grew rich enough to build towering gray Victorian houses along Preston, Chestnut, Brook, Second, Third, and Fourth streets. Across the Bluegrass, Greek Revival mansions reared façades amidst groves of ash, maple, and Scotch pine trees. Hemp, tobacco, and livestock farmers prospered as never before. Monthly court days brought mule, hog, and cattle traders flocking to jockey grounds about country courthouses. Livestock drovers delivered beef, pork, and mules on foot to the lower South. Roads swarmed with these droves and herds. In the spring mule drovers were everywhere in the cotton belt, and with them came slave traders driving their stock in trade in coffles as if they also were livestock.

This was in some respects the golden age of Kentucky. Since the late 1820's the state had been under the domination of Whig leadership, a political faith which was badly shattered with the passing of Henry Clay in 1852. As the nation was troubled in those turbulent years, Kentuckians were redirecting their political interests and maturing a new leadership. Democrats, however, were unable to woo old-line Whigs away from their traditional allegiance, but even so neither Whig nor Democrat wanted to see the bonds of union weakened.

Where Clay, by strong personal magnetism and political astuteness, had held the reins so competently, the task now fell to John Jordan Crittenden. His was a calm and steady leadership which recognized the strength of compromise in terms of bitter crisis. Though there were Kentuckians who favored differing points of view, the central mass agreed heartily with Thomas Riley's note to Crittenden on February 8, 1860: "The great, sound, conservative heart of the commonwealth, who are for the Union, the Constitution—the whole flag, every stripe & every star in its place. This party will struggle for the Union as it was." In November of that year Kentucky voters expressed their feelings. Even though two native sons, John Cabell Breckinridge, southern Democrat, and Abraham Lincoln, Republican, were candidates, Kentuckians rejected both of them. John Bell of Tennessee and his running mate Edward Everett of the Constitutional Union party bore the label, they thought, and maybe had the will to win the "struggle for the Union as it was." Bell received 66,000 votes, Breckinridge 52,800, and Lincoln barely scratched with 1,364.

Beriah Magoffin, a Harrodsburg Know-Nothing, was governor of the commonwealth. At best he was a weak leader, at worst he quibbled on the terms of Union. He had no control of the General Assembly, and under more quiescent circumstances he might have done little more than warm the gubernatorial chair and watch the political pot boil in Frankfort with zeal, which little and partisan men had so often done before him. Late in 1860, however, more was at stake. South Carolina had snapped one of the strings of union. John Jordan Crittenden's compromise proposal was soon to be rejected, and a tug of war had begun. Governor Magoffin could still plead ineffectively for sectional reconciliation by inviting delegates from the southern states to Frankfort to reconsider their acts, and he could send delegates to a peace conference in Washington in February, 1861. Too, he could make an effort to call a convention of border states to form a thick layer of neutrality between the squabbling sections. These things, however, required vigorous and decisive leadership, a quality which the governor did not possess.

The opening months of 1861 were frantic ones in Kentucky. The course for future action had to be set quickly and sensibly to prevent rash actions. As had so often been the case in Kentucky history, the fundamental political leadership did not center itself in Frankfort. There was the strong state press led by George D. Prentice of the Louisville *Journal* and Albert Gallatin Hodges of the *Daily Frankfort Commonwealth*. John Jordan Crittenden and Lazarus W. Powell as United States senators were as influential at home as they were in Washington. James Guthrie, the old Democrat wheelhorse of Pierce's Cabinet, along with John and Joshua Speed of Louisville, joined forces with S. S. Nicholas, Charles Morehead, Garrett Davis, Charles A. Wickliffe, and John Hopkins Harney to work with enormous influence to keep every star and stripe in its proper place in the national flag. Joined with these determined Unionists was Robert Jefferson Breckinridge, who was characterized by Governor Thomas E. Bramlette as a "weathercock in politics and an Ishmaelite in religion." From the outset this hoary old Calvinist fire-eater of many a religious battle thundered a righteous protest against secession. At Lexington, in January, 1861, he counseled his neighbors to follow a course of Moderation—a strange bit of advice to come from this intemperate man in the hotbed of southern sympathy and support and in a place where in earlier years he had attacked the papacy and boss slaveholder Robert Wickliffe with such fury.

Kentucky was vital to the fortunes of the Union, just as it was to the success of the rising Confederacy. When Abraham Lincoln told Governor Magoffin that, "I think to lose Kentucky is nearly the same as to lose the whole game," he understood the significance of the borderland. If Lincoln, a native son, was conscious of this fact, Jefferson Davis was equally perceptive. Davis knew that to make the Ohio the northern boundary of the Confederacy was to gain a sharp advantage for his section. Leadership in Kentucky itself was conscious that pressures to force Kentucky either way would result in civil war among the Kentuckians. There was no hope that the state could be made to join forces with the Union from the outset and to escape retaliation from the Southerners and their southern sympathizers. On the other hand, there was little danger that, relieved of unfortunate pressures, it would secede. To side with either Union or Confederacy would bring war to Kentucky soil. On January 8, 1861, Bell and Douglas partisans met in Louisville and agreed to unite to maintain the Union. In the immediate months ahead the General Assembly adopted a course of neutrality for the state.

Neutrality may have saved Kentucky from tremendous tragedy in terms of loss of human life and property. The historian can do no more than guess that, had the state decided to go either way from the outset, the first major battle line in the West would have been the Ohio River frontier. At no other place in the Union was the personal fact of a nation facing crisis more clearly revealed than in neutral Kentucky. Possibly this could not have taken place with greater personal force anywhere else in the Union. Craven humanity put profit above national security, and merchants, north and south, did a thriving business through the port of Cincinnati. Tremendous tonnage of precious goods of all sorts flowed southward over river and railroad. This was a moment for quick profit taking. Merchants, farmers, speculators, steamboat men of mixed sympathies, or with no sympathies at all, prostituted their loyalties and entered the market with goods.

Louisville became the entrepôt of southern trade. Unionists above the Ohio, and far enough away to raise a clamor without involving self-incrimination, charged that the Kentuckians' actions in this confused moment were actually giving aid and comfort to the enemy. The newly completed Louisville and Nashville Railroad labored under such a burden of freight that it was immediately shaken to pieces. Heavily laden steamboats careened with what Kentucky traders considered the legitimate fruits of commerce, but which nonprofiting Unionists called contraband.

The federal government was asked to regulate if not halt this trade. A blockade was placed on river traffic, but this was highly irritating to Kentucky neutralists, a fact which threatened to lead to political disaffection of the state. By early spring, 1862, the South had secured from the North by way of neutralist Kentucky an astonishing stockpile of products vital to the conduct of the war. For instance, processed meat from 3 million hogs in Ohio and Indiana was sent south. Other food supplies in like quantities glutted the southern market to such an extent that some shortsighted Southerners spoke slightingly of the northern source of supply.

While politicians and traders scurried about either alleviating or aggravating the various crises, individual Kentuckians found themselves in more or less emotional panic. Hot young bloods, bubbling with a sense of chivalry, born of no deep and clear analysis of the fundamental issues which divided North and South, prepared to join the Confederacy. They were loud in expressing their opinions, and their future actions more often than not were decided on a purely emotional basis. The army of the rising Confederacy had for them the tug of a Robin Hood romance. In Bluegrass Kentucky, especially, the call to action was medieval in its appeal to the hot blooded. Young men in Lexington, Harrodsburg, Danville, and other Bluegrass towns made quick decisions to side with the South. In Pennyroyal and Purchase, nearer the southern scene, decisions came even faster and more furiously for the southern cause. The course of events in western Tennessee and in the delta South inflamed the feelings and imaginations in this corner of the state.

Kentucky faced immediate difficulties. With prospects of war on both sides, and imminent danger of invasion, it was necessary to modernize a flaccid and disorganized peacetime state guard. Simon Bolivar Buckner, native son and a graduate of West Point with extensive military experience, was entrusted with the task of revitalizing the state militia. Both Governor Magoffin and General Buckner began a series of mysterious communications with the United States War Department. They sought federal arms to equip the guard. Buckner's hand in this is not clearly revealed. In a vague letter Governor Magoffin informed Secretary of War Simon Cameron that Buckner was an accredited agent of the state and that "he understands and will explain the position Kentucky has assumed in regard to our national difficulties, and the policy we have thought proper to pursue." Whatever this pair had in mind, Secretary Cameron was too wary to cooperate with them.

Almost immediately after Buckner's Washington visit it was evident that the state militiamen would be lost to Kentucky. In Lexington the swashbuckling blood-about-town John Hunt Morgan, grandson of Lexington's wealthiest merchant, drilled his Lexington Rifles. Other southern sympathizers prepared commands for future service. Buckner's command consisted of sixty-one companies, a force which dashed away from Kentucky by late summer of 1861 to fight for the Confederacy.

Kentucky Unionists correctly suspected Governor Magoffin of

being less than loyal to the state's neutral position. They knew of his secret requests for Confederate arms and they knew that he had entertained subversive messengers from the South. Too, they knew that to depend upon the state guard was to subject Kentucky to treachery. In May, 1861, the General Assembly provided for the organization of a second militia to be comprised of loyal Unionists and to be called Home Guards. It authorized the borrowing of $1.6 million to equip and maintain this new force. Attempts were made to recover state guard arms, but this only touched off a furious scramble for guns and ammunition. State unionist leadership, centered largely in Louisville and Frankfort, looked to Washington for aid.

Abraham Lincoln and Secretary Cameron, as well as Kentucky Unionists, knew that to openly support Union forces in the state or to commit an overt act which would violate Kentucky neutrality would drive the state into the Confederacy. Yet Kentuckians devised an ingenious scheme for securing arms. They understood the psychology of their people. Since the first frontiersmen had fended off Indian attacks, a gun was considered a necessary piece of domestic equipment. They persuaded President Lincoln to authorize in May, 1861, the issuance of 5,000 rifles to be given loyal citizens to be used in protecting their homes. These guns were brought into Kentucky by steamboat, rail, and wagon. They were distributed in Louisville and about Camp Dick Robinson in Boyle County. In transporting these guns halfway across the state, Unionists and Confederate sympathizers played a cloak-and-dagger game. From Maysville to Lexington Unionist Colonel Leonidas Metcalfe discovered that his wagoner was a treacherous southern sympathizer who stopped along the way to send news ahead to mobs that he was coming with a wagonload of guns. In Lexington, however, John Cabell Breckinridge and Madison C. Johnson counseled southern partisans to allow the guns to be carried on to Camp Dick Robinson south of the Kentucky River without incident. Perhaps they were influenced by the presence of Colonel Frank Wolford's mounted command. Thus it was that Abraham Lincoln, with the help of shrewd Kentuckians, succeeded in a covert way in invading the state without technically violating its neutrality. The people themselves had carried out the invasion.

Confederates gathered along the Tennessee banks were less subtle in their actions. Yankees were able to concentrate in force all along the river frontier in Union territory. At almost any point they chose they could thrust salients of invasion not only into the side of Kentucky but likewise into the widely exposed flank of the lower South itself. Three major rivers slashed gores of penetration to the very heart of the region, and Kentucky was a staging area at the top of this river system.

In the well-nigh indefensible geographical triangle formed by the Mississippi, Ohio, Cumberland, and Tennessee rivers, the Union command, poised along the Ohio and Mississippi, could take its choice of places to strike. The short waist of the Kentucky Purchase beyond the Tennessee offered no serious check to the march into western Tennessee to close the gap in the Mississippi and to open a deep channel into the heartland of cotton and secession. Neutrality in Kentucky in the face of these cold realities of war quickly became a matter of academics. Political liabilities involved in crossing an army into the state were great, but the military stakes were high. No one appreciated this fact more than those amateur Confederate strategists Generals Leonidas Polk and Gideon Pillow, who saw Columbus, Kentucky, on the Mississippi as a key to saving the river south. Across the Mississippi at Belmont, Missouri, Ulysses S. Grant and his Illinois Volunteers were getting their first taste of war. They faced the border South with an ominous threat. On September 2 and 3, 1861, Confederate troops under General Pillow moved up from New Madrid Bend in Tennessee to occupy Hickman, and General Polk joined them in Columbus. Thus overnight Kentucky's neutrality was destroyed. With Confederates concentrated at Columbus and U. S. Grant's inexperienced army pushing upstream from the steaming willow flats of Missouri, the southwest corner of Kentucky was ablaze with war. The Confederates quickly flung out a wavering line of attack from Columbus on the Missisippi to Cumberland Gap on the east. This line sagged, largely under its own weight. A thrust against it in force at any point would have threatened disaster all along the way.

Albert Sidney Johnston had resigned his commission as a Union officer and come home to Kentucky to command the volunteers located on the straggling line from east Tennessee to Arkansas. About Russellville and Bowling Green he gathered raw recruits and worked furiously to make soldiers out of them. He held the center position of the swaying western Confederate line in his position at

Bowling Green. On his east flank the relatively inexperienced journalist-politician General Felix Zollicoffer rushed from eastern Tennessee to occupy Cumberland Gap.

Lack of communications, stabilized supply, and unity of command all contributed to confusion of the Confederates. Zollicoffer was drawn away from his eastern anchorage to engage in October, 1861, in the futile skirmish of Wild Cat Mountain in Rockcastle County. He was caught in a second and fatal skirmish with George Thomas' Federal troops at Mill Springs. The Confederate line was broken. Grant and his new colleague, William T. Sherman, had not lingered to swap shots with the entrenched Polk at Columbus. Instead they moved with rapidity on Paducah and forced their way into the Cumberland and Tennessee rivers, and then moved southward. Behind them Louisville was made a Union headquarters town, and the Federal grip on Kentucky was tightened. No longer did a reluctant Lincoln in Washington, or a nerve-shattered William T. Sherman in Louisville, or an overcautious group of well-meaning citizens hesitate to take a positive action for fear of alienating the commonwealth. Polk had cast the die of invasion, but not until Unionists were able to consolidate their position and to gain control of political affairs in Frankfort.

For General Grant, the shrewd decision to force his way upstream along the Cumberland and Tennessee past Confederate strongholds was the beginning of a distinguished military career. Just as the eastern Confederate line had crumpled at Wild Cat and Mill Springs, Grant slashed in behind Polk at Columbus, threatened to maroon Johnston and his 28,000 troops at Bowling Green, and engaged his foe in well-executed recoil actions at Forts Henry and Donelson in February, 1862. Crashing these barriers from his path, he opened the Tennessee ahead of him. He headed southward in steamboats. With the fall of Fort Donelson Johnston withdrew from Bowling Green and moved on to Shiloh or Pittsburg Landing and to his death.

Behind the retreating armies Kentucky was left in the kind of calm which follows the first blow of a mighty storm. The war was gone from its borders so far as important fighting was concerned. Victory at Shiloh had sent Grant charging even more vigorously southward, and the threat to Kentucky was now clouded by uncertainty. That there should be a backlash of invasion following Shiloh was a keen possibility.

In July, 1862, John Hunt Morgan and his homesick command galloped across the state border near Tompkinsville on their way to harass central Kentucky. Behind them they left panic and before them they spread terror. Nothing Morgan did on this raid can be considered of great military significance. But this rollicking gallop into the Bluegrass gave a keen edge of drama to the war. As usual Kentucky was on the verge of a hot political election and the homecoming of the hard-riding raiders added spice, if not influence, to the perennial summer campaign.

Morgan and his men rode back to Kentucky partly as a homecoming visit, but more to frighten Unionists and to disrupt communication lines. Too, they no doubt were preparing the way for Braxton Bragg's subsequent invasion. At Harrodsburg and Lawrenceburg they enjoyed hefty meals of hot biscuits and fried chicken, country ham, and Shakertown preserves. At Shakertown itself they raised the wind. In that community of staid and sexless converts of Mother Ann Lee's frigid philosophy of love and life, the appearance of Morgan's voracious horsemen was a great deal more realistic and far less decorous than were those silent visitations of Benjamin Franklin, George Washington, and the Hebrew fathers, Abraham, Isaac, Jacob, and Esau, as described by the faithful community recorder. The brothers and sisters were sent scurrying about the yards catching chickens, slicing hams, opening jars of jam, and making biscuits. Hardly had the last greasy-mouthed horseman galloped from sight down the Harrodsburg Pike before the harried recorder was at his books. He scribbled a note of relief that the conscienceless horde of Confederates had come and gone. Now order could be restored and the horrible memory of the sweaty raiders could be erased by the more pleasant and spiritual visitations of Chief Tecumseh, Red Jacket, and General James Wilkinson.

Converging on the most unprepossessing military objective in all the land, Morgan's raiders captured sleepy little Midway in Woodford County and the telegraph office of the Lexington and Frankfort Railway. Here the expert telegrapher George Ellsworth created pandemonium among officials in Louisville, Frankfort, and Lexington. Though he was virtually surrounded by Union forces, Morgan was in command of the telegraph wires at least. His messages were intended to obscure his real objectives, Cynthiana and the Central of Kentucky Railroad. The result of Ellsworth's alarming messages was the awakening of President Lincoln and General William S. Rosecrans from their early Sunday morning slumbers. It seemed from the Kentuckians' messages that Morgan was about to pop up everywhere in central Kentucky. Troops were sent out from Lexington and Frankfort only to be recalled when Ellsworth sent his farewell message that Morgan was leaving Midway. If the Confederates were not fighting the Union troops and the Home Guards they were at least wearing them down by running them up and down the roads. While Brigadier General Jerry Boyle of Louisville and Governor James F. Robinson in Frankfort, several Union officers, and a host of private citizens planned feverishly to head off the raiders, Morgan dashed into Georgetown and aroused that peaceful county seat community just before churchtime. His handbills published in Glasgow had preceded him. Like a modern Napoleon or a grandiloquent Joan of Arc, he orated:

Kentuckians, I come to liberate you from a despotism of tyrannical faction and to rescue my native state from the hands of your oppressors. Everywhere the cowardly foe has fled from my avenging arms. My brave army is stigmatized as a band of guerrillas and marauders. Believe it not. I point with pride to their deeds as a refutation of this foul aspersion. We come not to molest peaceful individuals or to destroy private property, but guarantee absolute protection to all who are not in arms against us. We ask only to meet the hireling legions of Lincoln. The eyes of your brethren of the South are upon you. Your gallant fellow citizens are flocking to our standard. Our armies are rapidly advancing to your protection. Then greet them with willing hands of fifty thousand of Kentucky's brave. Their advance is already with you.

This was Kentucky oratory of heroic proportions, clichés and all. Like a young Tom Marshall standing high in his stirrups, Morgan rendered a peroration that remains unsurpassed:

THEN STRIKE FOR THE GREEN GRAVES OF YOUR SIRES!
STRIKE FOR YOUR ALTARS AND YOUR FIRES!
GOD AND YOUR NATIVE LAND!

Morgan did little more than strike his native land a glancing blow at Cynthiana Bridge. Colonel Thomas J. Landram's command of Home Guards and Federal cavalry was too strong for the small raider band under Morgan. A brief skirmish at the bridge and the old covered structure was to stand bullet-laden for the rest of its existence. Before the last screaming raider had turned and dashed over the hills along the very paths where a century before Shawnee warriors had come looking for scalps, the feather-bedecked Morgan was gone. The feint against Cynthiana had perhaps for its purpose the creation of the illusion that Morgan was headed for Cincinnati, but more specifically it was a thrust to give him an opportunity to make his escape from Kentucky.

For twenty-four days Morgan and his men had terrorized the land where rested "the green graves of (their) sires." The Kentuckians had disappointed them. They failed to flock into the Georgetown camp in large numbers to fight for the Confederacy. Morgan fled to eastern Tennessee, but not before Ellsworth had one final fling on the telegraph. At Somerset Morgan wired his old friend General Boyle, United States Commandant of Kentucky, the cheery note, "Good morning, Jerry. This telegraph is a great institution. You should destroy it as it keeps me posted too well. My friend Ellsworth has all your dispatches since July 10 on file. Do you want copies?"

Morgan had come like Zeus hurling telegraphic thunderbolts, majestic proclamations, and gathering fresh horses and fried chicken and ham as he went. Behind him galloped a second Confederate horseman at the head of a larger command. General Edmund Kirby-Smith invaded Kentucky on a mission of drawing the war back into the state. He led his command along the Wilderness Road from eastern Tennessee and through Cumberland Gap to prepare the way for Braxton Bragg's invasion. Less noisily than Morgan, this officer, on his first independent assignment, closed in on central Kentucky with 12,000 troops. He traveled hard and fast, his men galloped by old landmarks that were reminiscent of the great pioneer advance into Kentucky. At the crossroads village of Kingston, Smith's troops were fired on by Union pickets. On the humid last day of August, 1862, there opened the Battle of Richmond in which General William ("Bull") Nelson's poorly seasoned troops were driven back over twenty miles of Bluegrass farmland to Clay's Ferry crossing of the Kentucky River.

Taking his ease in Lexington, the mercurial Nelson learned too late that his command was being hard pressed in battle. He rushed over the Richmond Pike to the river, but the battle was over and his men were in disorderly retreat. He slapped angrily at fleeing men with the flat of his sword, but General Kirby-Smith's army was too hot on his heels and he too dashed off into inglorious retreat.

While Kirby-Smith was enjoying the first flushes of victory Morgan was in east Tennessee, and again issuing flamboyant handbills. With Kentucky safely beyond the Cumberland ranges, he addressed his command:

Soldiers: Your country makes a fresh appeal to your patriotism and courage.

It has been decided that Kentucky must be freed from the detested northern yoke, and who so fit to carry out this order as yourselves?

The road is well known to you! You have already taught the tyrants at Tompkinsville, Lebanon, and Cynthiana that where Southern hearts nerve southern arms, our Soldiers are invincible.

Again there was a wonderful saddle-stirrup peroration. Like an Alexander the Great or a Roman Hadrian fresh from conquest, Morgan literally shouted:

To an enemy be as tigers, to our Southern brethren be as lambs! Protect their homes, respect their property! Is it not that of your Fathers, Mothers, Sisters, and Friends!

Soldiers: I feel assured that you will return with fresh laurels to enjoy in peace the fruits of your glorious victories!

In the meantime let your avenging Battle-cry be: "Butler!" But shout "Kentucky" to your kindred and friends.

Back in Kentucky a less eloquent Jacob Cox of Ohio took a closer look at the raider and his men and appraised them less majestically:

> John Morgan's foot is on thy shore
>   Kentucky! O Kentucky!
> His hand is on thy stable door,
>   Kentucky! O Kentucky!
> You'll see your good gray mare no more,
> He'll ride her till her back is sore
> And leave her at some stranger's door,
>   Kentucky! O Kentucky!

Central Kentucky was a mire of quicksand for armies. Kirby-Smith might have attacked Cincinnati. He might even have struck a harder blow at Kentucky itself, but his actions were characteristic of Confederate indecision and delay. He seemed bent as much on a political as a military mission. Confederates still hoped to join Kentucky politically to their cause. While Kirby-Smith waited in Lexington for Braxton Bragg to arrive, a contingent of his command took Frankfort, but not before state officials had fled to Louisville.

Moving up from the neighborhood of Nashville along a most uncertain route, and for a most uncertain objective, General Bragg came with a command of 28,000 troops and an interminable wagon train. He lacked a sense of strategy, and his purpose seemed to have been lost during those days of grinding ponderously northward. At Green River Bridge he stopped to fight a costly and meaningless skirmish. Creaking on, Bragg turned his column inland away from Louisville and toward the militarily sterile country about Harrodsburg and Danville.

Bragg's objectives in Kentucky were not purely military. In a public proclamation issued from Bardstown he revealed his intent of once again trying to rally Kentuckians politically and economically to the Confederate cause. He wished to seat a Confederate in the governor's chair in Frankfort and to hasten Confederate representatives off to Richmond. For a brief moment he partially accomplished this objective when Richard Hawes posed as Confederate governor, but he was not in office long enough to have any impact on political affairs. The appearance of Colonel Sill's cavalry company above the capital on the western river hills sent the Confederates, including General Bragg, scurrying for safety.

By every standard of military strategy Braxton Bragg proved himself a poor general officer. He seemed to have taken no mature stock of either his objective or his situation in Kentucky. At the same time he labored under a political preconception because of his lack of factual information and judgment. Unionism was too strong in the state for any officer entrusted with the safety of human lives to take chances. His proclamation that he had arrived in Kentucky to free the people rang as emptily as a clapperless bell. The people were already free and wished to remain so.

Following Bragg out of Tennessee came that equally indecisive and ponderous officer Don Carlos Buell. General Buell was in pursuit of Bragg, uncertain though he was as to what point in Kentucky Bragg was headed. Sluggish and plodding Prussian that he was, Buell did credit Bragg with having enough imagination to select a major objective, and that was Louisville, and the Louisville and Nashville Railway line. At no time did Buell seem anxious to press upon the heels of Bragg or to frustrate his march.

Bragg's failure to drive with crushing speed toward the Falls of the Ohio gave Buell an opportunity to slip unhindered into Louisville with its strategic position and important sources of supply. With this major base of operation immediately at his back and now in command of 61,000 men, many of whom were Kentuckians, fresh for battle, Buell set out to confront the Confederates. Early in October and in the hot season in Kentucky the two armies stumbled thirstily through the rock- and brush-cluttered inner layers of the encircling Kentucky knobs. Water became a major need of troops on both sides, and soldiers hunted along the arid creek beds for stagnant puddles from which to slake their thirst. While wandering along the creeks the two armies drifted into battle. On October 8, 1862, there opened the bloody engagement of Perryville. In the peak of battle 28,000 men were under fire, and when the fighting ended 7,736 of them had been killed or wounded.

In battle Bragg was as hesitant and indecisive as he had been on maneuvers. Across the ridges from Confederate headquarters Don Carlos Buell was as timid and indecisive as was his foe. He had won the first element of victory but lacked the courage to push ahead for the rout and destruction of the Confederates. For him Perryville became the badge of failure, even though he won the battle. Bragg lacked the ingenuity and determination to pull his forces together to fight another day; instead he followed Morgan's trail southward to eastern Tennessee. Behind him lay defeat, hundreds of dead and wounded men. With him went knowledge of monstrous failure as a commander. He had learned a bitter lesson in his attempt to dabble in Kentucky politics.

In the van of the Confederate columns lumbered 4,000 wagons loaded with loot gathered in central Kentucky. Lexington alone supplied 7,000 barrels of pork and $90,000 worth of clothing. Other materials were commandeered in like quantities. It was said that it took two and a half days for the line of wagons to creep past a given point.

For Kentucky, Perryville ended the important fighting in the Civil War on its soil. It would perhaps not be too harsh a judgment to say that this bloody encounter had little or no decisive significance in the military decisions which took place in the war. Certainly it failed to change Unionist attitudes of a majority of the Kentuckians. But this was not the part of the war which pinched Kentucky. There was the eternal skirmishing. John Hunt Morgan's raiders rode once again back into the state along the Louisville and Nashville Railroad during December of that year. They played havoc with transportation facilities, threatened Louisville, and upset Kentucky generally. They captured Elizabethtown and its Federal garrison, burned the tremendously important trestle on the Louisville and Nashville at Muldraugh's Hill, and then turned back to Tennessee. Morgan's retreat to Tennessee by way of Bardstown, Springfield, and Campbellsville was a test of men and horses. The weather was bitter, and the Yankees were concentrated across his path and at his back.

In July, 1863, Morgan and his men were back in Kentucky, this time driving up from Burkesville, Columbia, again over the road to Campbellsville and Lebanon, and then making a wild ride to Brandenburg and the Ohio River. They were on their way to invade Indiana and to raid Ohio. Few times in the war did so few men undertake such an ambitious task. Morgan's true objectives on this raid are still veiled in mystery. His invasion threw Governor Levi Morton and his Hoosiers into a panic, and even stirred up the people of Ohio, but the raid ended in the capture of Morgan and his men and their imprisonment in the Ohio Penitentiary. Morgan was to raid again in Kentucky, but on this later ride his old fire had gone. There was no buffoonery on the telegraph lines and no throbbing saddle-stirrup oratory. His men, under the command of Captain C. A. Withers, robbed the Farmer's Bank of Mount Sterling of $45,000. Morgan was enraged at the actions of his men, and the Confederate cause suffered irreparable damage. A surprise attack by Stephen Burbridge against his troops at Mount Sterling decided Morgan to ride away once again to east Tennessee. He rushed through the eastern mountains to Greenville, Tennessee, and to death at the hands of a Federal trooper.

Morgan had caused much damage to property in Kentucky, his men had ridden many a horse away from the state without bothering to get the owner's consent, and his raids had created consternation time after time. But he was never able to gain a foothold in the state. His reputation far exceeded his permanent gains, and it grew in the future with the mellowing of those raiders who recalled the days when their swashbuckling leader had ridden at the head of his column with his feather-bedecked hat as a banner of daring.

There were countless other raiders who lashed at the border state during the war. Scarcely a community escaped some kind of clash of arms. Humphrey Marshall and James A. Garfield fought minor engagements in eastern Kentucky. Earlier in the war Frank Wolford's cavalry had struck in running skirmishes, and conflicts between guerrillas and Home Guards or between rival factions in local communities brought the war to the very doors of the people. In western Kentucky there were frequent fights which sometimes were more nearly outbreaks of local political rows than military activities.

The parts of the shooting war which struck the people the hardest were the heartless guerrilla raids. Almost no part of Kentucky escaped pillaging by these vicious scoundrels. They attacked defenseless families and Union and Confederate troops alike. Confusion early in the war between State Guard and Home Guards, the lack of positive action on the part of Governor Magoffin, and the excitement of citizens' groups were contributory to the organization of these lawless bands. Distribution of the Lincoln guns, though technically not a violation of Kentucky's neutrality, placed one phase of the struggle on a highly personal basis in the giving of guns to nonmilitary personnel.

The division of families in their loyalties created further tensions. As a neutral state Kentucky had largely dodged great physical injury, except to its railroads, but the war opened the way for monstrous internal social and political damage. In its newly formed militia, the Home Guards, there was lack of discipline, and in far too many instances willful men under the guise of public authority set out to regulate community affairs to suit themselves. They settled lingering private grudges and opened new ones. They were often unable to distinguish between necessary military action and murder or between supplying a military command and outright thievery of property.

Guerrillas appeared in almost every county in Kentucky. They ranged from malicious local regulators to highhanded and well-organized bands of thieves and cutthroats. There were Rowzee's Gang, Skagg's Men, Quantrill's raiders, Sue Munday's band, and those loosely banded villains led by "One Arm" Berry. News got around among the evil scum on the fringes of the war in other states that neutral Kentucky was fair hunting ground for thieves and brigands.

Already local sons were demonstrating this to be true. During the last two years of the war Kentucky was threatened with social and political anarchy because of the brigandage within its border. Union commanders claimed that guerrillas operated as arms of the Confederate Army and Confederates charged they were Union sympathizers.

On January 4, 1864, Governor Thomas E. Bramlette (elected in August, 1863) issued a proclamation in which he proposed to hold Confederate sympathizers responsible for damages arising from guerrilla raids. In cases where loyal citizens were kidnaped, five of the most active rebel sympathizers were to be arrested and held as hostages. General Stephen Burbridge, who never did anything halfway, not even to stealing profits from the sale of hogs, issued his stringent "Order 59" in which he proposed to arrest rebel sympathizers within a radius of five miles of the places where guerrilla crimes were committed. Rebel property was to be seized, and when loyal Unionists were murdered, five guerrilla prisoners were to be shot in public. In October, 1864, General Burbridge ordered Union officers to receive no guerrilla prisoners of war, but to have them shot immediately as traitors. In other orders rebels were to be assessed levies to restore losses suffered by their loyal neighbors at the hands of guerrillas.

One of the native sons who became notorious bandit leaders was Sue Munday (Jerome Clark), from Franklin in Simpson County, who took civil affairs into his own hands. In May, 1865, he was captured at Webster in Breckinridge County, and in quick order this simpering coward was tried, converted to the Episcopal faith, and hanged in Louisville. One Arm Berry was more fortunate, but no less offensive in his raids. He escaped the harsh fate of other guerrillas.

From outside the state Champ Ferguson, guerrilla and possibly Confederate spy, came to harass communities along the Tennessee border. Fresh from the sacking of Lawrence, Kansas, and its wholesale murders came William C. Quantrill. Quantrill was a western bad man who carried on his own private war against border society until things got too hot for him. He trailed across Missouri into Kentucky early in 1865. Once east of the Mississippi he began to blaze a trail of terror and robbery toward central Kentucky. Near Taylorsville, at Wakefield Station, he was shot and captured by Captain Terrill's Union company, and was hauled off to Louisville to die far too decent a death in a military hospital.

Two of the most notorious guerrilla warriors were gone. Behind them they left scores of nameless raiders who inflicted great damage on people and property. By the closing year of the war rural Kentucky was aflame with local hatreds. Every eastern mountain county was victimized by raids, but none was more embittered than those along the Big Sandy River. In this rugged and isolated land both Confederates and Unionists had struggled to free themselves of threatening land entrapments, and had fought each other in skirmishes in doing so. At the same time vicious men, associated with neither army, cut down neighbors in cold blood while passing themselves off as soldiers of one of the armies. They ransacked houses and stores, attacked defenseless women, and stole thousands of horses, cows, hogs, and sheep. For a quarter of a century after 1865 circuit court dockets in the Big Sandy counties were cluttered with suits seeking redress for losses suffered at the hands of thieving guerrillas.

Hatfields hated and shot McCoys for many reasons, but an important one was injury inflicted by guerrillas. Names of these families, especially of the McCoys, appear in court cases involving war damage. A McCoy was a member of a gang which robbed a country store in Pike County. They took everything in sight including a bag of goose feathers. One of these medieval thieves mounted his horse, already swaying under the weight of loot; about his neck he had piled several layers of hoop-skirt bands, and on his head he had stacked several ladies' hats, and as he rode away he shouted jubilantly, "I'm going home to my ducky!" Sullen but defenseless mountaineers watched these vandals pillage their property but they marked the future day when they would bring them fair between the sights of a hog rifle.

Great was the physical damage done railroads and some property in Kentucky during the war, but none was more intense or lasting than the personal hatreds that were incurred. An innocent man who was either imprisoned or assessed for damages done in his neighborhood refused to forget his injuries in later years. Schools were virtually disbanded. In Lexington Transylvania University was vandalized by soldiers. Canals, rivers and locks and dams, factories, and highways suffered serious injury or were destroyed. No one could estimate the damage done morale; even future political growth was stymied. A generation was forced into ignorance to await reorganization of the schools and colleges. Although a part of the state's economy had actually profited from the war, the phenomenal shrinkage of live-stock, farm products, and other forms of wealth was revealed in the census count of 1870.

The highhanded acts of Union military officers in their interference with political affairs in Kentucky were among the most disgraceful in American history. Beriah Magoffin was forced to resign the governor-ship in August, 1862, in favor of the more conservative James F. Robinson. By this time discontent with President Lincoln's policies, especially those relating to use of Negro troops and interference with slavery, was great. Federal military officers took it upon themselves to stamp out opposition to administrative policies. They refused to allow political groups to meet in public assembly or to explain their pur-poses. They ruled the names of candidates off ballots and openly intimidated voters. Thomas E. Bramlette was elected governor in 1863 under the most undemocratic circumstances imaginable. Laza-rus W. Powell, United States senator, found himself under the mili-tary surveillance of Generals Halleck and Burnside because of his independent assertions. The number of votes cast in Kentucky be-cause of this intimidation was greatly reduced.

The name of Chief Justice Alvin Duvall was removed from consid-eration as a candidate for the United States Senate by that masterful hog thief Stephen Burbridge. President Lincoln himself interfered shamefully with free elections in Kentucky by declaring martial law and removing the writ of habeas corpus during the local elections in August, 1864. Burbridge further intimidated voters by saying prior to the presidential election of that year, "Now, gentlemen, you all want pay for your horses and niggers and corn, and your hogs. Be cautious what record you make."

Even Governor Bramlette, who owed his own election to voter intimidation, was angered by Federal action. He wrote President Lin-coln, "We are dealt with as though Kentucky was a rebellious and conquered province, instead of being as they are, a brave and loyal people." Interference with free political expression in Kentucky from 1863 to 1865 was indeed a stain on President Lincoln's administra-tion, and it was a provocation of internal suspicions and resentments which have endured a century.

At one stage of the earlier phases of the sectional dispute Ken-tuckians hoped Congress would compensate them for their 230,000 slaves to the extent of $34 million and thus bring an end to that institution without financial loss. This was never accomplished. As early as 1862 the United States Army began recruiting Negroes into its ranks and almost 30,000 ex-slaves found their way to freedom by this route. The Army employed others in work gangs which meant freedom for them, and, after March 3, 1865, for members of their families. General John M. Palmer of Illinois replaced the highhanded Burbridge as military commander in Kentucky in February of that year. He began immediately to destroy the last vestiges of slavery. He issued the famous "Palmer's Passes" which sent thousands of slaves scurrying across the Ohio to freedom, and by midsummer he had made the former exodus of slaves through the old underground railway seem a pleasant trickle compared with his floods. By October the institution of slavery was so badly crippled that there was little left to be accomplished in Kentucky by the adoption of the Thirteenth Amendment.

In two areas the Civil War in Kentucky exerted a deep and lasting influence. Fathers and sons were divided in their loyalties. Brother opposed brother and neighbor was set against neighbor. A brother, three half brothers, and the husbands of three half sisters of Mary Todd Lincoln fought in the Confederate Army, while a brother and a half sister remained loyal to the Union. Robert J. Breckinridge, as keynote speaker in the Republican National Convention in Baltimore in 1864, said that "The only enduring, the only imperishable cement of all free institutions has been the blood of traitors." He had two sons, a son-in-law, and his nephew John Cabell Breckinridge in the Confederate Army. These were among the traitors whose blood the fiery preacher was ready to spill. One of his sons was in the Union Army, and another was a cadet at West Point. James Brown Clay, son of the ardent old Unionist Henry, and four Clay grandsons fought under the stars and bars. John Jordan Crittenden's sons were divided, one of them resigning a United States Army commission to serve with the Confederacy; both of them became generals. The sons of George D. Prentice followed the Crittenden example by dividing their loyalties from their father's, and later the father pleaded with Abraham Lincoln to allow his son Courtland to be exchanged from a Union prison.

Sixty-seven of Kentucky's native sons served the Union cause in the rank of general, while thirty-eight attained like rank in the Confederate Army. In fact, native son Robert Anderson was in command at Fort Sumter when it was fired on in April, 1861. The impact of war on Kentucky was to be measured more precisely in terms of men who served in the two armies and in the Home Guards than in terms of action on its soil. Despite the campaigns of the Confederates, and subsequent irritation over the enlistment of Negro troops into the Union Army, Kentucky filled its draft quotas. In all, 76,000 men served the Union, while approximately 25,000 went to the Confederacy. At Shiloh, Perryville, Stones River, Chickamauga, and with Sherman before Atlanta and on the march to the sea, Kentuckians fought Kentuckians. At Perryville eight regiments of native sons fought on the side of the Union. Perhaps one of the most rugged fighting units in the whole Civil War was the 1st Kentucky Confederate, or "Orphan Brigade," which was organized at Bowling Green on October 28, 1861, and was disbanded in North Carolina in April, 1865, when Joe Johnston surrendered to William T. Sherman. It fought in every major engagement in the West from Shiloh to Atlanta. Before Atlanta it lost 860 men in a hundred days. Out of 1,065 men before Atlanta only 240 endured to the end of the war. Of all Kentucky sons engaged in war, 10,000 died of battle wounds and another 20,000 fell victims of disease and exposure. Approximately half the Kentuckians who reached manhood during the decade 1850-1860 were either destroyed or disabled by war. Thus was the "neutral" borderland caught in the hard bind between warring sections. It paid a high price to keep every star and stripe in place in the flag. Kentucky blood spilled in the war was bitter and black. Hatreds and enmities ran deep—and ruins, spiritual and physical, crippled at least two future generations emotionally.

Just as Kentuckians in 1861 found themselves divided in their loyalties, so they were again divided in 1961. Two Civil War Centennial Commissions, supported by the state, set out to celebrate four years of remembering. Men at Civil War round tables in Louisville and Lexington fanned the embers of memory by listening to gentle, and sometimes not so gentle stories, of the war, and by dressing up like sleek overfed Union and Confederate soldiers playing at battle, rather than thinking in the grisly terms of 30,000 Kentuckians whose lives had been snuffed out. Despite the fact that 76,000 Kentuckians in all were drawn into the war and sixty-seven native generals were in and out of battle, the facts of economic and social history of this period seem too unromantic and dry. The arguments of Clay and

Crittenden now appear too technical or too boring to be discussed by a speaker who comes armed with maps, charts, and a devotion to second-guessing the strategist. It is exciting to ride vicariously with Morgan and Kirby-Smith, and even to straggle along with Buell and Bragg, but the hard facts of the Civil War in Kentucky had fundamental meanings in their long-range importance.

By Their Works
Ye Shall Know Them

Three things can be said with assurance about Kentucky politics and politicians. First, politics is the oldest practical art form in Kentucky history. It was brought across the mountains by the first settlers and it has flourished ever since. Second, it is perennially a topic of conversation which keeps the boys talking and arguing at the crossroads, around the courthouses on Saturdays, about the churches on Sundays, and up the creeks and in the newspaper offices every day. Finally, nobody can tell for certain today who will be "sleeping together" politically next campaign season.

Politics is played in Kentucky as a game, but it is played with vengeance between the "ins" and the "outs," and the hunger of the outs for office and patronage is insatiable. Ever since the first Virginia sheriff arrived in a backwoods county to keep order there has been a yearning for public favor in Kentucky. The sheriff brought with him as chief item of his official baggage the germ of politics. Aside from performing his constabulary duties he courted the voters to ensure his re-election. This has kept up; but the interesting thing about political campaigning in Kentucky is the intensity of the ardor with which an ignoramus seeks election to a rural constableship and that of a candidate seeking the governorship. Perhaps the only discernible difference is that the gubernatorial candidate covers more territory, eats more poorly barbecued meat, gives more speeches, kisses more babies, offers more promises, and screams louder in favor of God, home, and mother.

Some Kentucky campaigns have generated a tremendous amount of heat from mudslinging and character assassination. If the people took really seriously such charges and countercharges they would disband the state's government, throw the capitol into the Kentucky River, and lock all the politicians behind jail bars. To hear the opposition tell it, the people elected four years before a band of pirates, horse thieves, thugs, embezzlers, and dumbbells to office, chief of whom was the governor. It has been many a year since a man occupied the Kentucky governor's chair without some time or other being charged with building an "administration machine," with being power mad, venal, incapable, naïve, and a captive of special interests.

Under the provisions of the Constitution, the governor has only four years in which to make his magic. A new governor coming into office scarcely has time to doff his rented plug hat, shuck his morning coat, and pull off his striped inaugural britches before the political pundits begin picking his successor. That is how he himself was projected before the people. If a new governor hopes to honor a reasonable number of his glibly uttered campaign promises, then he has to get down to business with a widely ranging program at the first of the biennial legislative sessions, or he will be caught the second time around with empty patronage pockets and a willful legislature on his hands, and there is nothing more flatulent than a governor short on political favors.

Being governor of Kentucky at times must be akin to having the itch. The man is never free from the self-seekers. They spring up like India's poor from the streets holding out their bony hands crying for baksheesh. They clamor for jobs for themselves, their sons, and their daughters, they want pardons for wayward husbands, brothers, and cousins, improved roads past their doors (some have been accused of seeking hard-surfaced drives onto their farms), they seek appointments to boards, the creation of state parks, and the location of state garages in every county, or to get a son graduated from a state college. They never give up.

Somewhere in the dark past a reckless governor favored a friend by making him a colonel of nothing really. This was one of the most annoying blunders in Kentucky history. The governor may have salved the ego of a friend but he opened a floodgate to favor seekers. Almost everybody wants to be a colonel or an admiral of a muddy branch. Every time a convention meets or someone visits Kentucky, a friend besieges the governor's office begging for a commission. The governor's anteroom is never free of the seekers who no doubt are as politically threatening as were the long and hostile Shawnee gantlets of pioneer days.

One revered old governor told a group of intimate friends at a meeting of the Kentucky Club in Washington that there were two things he never wanted to have again. One was gonorrhea, and the other the governorship of Kentucky. Remarkably few of his listeners shared the old man's views of the latter honor. Some of them at the moment were scheming to return to the wheel of Frankfort and the endless supplications of the "deserving." They still seek in Kentucky to better Isaac Shelby's two-term record as governor, 1792-1796 and 1812-1816. Thus it is that the political fabric of Kentucky is woven, dyed, stretched, and torn by those who live to seek public office.

Creating a new state out of a sprawling and poorly defined piece of backwoods territory in the latter quarter of the eighteenth century was a bold undertaking indeed. Here in an unspoiled western wilderness it seemed that the natural man could form a perfect political compact with himself. Here he could prepare the pattern for the extension of the great republic westward, and give his people an open chance at their "second redemption."

Riding on the tail of Daniel Boone's trail-blazing party to Boonesboro in 1775, Richard Henderson matured a political scheme to assume control of a good block of western country. He called together a legislative assembly in that year at the seat of Transylvania and introduced the fascinating Kentucky pastime of making laws. George Rogers Clark and the Virginians led by Thomas Jefferson, however, offered not so loyal opposition to Henderson's grandiose plans. In remarkably short time they tripped the judge and sent him packing southward to occupy a less princely domain near Henderson.

Instead of the natural man breathing deeply of the virgin air and striking at the land and ancient political ills with the pure motive of building a free and unintimidated society, he sat down and felt sorry for himself. To himself he was the forgotten man of Virgina. He complained and whined endlessly. The stream of his petitions to the

Virginia Assembly rose, in the latter part of Kentucky's attachment to
that state, to flash flood proportions. The picayunishness of many of
these requests indicated anything but a free and independent aggressive society. The new country was politically dependent upon the
mother state. Though Kentuckians have always referred affectionately to Virginia in the feminine gender, Virginia's responses to the
daughter were often strongly masculine in tone.

One would be rash to say that Kentucky politics has been largely
issueless over the years since 1785. This is far from the case. What
has occurred has been a tremendous dodging of issues. There have
been problems aplenty. First, that of gaining independent statehood
and devising a constitution which would protect the people from
themselves involved no end of emotion and maneuvering. With the
corrupting force of cheap frontier land, on the one hand, and an ever-
boiling international caldron of intrigue, on the other, there was no
cessation of conflict and turmoil. The Spanish conspiracy alone came
near to unsettling the Kentucky political mind. It did separate the
political goats from the sheep in the area of national and Virginia
loyalties. James Wilkinson and his cohorts were the bad ones. They
proposed to woo the western country away from its natural loyalties
into an alliance with Spain. They offered rich advantages in downriver trade as a reward for disloyalty. Scarcely had the last echo of
the Spanish fiasco died away before Kentucky was caught in the great
burst of fervor for the French revolutionaries in 1793. To men on the
western waters it seemed that as freemen they were morally bound to
assist the revolutionary Frenchmen. They assumed that revolution to
be closely akin to backwoodsmen fighting the cause of universal
human freedom. Democratic clubs were organized in several Bluegrass towns, liberty poles were erected in courthouse squares, and
western citizens donned the cockade of Revolutionary France. So
noble a Kentuckian as George Rogers Clark became entangled in this
conspiracy, and Isaac Shelby might well have been taken in by the
French plea had not President Washington's stern letter reached him
in time.

The procession of political issues has been endless: the opening of
the Mississippi to free navigation, removal of the British from the
posts in the Northwest, quieting the Indian menace, the whiskey tax,
the Alien and Sedition Laws, the rise of a landed aristocracy, and the
Old Court-New Court fight. So it has gone through the years.

A burgeoning Jeffersonian republicanism sent Kentucky's young political leadership into the breaches shouting the glories of the common man. They had plenty of ammunition. The whiskey tax was pure distilled Hamiltonianism, Jay's proposed treaty with Spain in 1784 to close the Mississippi was eastern mercantile chicanery, and failure to end the Indian attacks along the Ohio was a Federalist conspiracy.

John Bradford's *Gazette* and Stewart's *Kentucky Herald* tingled with the indignant outcries of humble citizens who all but predicted the end of time if the Alien and Sedition Laws were not repealed. Thomas Jefferson quickly became a father image about whom western political leaders could gather and consolidate their forces. John Breckinridge, with his seductive oratory and legal skill, and George Nicholas, whose deep political wisdom made him a powerful ally, joined forces with Isaac Shelby, James Garrard, Benjamin Logan, Caleb Wallace, and others. By 1796 the political stage in Kentucky was set and the actors waited in the wings eager to speak their parts.

There was a deeply disturbing element in all the backwoods political drama; that was the power of the mob, of the faceless people. Earlier they had invested themselves with powers which were frightening to the rising conservatives. To draft and accept a constitution has always been a fearful thing for Kentuckians. A majority of them have doubted they had enough wisdom and self-control to accomplish such a thing. With the country filling up with a raw and uninhibited population perhaps there were some reasons for internal fears. Too, Virginia in her anxiety to check her headstrong Kentucky weanling hedged the movement for independence with binding restrictions. She acted like an overly protective mother giving reluctant consent to a favorite daughter to embark upon marriage with a river pirate. Strict provisions were made, and Virginia was assured her western offspring would be nestled safely in the arms of the Union before she finally agreed to separation. By doing so she no doubt raised in the Kentucky political mind fears and misgivings which have not yet been dispelled.

There has seldom been a time since 1780 when Kentuckians have not been involved in debate over the technical issue of constitutional adequacy. To them great sanctity resides in an ancient written document. They have attributed a spiritual quality of wisdom to the patriarchal hand that once writ and having writ moved on leaving no successors to repeat the act. In perennial struggles to revise and adapt constitutional government to Kentucky's changing needs negative campaigners have periodically generated enough fog to blind the people forever to the real issues involved.

It has not been the issues, however, which have highlighted Kentucky politics so much as political personalities. With the passage of time Kentucky's gallery of political personalities has grown populous. From Isaac Shelby in 1792 to the latest occupant of the governor's chair, the illustrious have multiplied, and so have the unillustrious. In large measure Kentucky's shining knights of memory have been politicians—or politicians first and military heroes second. And of all the personalities who have enlivened Kentucky political history none was more forceful or dramatic than Henry Clay. A callow youth of twenty and fresh from the instructional watch-care of George Wythe, he rode horseback over the Wilderness Road in 1797 on his way from Richmond, Virginia, to Lexington to hang up his shingle as lawyer. Quick-witted and adaptable, the Virginian fell quickly into the swing of western ways. Oratory, Henry Clay learned at the outset, was the finest blade a rising lawyer could take into the courtroom or onto the political stump. Imitating the masters of Old Virginia, he engaged the publicans of the Bluegrass in debates over revising their constitution and the freeing of their slaves; two sensitive nerve ends which conservative landlords wished to preserve both untouched and unscarred.

Clay was primed when his real chance came in July, 1798, to click his cockspurs at Maxwell Spring. Already an ardent Jeffersonian, he was allowed the honor of following the venerable George Nicholas in a rousing assault upon the Federalists, in both Kentucky and Philadelphia, for their ill-conceived Alien and Sedition Laws. Mounting the "stump" with the confidence of a terrier, Clay made the grove resound with his cry for individual freedom and liberty. In short order he convinced his audience that he was not only a good Federalist whacker but that in the future he was going to climb far up among the branches of Kentucky political favor.

Established Kentucky lawyers like Caleb Wallace, John Breckinridge, George Nicholas, and John Brown quickly saw that Clay, the "Mill Boy of the Slashes," was as masterful in the courtroom before a jury as he had been at Maxwell Spring before a noisy mob of the "great unwashed." So impressive was lawyer Clay that soon United States Attorney General John Breckinridge entrusted him with his own legal problems.

The Kentucky country courtrooms, with their sordid processions of drunkards, assaulters, batterers, horse thieves, adulterers, wife deserters, damage seekers, and land-grabbers, were green pastures where an eloquent lawyer could drown out even a preponderance of adverse evidence. These loud outcries, however, were intended to ring out well beyond the confines of the jury boxes. There was more at stake than mere legal success in the rescue of the man charged with murder, the yeoman farmer from the cancer of overlapping land boundaries and conflicting claims, and the assaulting bully from his just deserts. No finer reputation could have been established in early Kentucky by an ambitious young politician than that of being a clever land lawyer able to straighten out what Henry Clay called "fireside surveys" and of defending successfully the criminal called to the bar of justice.

Within a decade after his arrival in the West, Henry Clay, then under the constitutional age of thirty-five, was on his way to the United States Senate to fill out the unexpired term of John Adair. Adair had resigned in a fit of temper because the legislature had not re-elected him to the post. This opened for Clay the long road to Washington which he would travel many times in the future as congressman and United States senator, and as Secretary of State. Four times he aspired to go that way to the White House, but fortune deserted him each time.

In his earlier political years it was as a state legislator that Clay tempered his political metal within easy view of the home folks. In the overcrowded house chamber of Kentucky's tiny statehouse he lashed his foes with a manipulative deftness unknown up to that time. He shouted down and outmaneuvered Felix Grundy, white hope of the Green River back country, to get the first bank west of the mountains chartered. In the interim period between his services in the United States Senate and his election to Congress, the Bluegrass lawyer carried on a furious anti-British campaign in the General Assembly, using the weepy-eyed old Federalist curmudgeon Humphrey Marshall as a foil. Marshall in turn branded his brash republican tormentor "a flaming jacobinic demagogue." Jacobin or not, Henry Clay was a relentless antagonist. Clothed in coarse homespun, grown and woven at Ashland, he badgered his colleagues into voting 64 to 1 in favor of a resolution supporting the Madison administration in its blockade against the importation of British-made goods. The lone negative vote was that of Marshall.

In a heated debate in the Assembly, Clay accused the old lion of infidelity to his country's best interests. Marshall in less subtle terms called the young upstart an outright liar. This exchange of compliments turned the crowded House of Representatives into a scuffle in which one of Clay's blows landed on aged ex-Governor James Garrard with what Marshall said was the "force of a ball of soaped cotton."

His honor was wounded and the only recourse for Clay was to challenge Marshall to a duel to be fought beyond the Ohio in Indiana opposite Louisville. On the dueling ground, and within the sound of the Falls of the Ohio, the Kentucky legislators shot at each other three times. Clay grazed Marshall's belly and Marshall wounded Clay in the fleshy part of the thigh. As Clay wrote James Clark, January 19, 1809:

I have this moment returned from the field of battle. We had three shots. On the first I grazed him just above the navel—he missed me. On the second my damned pistol snapped, and he missed me. On the third I received a flesh wound in the thigh, and owing to my receiving his first fire, &c, I missed him. . . . My wound is in no way serious, as the bone is unhurt, but prudence will require me to remain here some days.

This duel set Frankfort afire with political anxiety. For Speaker Clay, however, it was a personal triumph which could have been much greater perhaps if he had killed the Federalist troublemaker.

As a "war hawk" candidate for Congress, and begging for the immediate conquest of Canada and Florida he conjured up visions for his land-hungry supporters in the Bluegrass. He even lifted the eyebrows of the conservative administration in Washington. Arriving on the banks of the Potomac fresh from the western hustings (where, as John Randolph of Roanoke said, Clay had cried with whippoorwill-like monotony, "Canada, Canada"), the young Westerner was now ready to take on the bigger challenge of shouting the country into war.

In Lexington John Bradford, through the *Gazette,* commended the local political hero to the country "as [being] all that becomes an

American Republican—[he has] a sacred reverence for the public liberties; love of country, and ardent zeal, tempered with prudence and wisdom for its honor and welfare. His soul is Roman but his oratory is that of Demosthenes."

That was the stuff Kentuckians liked, a politician with the soul of a Roman and the eloquence of a Demosthenes. In this Henry Clay never disappointed them, in and out of office, in success and defeat, he was their ideal of political excellence. They named sons, horses, dogs, villages, schools, a county, telephone exchanges, laundries, barbershops, and everything else for him. Joel T. Hart, Kentucky's famous sculptor, carved his likeness in stone; Matthew Harris Jouett painted his portrait in oil, and an army of print makers placed him on steel engravings. Most of the older law offices in Kentucky were adorned with the popular steel engraving of Clay's "Farewell to the United States Senate." No doubt many a barrister has gazed on those outflung arms and dreamed of making a jury sit up and take notice.

Even yet a fledgling legislator promoting a local bill recalls the grand gestures of the old engravings and takes off in oratorical flight only to fall ingloriously to the ground, out of words and out of images. This was not so, however, with the great John Jordan Crittenden, who patiently remained in the background. He climbed the steps to legal and political fame, to being governor and United States senator, without once having grazed the naval of an opponent with a duelist's bullet, worn the homespun of anti-British America, or kissed Kentucky babies "from Mills Point to the Breaks of Sandy." Yet he too set a political mark which has not yet been forgotten. Crittenden, as much as Henry Clay, sought a reasonable compromise solution of the nation's grim problem of trying to save the Union.

John C. Breckinridge and his cousin William Cabell Preston Breckinridge were fit successors to Clay and Crittenden. John C. became United States senator and Vice-President, and he served as a general in the Confederate Army. He had the oratorical gift and bearing to arouse a tipsy, burgoo-stuffed audience to the point of weeping over the lost cause in the immediate postwar years. John and "Billy" made southern partisans out of many a Kentuckian who had worn the blue in battle. There were many occasions in those days for glorifying the cause when the remains of Confederate soldiers were brought home to be reinterred in Kentucky soil.

The list of Kentuckians who enlivened the political hustings during the postwar years of "redemption" was long. An outstanding personality among them was J. Proctor Knott of Lebanon. He served three terms in the United States Congress during the 1870's and 1880's and was governor of the commonwealth. As a member of Congress he nailed the lid of the "pork barrel" to the door of public ridicule. In his famous speech in opposition to the juicy Saint Croix Railroad grab he exposed the special interests of Duluth to a public airing. Repeating the refrain "Where is Duluth?" he delivered one of the finest pieces of ironic oratory in Congressional history. This speech backfired for the Kentucky congressman. Never again was he able to mount the rostrum without his audiences expecting him to be humorous. Duluth, however, surrendered its pride and invited him to come as a guest of the city.

Scholarly integrity and deep devotion to rhetoric never bothered J. Proctor Knott's breezy contemporary James Bennett McCreary. This son of Madison County entered the Kentucky political arena under the happy political nickname of "Gentleman Jim." In 1875 he was elected governor, and was re-elected in 1911. McCreary had resided in Frankfort only a brief time before "Gentleman Jim" became James "Bothsides." A charitable historian wrote of him that there "was no good reason for the nickname except the 'Old Roman's' always polite and agreeable way of being on both sides, or neither of any controversy—or rather his disposition to not take sides, where there was neither necessity nor good taste and reason for doing so." This was a friendly view indeed. Under the conditions which prevailed during his administrations the "Old Roman" proved to be a gentleman of superb taste and rare judgment who ignored the earthy matters of the commonwealth which would generate criticism and stain a record. No doubt it was a happy thing that so smooth and eloquent a son represented Kentucky in the great centennial celebration in Philadelphia. McCreary and his fellows dispensed the essence of cheer from the Elkhorn bottoms, and pleaded ardently with fellow Americans to forget the recent unpleasantness. McCreary, like an Oriental father offering a daughter in trade, described the virgin resources of Kentucky which awaited the ravaging hands of the exploiter with money.

What Governor McCreary did not tell the people gathered in Philadelphia for the centennial celebration was that he and his predecessors had swept under the commonwealth's public rug enough unsolved problems to sink the state. They had ignored education, correctional institutions, the penitentiary, highways, corporations, and almost everything else that could be put out of public view. Oratory and anecdotes were substituted for social planning, and congeniality substituted for foresight and sound administrative policy.

The Breckinridges, McCrearys, Hardins, Crittendens, and Clays were not alone in their praises of the ancestral gods of Kentucky. No one was more masterful at this than was Joseph C. S. Blackburn of Woodford. The colonel served a term in the United States Senate, and had pleaded the causes of culprits at the bar throughout central Kentucky, but his real impact was as an articulate personality in the forefront of Kentucky's troubled political years at the turn of the century, and especially in the debacle which William Goebel helped to brew.

Blackburn, like Clay, was masterful before a jury in court. He was a defense attorney in one of Kentucky's most famous criminal trials. In 1883 "Little" Phil Thompson of Harrodsburg shot and killed Walter Davis over an alleged rendezvous with Thompson's wife in a Cincinnati hotel. This trial brought to the bar such lawyers as Senator Daniel Voorhies of Indiana, J. Campbell Cantrill, Judge Jere Morton, and George Denny. Everywhere in Kentucky people followed the Harrodsburg court proceedings with the same interest they followed a political campaign. Blackburn both angered and saddened hearers with his ringing oratory. How close he came to following the law and the evidence was another matter. As a political campaigner the old master kept his manipulations well concealed. His public statements were usually as frothy as the suds gathered at the Falls of the Ohio.

With all his sweet suavity Blackburn lacked the wit and humor of his Republican protagonist William O. Bradley of Lancaster. This home-bred and coarsely spun Republican was descended of pioneer stock who had supported Jeffersonian Democrats and dandified Whigs for generations, but the mixed loyalties of the Civil War era swept the youngest scion into the national party's fold. Bradley was a masterful storyteller, and his store of local anecdotes was inexhaustible. In 1895 his persistent campaigning was rewarded by his election to the governorship and the honor of being the first Republican to hold that office. Few men have served Kentucky during a stormier time than did "Billy-O B." He succeeded the Democratic faithful John Young Brown, who in four years had done nothing to quiet the storm of civil disorder in Kentucky; in fact he had helped raise the winds himself.

John Young Brown no doubt was a partisan if not a tool of the conservative special interests of Kentucky. In his personal demeanor he was not as discreet as the office of governor demanded him to be. There is a letter in the Lindsay collection of papers in the University of Kentucky Library in which Governor Brown requested that his friend and political ally Judge William Lindsay, chief justice of the Court of Appeals, go to Henderson and placate the citizenry of that town. The governor had become a bit overstimulated in that place and in good mountain style had jerked out his revolver and fired a rousing salute to conviviality on Main Street.

The assassination of William Goebel in 1900 (described in Chapter XV) largely chilled the old Kentucky orators' ardor. Politics in Kentucky became too vengeful and bitter for them. Time, however, healed many of the wounds, and by the outbreak of World War I a new crop of "glorious stump speakers" came on to renew the moods of the past. Primest cock of this new flock was Augustus Owsley Stanley of Henderson. Bald as a turnip, with piercing dark eyes, brassy and courageous, and possessed of a foghorn voice, this young politician was ready to debate the mighty. He even challenged the great William O. Bradley with telling effect. A comic on the stump, at heart Stanley was a poet and a scholar. His well-worn copy of Sarah Josepha Hale's *A Compiled Dictionary of Political Quotations* with its dog-eared pages and marked passages indicates how assiduously Stanley hunted for a precise quotation with which to soften his hearers. Sufficiently fired up with Old Crow, he could almost make himself heard across the narrow waist of Kentucky. He played on the emotions of audiences with the deftness of an Ohio River calliope player. He never allowed an annoying or confusing public issue to clutter his campaigning when a few well-chosen poetic quotations would lift the souls of the voters or when an attack on his bosom friend Ed Morrow, leading Republican contender, would better serve his purpose.

Edwin P. Morrow, a mountain Republican from Somerset, was a perfect foil. He, too, was eloquent and a master of sweet words of nothingness. Unlike Stanley, he had an issue which was near and dear to his highland constituents' hearts. He advocated removal of the dog tax which Bluegrass sheep raisers and Democrats had imposed on hill

men. Morrow wept uphill and throughout the coves over the cruel
fate of "Old Dog Ring." Why, Old Ring had helped settle the country. He had come into the mountains with the pioneers, and every
squirrel season knitted tighter the bond between man and dog. "Turn
him free, give every man a free dog or two!" shouted Morrow. Old
Ring bothered Stanley not at all; in fact on one occasion when both
men were speaking at the same time in the Madison County courthouse, Stanley downstairs, and Morrow up, Stanley cupped his hands
and howled at his opponent like a hound dog.

Stanley and Morrow bemeaned each other on the stump, traveled
together, slept together, and drank generously out of the same bottle.
On one occasion they appeared on the same stage. Stanley had eaten
too much burgoo and had washed it down with too much from the
"spring," and became nauseated and vomited before the crowd.
When his time came to speak he apologized profusely for his unfor-
givable act, but, he explained, every time he heard Ed Morrow make
a speech it made him so sick at his stomach that he lost control of
himself.

The fund of Stanley and Morrow stories is inexhaustible, and no
one enjoyed telling them more than Stanley and Morrow. Stanley had
a final fling at politics. Franklin D. Roosevelt appointed him a member of the International Boundary Commission, and, as he said, he
met once a year with his Canadian counterpart to determine whether
or not the boundary had wintered well. Having satisfied themselves of
this fact they toasted another year of international friendship in the
offerings of their respective nations.

As a member of the Boundary Commission, however, Stanley
found his political wings clipped by the restrictions of the Hatch Act.
In the middle 1940's the Democratic candidate for governor in Kentucky needed the assistance of an experienced cannoneer like Stanley
to fire the Democrats with vote-getting zeal. Stanley agreed to come
to Kentucky, but he could not speak because of the Hatch Act. On
his way down from Washington he stopped in Morehead to greet a
throng of faithful who had come out to meet him. He explained
sorrowfully that he was gagged by the antipolitical act and he did not
want to be removed from the Boundary Commission, but if it were
not for the Hatch Act he would tell them what to do. In a rip-roaring
old-time speech he watered his hearers' eyes and stirred their souls.
When he was through he explained that it was with great sorrow that

he could not speak, but if he could that is what he would have told them.

Later the old warrior returned to the scene of battle on the Kentucky hustings, this time on Cheapside in Lexington, but the old fire had smoldered away and he lacked enthusiasm. He realized this and explained in the middle of his floundering speech that he had no more spirit. Ed Morrow was dead and he carried with him to the grave the old provocations and inspirations of the great days when the dog tax was a greater issue than public education.

Stanley was to have one more chuckle at the expense of the Republicans. When Dwight D. Eisenhower became President of the United States the Republican faithful were hungry for the crumbs of patronage. One of these rich crumbs was the Boundary Commission sinecure. President Eisenhower in an attempt to reward a faithful supporter mistakenly fired a Stanley, but he turned out to be a Republican and not the old "yellow dog" Kentucky Democrat. Stanley was still guardian of the national boundary to the amusement of the national press and the Kentucky Democrats.

In Stanley's place in Kentucky there came a young charger from Paducah, Alben W. Barkley. A master of native wit and anecdote, Barkley was born a ready campaigner. After serving a long and arduous apprenticeship in his progress through several county offices and in Congress, Barkley sought the governorship in the early twenties on a platform of revising two of Kentucky's sacred images, liquor and horse racing. He received a practical lesson in the influence of the Bipartisan Combine, made up of Democrats and Republicans, and the Kentucky Jockey Club. To tackle liquor and horses at the same time in Kentucky was to drink deep indeed of the political hemlock.

Undaunted by his first defeat, Barkley had learned the ways of state-wide campaigning. Driving over the rough roads of Kentucky with his son David, he, like the pioneer circuit riders, had time to think through his mistakes. His second time around he was elected to the United States Senate, where, like Henry Clay earlier, he quickly became a national figure. No one, not even Clay, could make the eagle scream louder for democracy than Barkley. He mixed the homely humor of William O. Bradley with the dulcet oratorical melodies of Joseph C. S. Blackburn and Augustus O. Stanley to bring the crowds up close. In fact, it is to be doubted if any other Kentuckian ever warred so gallantly for his party. So long as historians comment on the miracle of Harry Truman's election to the Presidency in 1948 they will recall that it was the indestructible Barkley who thundered the Democratic Convention in Philadelphia into something resembling unity. Later as Vice-President he gave the office a sparkle and usefulness which it had never had before.

Back home Alben W. Barkley was as skilled at playing courthouse politics as the best of the craftsmen. In 1938 he found himself challenged by Governor A. B. Chandler and the support that the governor had throughout the state. In this campaign it was the patronage and highway boys versus the WPA and other federal public works agencies. No one knows how much political shenanigans went on in this campaign, but one thing is certain—"Bloody Harlan" added considerably to its unsavory reputation because of the Barkley-Chandler feud.

When Barkley's term as Vice-President expired and the Republicans flocked to Washington he had reached an age when most men would have retired to enjoy reminiscing on the front porch of the Angles Estate in Paducah. Not so Barkley. The old charger was still anxious to do further battle, his ambition as stout as ever. Once again he took to the Kentucky hustings to make the shingles on every courthouse ring as of old, and the people helped him start a senatorial career all over again.

Barkley's last great oratorical triumph came at Washington and Lee University. At the end of a long speech in which he reviewed politics as a career, a student asked him if he suffered disappointment at not being elected President. Garbling the Scriptures he replied in that wonderful peroration, "I would rather be a servant in the House of the Lord than to sit in the seats of the mighty."

This was the end. The passing of Alben Barkley broke the golden strand of Kentucky eloquence. No Roman was left who could eat his fill of burgoo, never lack for a fetching anecdote, shake the hands of an army of constituents, and hold a rowdy audience spellbound for two hours. There may never be the like of him again because political campaigning in Kentucky has been mightily dulled by modern technology. Who could take time on radio or television to wind up telling a juicy anecdote? Anyway these media have created a kind of public squeamishness that has removed the earthy folksiness from public speeches. No matter how broad the humor or language in the old days the crowd yelled to their favorite candidate to lay it on his opponent. There's no one around to yell and laugh on television.

Behind the colorful political personalities in the post-Civil War era there were the grim Kentucky "troubles." The cards fell poorly for the commonwealth as it struggled to find stability and maturity. The feuds, the tollgate war, the Goebel assassination, the railroads, a general crime wave, and social maladjustment bothered the people. In Frankfort political heads often rested uneasily, and politicians tried hard to ignore their basic responsibilities. Of all these ordeals, however, none was more shocking than the disappearance of the state treasurer, and with him the state's public funds. This incident tarnished the image of the brigadiers and made every ingratiating politician highly suspect.

In a remarkably short time after the war the Democrats were back on their feet and seeking the seats of power. In 1867 they offered a full slate of candidates to recapture Kentucky for the virtuous. John W. Stevenson was chosen to lead the faithful back to the barbecue. James William Tate was slated for the treasurership. In personal appearance Tate presented the truest image of sand rock honesty. His broad forehead was shocked with black hair, he had keen but kindly eyes, and a turned-down mouth well concealed behind an extraordinarily thick coffee-strainer mustache. What was more, "Honest Dick," as he was affectionately called, had an ancestry well anchored back in Virginia. A maternal grandfather had trudged across the mountains as a pioneer traveling churchman to plant the Baptist faith in the land and he wrote of these struggles in *Ten Baptist Churches*.

Honest Dick Tate was born on the Elkhorn, and almost from the cradle up he was schooled in the art of politics at the capstone in nearby Frankfort. Since early antebellum days he had observed the comings and goings of the motley army the people sent there to represent them. He knew the governors, and even the state treasurers. Now it was his time to take his place at the great public trough.

The "redeemer" election of 1867, said a bitter Republican observer, had mixed meanings. To him it resulted in returning the Kentucky rebels to power over state government. He believed it must have pleased the heart of every traitor south of the Ohio River. This observer knew not how well Democratic faithful had done their job because the precise statistics of votes cast in the counties were not readily available to him. Never before, and only a few times since, have so many delinquent voters been so faithfully represented at the polls by "friends." Without quiver of voter conscience the "ticket" was swept into office.

For the next two decades the Honorable Dick Tate was to create a host of loyal supporters by being a most obliging man as treasurer. When a deserving constituent came with worthless check in hand Uncle Dick asked no needless embarrassing questions; he did not need a check—in fact, he would take an equally worthless promise to pay as sufficient collateral. In time he accumulated a pile of "cold checks" and worthless promises to the amount of $150,000. This, reasoned the treasurer, represented a mere oversight on the part of honest debtors and loyal voters who would go on forever returning Honest Dick to office to prevent the exposure of their own defalcations.

By mere accident the wheel of political fortune took a backward turn for the thieving treasurer. Freshman legislators who came to Frankfort in 1888 believed the political gossip they heard whispered in the corridors of the capitol. One of them, before he could be properly "instructed and obligated," introduced a resolution to institute "a sort of a general investigation of state affairs, beginning with the treasury." George Willis, historian of the Democratic party, said, "Such a flash of lightning, and peal of thunder as was never heard before or since heard came out of a clear sky, and rocked the state and the Democratic party as nothing had done since the war."

Honest Dick quivered on the verge of exposure. This was too much for the old fraud who had enjoyed so much acclaim as the most dependable officer ever sent to Frankfort. He departed Frankfort under cover of darkness, and to smooth his way he took along more than a quarter of a million dollars of public funds, and left behind $100,000 in uncollectable debts. In a single act he both stunned and bankrupted the people. The more trusting believed Honest Dick would come back, that he had just gone off with the money to keep it safe. The informal debtors hoped he would return to save them.

There was no doubt about it, the treasurer's vault was empty except for a child's purse. A cherished daughter, Edmoina Lloyd Tate, had died and her father had placed her tiny purse with its child's trinkets in the public depository for safekeeping—a sorry bit of collateral indeed to offer a materialistic state which valued more its $350,000 of embezzled funds.

Where Honest Dick went no one has ever learned. How he spent the money is another secret he took to his grave on some alien soil. Perhaps he spent a good part of it entertaining other southern treasurers who had run off with the public funds of their states at about the same time. Behind him the absconding treasurer left an angered people who determined never again to place so much trust in a common politician. Three years after the state treasury was rifled, delegates wrote into the state Constitution a provision that no official could succeed himself. In this way every four years they could count the "cold checks" and vapid promises to pay. Thus the restless ghost of Dick Tate lingers on in the corridors at Frankfort to remind Kentuckians of the folly of a permanent love affair with a public servant.

The grass-roots source of power of political decision in Kentucky rests largely with the courthouse rings. In the opening of the nineteenth century an unwashed but deserving backwoodsman said his people wanted a new county so they could do as they pleased and have opportunities to get themselves elected to offices. Legislators obliged these hungry office seekers by exhausting the state's geography creating new counties. Early in the seventeenth century Englishmen shipped their county system off to Virginia, where gentlemen freeholders became magistrates, judges, sheriffs, county lieutenants, and clerks. The pattern was struck—the county became "the" government for the people. Magistrates fined or favored them with openhandedness, sheriffs tracked down criminals, taxpayers, and jurymen for fees, and clerks registered deeds, wills, and issued marriage licenses with equal zeal. All of these officials were careful to curry favor with the people. Thus it was that "courthouse rings" came into existence while Virginia still held sway over the western country. Among the Old Dominion's castoff gifts to Kentucky was not only an antiquated English county system but also a deep reverence for it.

Down to this moment remarkably little change in county political structure has occurred. The rural Kentucky courthouse is by no means a unique American institution, but it does have a character of its own. It adorns the main squares of towns across the state, sometimes even sitting astride main highways. It is used and abused with equal vengeance. In many places the temples of justice long ago became king-sized spittoons. They give off odors of unwashed bodies, tobacco juice, and public toilets. It takes a lot of loafing and the passage of time to produce the mellow aroma of a rural Kentucky courthouse.

There is never a moment in Kentucky when the courthouse rings lose consciousness of their political missions and interests. As certain as the next primary election date rolls around there are always long lists of candidates. Office seekers swarm the roads and bypaths in search of voters. They litter the countryside with placards, handbills, and cards proclaiming their unusual capabilities for feeding at the public trough. Almost every utility pole and roadside tree offers the passer-by an assortment of expectant faces. Modesty has no place in the campaigning for county office. As an example a candidate in a Cumberland Plateau county recited a lengthy pedigree of highly respected pioneer ancestors and immediate kinsmen as a basis for his claim to office, but he weakened this solid position a bit by saying, "I am descended from the best people in the mountains on my wife's side at least."

The scramble for local offices seldom projects issues of greater moment than "turning the rascals out" so a new crop of rascals can batten during the next four years. Turning the rascals out of county offices on the Jacksonian principle of rotation in office has often been hard to accomplish. In past decades vast discrepancies have appeared between the number of voters registered and the votes cast. In an analysis of a century of Kentucky voting behavior in presidential elections, J. B. Shannon and Ruth McQuown found that it was not at all unusual for a county to return 110 percent or more of its potential vote, and there was no telling how much in excess of voters registered. It has been said that some election boards in selected counties have held up the count until they could learn how big a vote was needed to achieve victory. The gossips have even said that some of the more constructive amendments to the Constitution itself were "counted in." That is, election officials in some counties have returned enough favorable votes to make a majority. This much is certain, defeated candidates perennially send up howls that they "were counted out," and maybe they were. It is deemed necessary to keep friends present at all vote counts. In earlier days a discreet distribution of dollar bills and the use of "chain ballots" accomplished wonders. A local boss secured a blank official ballot, maybe from someone sacrificing his vote; the ballot was marked and traded all day for unmarked ones. The venal voter got a dollar for his vote, but only if he fetched out a blank ballot to keep the chain continuous. Old politicians love to reminisce about the days when they won elections by clever subterfuges. Now a new generation has to start all over. The age of electronics has caught up with the courthouse gang and vigilant machines guard the right of the voter, but even some of these have been tampered with.

Whether they have operated at precinct, county, or state level, Kentuckians have played politics as a fascinating game. There never entered into Kentucky politics the Pollyanna philosophy that it was not the victory that counted but how well the race was run. Victory was the only end result that counted, and without it a politician was a lost soul. This has been the code, and Kentuckians have always lived politically by the code. They have been dramatically successful not only in wielding an enormous influence over the lives of Kentuckians but have made their greatest impact nationally in the area of political affairs.

→》》 *XIII* 《《←

A Run for the Glory

Nestled inside the space of approximately a thousand square miles in central Kentucky is a region where grass and trees grow in lavish abundance and where cattle, fine sheep, and blooded horses also thrive. In gently rolling pastures bordering tiny limestone streams which drain off into the Kentucky River the bluegrass grows best. Few small areas are so well known for the quality of land and products—not even picturesque Suffolk, the Cotswolds, and Devon. This is the place where the Kentucky horses have made breeding and racing history.

The horse world of the Bluegrass lives apart. The course of its life is guided by its own folk mores, an unorthodox kind of economics, and its peculiar needs are served as they arise. This landed island even exerts its peculiar pressures on its counties, and upon Frankfort. Horsemen use their own semantics, and an outsider can commit no greater folly than to misuse their terms. To live and thrive in the horsy community offers social prestige, but demands a sizable backlog of ready cash to do so successfully. To be a really big horseman, breeding and racing glamorous stake winners, necessitates phenomenal expenditures of money, so much in fact that since 1880 fewer native sons have been able to stand the gaff. Perhaps nowhere else in this country, except around Newport, Cape Cod, Miami, Palm Springs, and, possibly, Low Country South Carolina, can sporting landlords exist so pleasantly as in Bluegrass Kentucky.

Thousands of everyday Kentuckians living within a stone's throw of the great farms know little at first hand about the intricacies of horse breeding and training. Yet their lives are in some way influenced by the presence of the horse and the sport of racing. The closest most of them ever come to a thoroughbred is in the saddling paddocks of Keeneland and Churchill Downs, the $2 pari-mutuel windows, or staring at them from their automobiles along the roadsides. Most of them have never bridled or saddled a horse, and Bluegrass Kentucky is the most unpromising place in the land for one to take a casual horseback ride about the countryside. There are few horses which inexperienced riders can handle, and no public bridle paths on which to ride.

Nevertheless, it would be appropriate to include a portrait of a horse's head in the state seal. When one enters Kentucky he is greeted by billboards portraying a gracious colonel tipping his hat in welcome, against a background of pasture, mares, and foals. A little farther on he is told Kentucky is fun, and the fun is a galloping thoroughbred. This seems strange indeed in the isolated rural spots far removed from horse country where the roads enter the state. Publicity agencies spend large sums of money annually in proclaiming the horse king in Kentucky. They offer prospective visitors great swales of carefully clipped meadowlands, miles of white plank fences, and countless mares and foals wandering lazily over the landscape as bait.

Bluegrass newspapers run endless columns of horse news ranging from race results to the pleasant tenor of life on the lush gardenlike farms. Once a year the Lexington papers produce Bluegrass editions which devote much space to the breeding and racing industry. Advertisements proclaim the attainments of farms and their stallions. Louisville papers, just off the edge of horse country, boom the opening of Churchill Downs and the running of the Kentucky Derby. Sports announcers on radio and television re-create the excitement of the grandstands by reviewing daily race results over the country, including the vital matter of prices paid by the pari-mutuels.

Horseless Kentuckians enjoy vicariously the joys of being big horsemen. They pay all sorts of little tributes to the thoroughbreds. No one could estimate accurately the amount of money these people spend on horsy bric-a-brac such as prints, mounted horseshoes, horse's heads, bridle bits, riding crops, stirrups, color standards, and horse statues.

It would be nothing short of sacrilege for the lord of a pine-lined den to be without his mounted relics, even if he has never straddled a horse or entered the winner's circle. No one, however, pays greater tribute to the Kentucky horse tradition than those modest urban dwellers who strew their lawns with color standards. Even the cut of clothing sometimes expresses a horsiness. It is not unusual at all to walk down the streets of Lexington and see a dead-game sport strolling along in his race-track garb. Even automobiles are adorned with horse emblems. Thus a sportsman can retire to his den as if it were his tack room and imagine that it is a repository for the country's flavor and a storehouse of ribbons and silver trophies.

There is more to the horse country, however, than pine dens, color standards, white fences, big barns, gracious manor houses, priceless horses, and race tracks. The whole social and economic fabric of the Bluegrass is colored by the industry. Hundreds of people earn their livelihood directly from the farms. An army of veterinarians look after the physical welfare of horses. Auctioneers and horse brokers are indispensable in the buying and selling of stock. Feed millers and dealers do thriving businesses, so do lumber and fencing salesmen. Not all the hill-grown white oak goes into the manufacture of liquor barrels. Paint stores thrive on keeping pasture fences shining, and harness makers and farriers prosper in the Bluegrass long after the tools of their trade have come to repose in museum cases in other places. An army of editors, writers, statisticians, pedigree searchers, librarians, and other specialized personnel serve the horse. Printing bills of horsemen and related tribesmen supports journeymen printers. A long retinue of grooms, swipes, exercise boys, jockeys, and farm laborers serve as necessary retainers. Even Bluegrass "dirt" farmers profit from the sale of feed, hay, and bedding straw.

On the debit side of the horse industry, and especially in racing, are the undesirable hangers-on who infest the country in and out of season. Like maggots touts seem to spring out of the ground. In both personal appearance and oily mode of approach they present themselves as impossible sources of reliable information or trustworthiness; nevertheless they gull an army of greenhorns year after year. The innocents who seek the end of the rainbow in pari-mutuel cash drawers are willing to accept tips from anyone. Colonel Matt J. Winn, manager of Churchill Downs, described a hypothetical meeting between a business tycoon and a Negro swipe:

The tycoon had picked "Silver Thaw" after careful consideration of all the facts. The Negro swipe said "Axeltone" was the horse. They argue. And 99 times out of 100 the industrial tycoon, who wouldn't consider the darkey bright enough to shine his shoes outside the race track, yields to the mind of the swipe and bets on Axeltone, only to see Silver Thaw win by 4 lengths, eased up.

It has happened a few million times, and it will happen as often again, for no other reason than that a horse player, once inside the gates, is hypnotized into thinking that because another man smells faintly of horse barn odors, he is an oracle on horse racing.

There are habitual gamblers who live in perpetual hope that fortune's tide will favor them in the next race, a thing that almost never happens. Perhaps they are no worse than the naïve Saturday afternoon suckers who slip away to Keeneland, the Trotting Track, or Churchill Downs with the bubbling hope they can parlay the rent and grocery money into a sizable stake. Gossips about Lexington say that many monthly store and service bills go unpaid during the racing seasons.

The tug goes on constantly between Lexington, Louisville, and northern Kentucky police and the bookmakers. Newspapers describe the sacking of elaborate establishments by raids. These places have complex telephone connections, great racks of file cards, track information, and betting forms. Bookmakers are hangovers of the old days of betting and before the pari-mutuel machines were introduced to the tracks. These footpads, with their hats for offices, operate in any hospitable public place where customers can find them. Frequently they fall into the clutches of the law, but they are soon back in business after the next session of police court. Apparently the bookie is one of the most tenacious leeches in American society. In spite of his clashes with police and some public disdain he survives everywhere, and his "two-dollar" customers always know his whereabouts. As certain as horses enter starting gates there will be bookies—little ones afoot and big ones with elaborate parlors and under mobster control. Gamblers are not interested in a huddle of graceful animals performing magnificently on a well-prepared track. To them a horse is a number, and a well-bred and graceful horse is the one which reaches the finish line first and pays off well. The only times gamblers are interested in bloodlines and breeding is when they pore over the *Racing Form* in bars and hotel lobbies. All of this is part of the Bluegrass way of life.

During the racing seasons fans by thousands gather in hotel and motel lobbies, in restaurants, filling stations, shops, and local stores. For over a century main-street businesses in Lexington and Louisville have enjoyed a second Christmas trade during these gatherings. To talk of restricting the horse business or in any way unsettling it would create a terrific furor. It would bring from horsemen frightening threats of moving away to Florida and California. Losing its horses would be a serious injury to the Bluegrass. A single big stake-winning horse retired to stud on a Bluegrass farm is worth almost as much to local businesses in income from tourists as that from a small industry.

No one knows how much income Man o' War brought to central Kentucky. Few visitors came to Lexington without calling upon him at his stable on the Far-away Farm. The moment a prominent visitor landed in Lexington he was rushed out the Russell Cave Pike to pay his respects to this famous horse and his personable groom Will Harbut. Now that both horse and groom are gone, visitors still drive to the farm to see Man o' War's grave and statue, and to be impressed by the expenditure of so much money to commemorate a horse's memory. They also visit the graves of Domino, Nancy Hanks, Fair Play, and the Calumet horses.

Devotion to the horse in Kentucky has contributed positively to the preservation of the natural beauty of much of the inner Bluegrass. Rolling acres of vivid green meadowland enclosed behind miles of glistening fences give the region the appearance of a luxuriant garden. On lazy spring days when the yellow locust and catalpa are in full bloom, and mares and foals graze in the pastures, and bumptious stallions pace arrogantly up and down paddock fences, one can dream that everyday Kentucky is far away. That is, he can dream until the roar of the bulldozer and the onrush of suburbia startle him into realization that the farms are disappearing.

Such manorial estates as Calumet, Dixiana, Greentree, Almahurst, Claiborne Stud, Hamburg Place, Spendthrift, Walnut Hall, Circle M, and Elmendorf seem idyllic places in which to live the good rural life. They contrast sharply in appearance with neighboring tobacco farms sandwiched in between, where farmers wrest a living from the soil and where there is a lack of capital to build and paint fences, to prune trees, and to clip grass.

Visitors have gone away from the Bluegrass with the mistaken notion that horse farming is almost a normal way of life. Many an urban Kentuckian has dreamed of buying a tiny piece of land and living in a limited way the exciting life of the successful horseman. Maybe he could even have a back-yard stable in which his filly might someday foal a stake winner—novelists have said this happened. This dream, even of acquiring the farm, seldom comes true.

Few people can afford to keep in style a Bull Lea, Native Dancer, Citation, Bubbling Over, Whirlaway, Man o' War, or a Nashua. These stallions were not foaled in humble "dirt" farm stables, nor were they bred and raced by amateur back-yard farmers. Remarkably little of the capital which sustains the picture-book Bluegrass estates originated in Kentucky, and relatively few native sons own famous farms. Yet the horse farms make a high return to Kentuckians both as beauty spots and as attractions to money-spending visitors.

Behind the growth of the horse industry in Kentucky is a long and involved history which runs parallel to that of the state. Historically the sporting horse business was not originated by rich outsiders. Kentucky's earliest pioneers owned good horses, and their descendants improved their breeding and racing stock by far simpler procedures than the modern ones. Up until the giddy 1870's and the accumulation of the great American fortunes, breeding and racing Kentucky horses was largely a sideline with the "colonels" and politicians. However, once new rich Easterners of the post-Civil War era adopted the sport of racing, in imitation of British sportsmen, they turned to the Bluegrass for racing stock, breeding lines, and pasturage. The millionaires brought revolutionary changes to both New York and Kentucky. The fact that the island of rich pasturage north of the Kentucky River was a breeding and conditioning ground which rivaled Britain and Virginia was a gift of nature; geography and geology contributed generously to the success of this country.

Below Frankfort the sinuous little Elkhorn long ago gnawed a hole through the tough limestone beds and over the forbidding cliff along the Kentucky. Its two prongs meander across the Bluegrass and drain a most fertile stretch of farmlands. Laterals flow over shallow limestone beds to mold this luscious country into rolling slopes and valleys. There are great oaks, black cherries, ash, coffee trees, sycamores, some of which no doubt dotted the landscape when the first settlers appeared to claim the land which lay along these streams. In a largely unrecorded past Indian hunters came to regard this as prime hunting territory. Its rich canebrakes, grass meadows, and streams attracted buffalo and other herbivorous animals in great herds.

Northern and southern tribesmen contested furiously for possession of this country with its animals and grass.

Unhappily no visitor in mid-eighteenth century set the record straight as to whether or not bluegrass grew in the Elkhorn country. A single paragraph would have avoided future controversy as to whether or not this grass is indigenous to Kentucky or was imported from Britain. As it is, the argument may never end. That it produces fine livestock is an established fact.

Knowledge of the first white visitor is as foggy as the origin of the grass. He might have been one of George Croghan's wandering Pennsylvania traders, a Virginian, or a captive of the Indians taken in the Carolinas. Sometime early in the first part of the eighteenth century men east of the mountains heard about the area.

For thousands of years decaying vegetable growth atop the soil and rotting limestone underneath formed a hospitable seedbed for cane and grass. Decaying stone has impregnated an ever-thickening layer of mineral soil rich in phosphorous and calcium. Plants enriched by these minerals in turn strengthened the animals that ate them. It was here that nature prepared the Elkhorn country to sustain a flourishing livestock industry, and especially to sustain stout-muscled, light-framed sporting horses.

In 1880 an enthusiastic son of the region wrote, "As a stock raising district, Kentucky has not its equal in the world. Her horses, mules, cattle, sheep and hogs are produced in the most perfect form of development. . . . The South and West look to its great annual sales of shorthorns for their supplies of breeding animals, and the East to its annual horse sales for their supplies of fast trotters and fleet-footed coursers. Many of her best bloods have found their way across the ocean, with a view to improving the studs and herds of Great Britain."

Benjamin Bruce, an early editor of a local breeding periodical and an authority on Kentucky bloodlines, stoutly claimed that the presence of limestone in Elkhorn grass and water made the difference between Kentucky soil and that of other states. He said an inch cube of bone from a Kentucky horse when compared with a similar specimen from Pennsylvania revealed a marked difference. The bone from the Bluegrass was like fine-grained ivory, while the Pennsylvania sample was "porous and calcareous, resembling pumice stone." The muscular system of the Kentucky horse, said Bruce, was sinewy and strong, his barrel was full and round, and his stamina greater. When Kentucky breeding stock was carried to other parts of the country, he said, it tended to breed downward in bone and muscular qualities.

Thus the horse has been an enduring part of the trinity of Kentucky pride, and in some respects the paradox of its social and economic history. If Kentuckians themselves had achieved as much fame in public and intellectual affairs as their horses have in racing history, their state's history would have been greatly enriched. Perhaps no Kentucky physician, not even Dr. Ephraim McDowell, has attracted so much general public attention as did the great stallion Lexington. No university professor has achieved within Kentucky so glowing a fame as did Man o' War. It is to be doubted that, with one or two exceptions, any Kentuckian has sired so many successful offspring or was so fortunately mated as were a host of famous stallions.

Historically Dr. Thomas Walker and Christopher Gist were mounted on horses when they broke trail into Kentucky in middle eighteenth century. After them came mounted long hunters in search of skins and furs. Daniel Boone's long-hunting party came mounted; in fact their horses were the cause of some of its difficulty with the Indians. In 1775 William Calk described the unruliness of his party's horses. For the early settlers horses were of primary concern, as was reflected in legislation adopted by the Boonesboro Assembly. One of its nine laws sought to improve the breeding of horses.

The forerunners of today's horses packed their owners' goods across the Appalachians from Virginia and the Carolinas, and once in Kentucky they helped put people beyond troubles in Indian raids. For almost a quarter of a century Indian and settler alike were obsessed with stealing each other's horses. The lingering conflicts of the border degenerated after 1782 into nothing more than horse-thieving raids in which both sides profited.

Kentucky's earliest horses, somewhat like its first settlers, were not descended from distinguished ancestry, nor did they produce progeny of distinction. They were, however, tough, dependable animals endowed with endurance and speed. Their owners boasted of their capabilities in the same manner they bragged about their rifles and shooting capabilities. No doubt the first horse races run in Kentucky resulted largely from boastfulness and banter of owners. These races were largely "main street" affairs in which noisy and profane horsemen ran their nags down the only open stretches—the village streets.

So obnoxious did this practice become in the early Kentucky towns that the legislature expressly forbade street racing in granting new town charters after 1810. Forced off the streets, horsemen developed race courses of their own. A purse race was run on Water Street in Lexington in 1789, but almost immediately a race course was laid out on top of the Broadway Hill.

Following quickly after its initial publication in 1787 the *Kentucky Gazette* carried advertisements of stud horses. By the end of the century the sporting horse industry was well established in the Bluegrass, and notices of stallions were as commonplace as political news. Like their owners, the early stallions had a proud Virginia ancestry. Dating from the importation of the stallion Bull Rock, who was descended directly from Darley's Arabian and Byerly Turk, this horse combined Arabian and British bloodlines. Eighteenth-century Virginians imported other Arabian and British stallions, among them Buzzard, Diomed, Herod, and Dare Devil. Diomed contributed most to establishing the thoroughbred base in Kentucky. Many of his offspring were publicized as sires of superior quality. Following 1797 the list of names of stallions standing at stud became almost as lengthy as those of candidates and militiamen. Such famous pioneers as Weazel, Dare Devil, Mogul, Bacchus, Spread Eagle, and American Eclipse were among those advertised.

It was, however, the great Buzzard who contributed most to the establishment of the thoroughbred industry. He was foaled in New Market, England, out of Misfortune by Woodpecker, and back of this mating was the dam Snap whose memory is still green. Buzzard was bought in 1806 for $5,500 by Henry Clay from Colonel John Hoomes's estate in Bowling Green, Virginia. A year later Senator Clay wrote Colonel Thomas Todd that Colonel John Taylor of Mount Airy, Virginia, had proclaimed Buzzard "the finest horse upon the continent." This may well have been true. Buzzard had won thirty-four races at New Market, and his colts claimed more than two hundred prizes. He was one of the first stallions to be syndicated in Kentucky. A year after his purchase Henry Clay sold shares in him to four other Bluegrass breeders, including Colonel Ambrose Buford. There is a marked difference between the fee of $50 a "leap" charged by the Buzzard syndicate and that charged by the owners of the modern Nashua.

In many respects the rise of the thoroughbred industry in frontier

Kentucky refutes some of the concepts of a plain sweaty social democracy. True, talk about breeding stalls, stables, and race grounds was as earthy as the banter at logrollings. Early horse breeders and racers were also everyday farmers. In time racing rules were formulated, but noisily contested heat races tempted the devil to take the hindermost. Many races were run amidst so much swearing, rowdiness, drinking, and fist fighting by owners and bystanders that it was a marvel that horses were brought near the finish lines. An early backwoods classic, "A Quarter Race in Kentucky," describes such an informal race match in which the central character was "bamboozled, whipped, and skinned."

In time the western frontier environment generated a love of sports, and such physical contests as hunting, shooting matches, cockfighting, and horsemanship became as usual as Indian fighting. None of these, however, involved as scientific a sophistication as did horse racing and breeding. This literally sprang from the land in subsequent years, and as an importation from Virginia and England. Few things reflected so fully Kentuckian desires to assume the manners of landed gentry as the interest in breeding fine horses.

Thus it was that many Kentuckians became gentlemen and colonels on the reputations of their stud horses rather than upon their own personal accomplishments. Reading Kentucky horse history is a challenge in the appreciation of genealogy—even more so than in human history. Frankly it is an area where the uninitiated soon becomes lost. He wanders through bewildering lists of names, of matings of sires and dams, of grandsires and granddams until he is baffled.

Behind the history of the horses, nevertheless, were colorful men, many of them prominent Kentucky and national politicians. Most distinguished of these was John Breckinridge, Jefferson's attorney general, who owned Cabell's Dale (Castleton). Here he bred and raced some of the best horses in the early 1800's. Almost from the beginning of his career as an attorney in Kentucky, Henry Clay was interested in horses. As a matter of fact he had ridden a good mount across the Appalachians to Lexington. His name appeared as early as 1809 as owner of a stake horse entered in a public race meeting. Besides Buzzard he owned the imported stallion Yorkshire who sired a string of successful progeny. Clay was a master at giving horses bizarre names, among them Allegrante, Phantomia, Argentile, and

Zenobia. The master of Ashland seemed, however, to be more interested in breeding horses than in racing them. This he left to his
sons.

Within a few months after Henry Clay's arrival in Kentucky a local
jockey club was organized. Sportsmen meeting in Postlethwaite's
Tavern formulated rules for their conduct. Clay was an active member of this organization, and for almost a century the name of Clay
was an impressive one in the breeding of horses; during this time Ashland was an important thoroughbred and trotting horse nursery.
Three sons, and a grandson-in-law, Henry Clay McDowell, carried
on the tradition.

Among Henry Clay's Bluegrass neighbors who bred and raced
thoroughbreds were Colonel William Scott Buford, Colonel Ambrose
Buford, J. M. Gatewood, J. M. Garrard, and Elisha Warfield. The
Bufords perhaps were the most important breeders and racing men of
their time. Dr. Elisha Warfield developed the magnificent Meadows
estate on the north side of Lexington where his holdings spread
across the rich canelands of the North Elkhorn country, and from his
meadows came many notable horses.

If Dr. Warfield ever achieved a reputation as a physician, it was
long ago forgotten. He tried his hand as a merchant, but at this he
was less than a success. Horse breeding and playing the role of important man about Lexington was more to his liking. He abandoned
the routine affairs of trade and became a gentleman farmer, and
quickly his Meadows gained the reputation of being one of the most
hospitable homes in Kentucky. Its great hall and twin parlors were
frequently crowded with guests. If there was anything important happening in Lexington, Dr. Warfield's name was sure to appear among
those of the public committeemen. He helped welcome Lafayette to
the town in 1825, he organized and promoted the pioneer railroad to
connect the inland town with the Ohio River, and engaged in local
politics. No social event was worthy of the name if the Warfields were
not present. When a prominent visitor came to the Bluegrass Dr.
Warfield's Meadows was open to him.

Despite all of his public activities, however, Dr. Warfield has written his name in history more clearly as a horse breeder. One exuberant historian has said of him that he was "a man of culture and
fortune, retiring from mercantile life while yet in the full vigor of
manhood, with an enlarged capacity for the active, stirring past time,

more particularly relating to the high-bred horse, his attention was devoted to the turf, and no man ever did more to contribute to its elevation." The latter part of this extravagant statement contained much truth. Among Dr. Warfield's horses were Alice Carneal and her famous colt Lexington. This pair exerted an influence on Kentucky breeding far beyond the life span of horses and man.

Urban expansion has overrun the Meadows Plantation and has destroyed the great hall and the parlors. Gone are Dr. Warfield, his daughter Mary Jane, her husband, Cassius M. Clay, and their children. Almost forgotten is the double tragedy of two Clay children being poisoned to death by a slave; their corpses lay in state in one of the Meadows parlors. The memory of Alice Carneal, Boston, and Lexington, however, remain fresh wherever men talk of great American horses. The bloodlines of Boston-Alice Carneal-Lexington long ago passed beyond positive identification, but their standards of excellence survive.

Lexington's long history was only partly confined to Dr. Warfield and the Meadows. In 1853, under the classic name Darley the colt was sold to Richard Ten Broeck for $5,000. Ten Broeck took the colt south to challenge the best horses of Alabama, Mississippi, and Louisiana. He sought especially to conquer the Glencoe filly Sallie Waters, which he did that year. He then challenged Colonel T. J. Welles's LeCompte, Alabama's Highlander, and Mississippi's Arrow in matched heats on the Metaire Race Course in New Orleans. In a rematch with LeCompte Lexington was defeated, but in a third challenge the great Boston colt showed his heels to LeCompte and the South. This third match of three miles, run April 7, 1855, was one of the most exciting sporting events of the antebellum South. It was Kentucky against the South in the three-heat race, and this time Lexington won, setting a world time record of 7:23 ¾ in the first heat.

Nearby in Woodford County in the very heart of the Elkhorn country, Robert Alexander, a Scots lad and Cambridge University graduate, established his famous Woodburn estate on 2,000 acres of virgin land purchased from General Hugh Mercer. With a long rifle slung over his shoulder this young friend of Benjamin Franklin crossed the mountains to develop one of the finest breeding farms in Kentucky history. Once in Kentucky young Alexander followed a Scotsman's bent and engaged in banking, trade on the Kentucky River, and the development of Woodburn's acres. The natural fertility of the land dictated the breeding and grazing of quality livestock almost as naturally as it grew oaks and sycamores. In the post-War-of-1812 years, when central Kentucky farmers reaped profits from the flourishing cotton market in the spreading South, Robert Alexander brought his lands into production. His interest in livestock, however, ran to cattle, sheep, hogs, and work stock. His importations of English brood animals were in keeping with the excitement then prevailing in Kentucky.

It was Robert Aitcheson Alexander, a nephew, who actually began the breeding of thoroughbreds and trotters at Woodburn. Like his Uncle Robert, the new master of the famous estate kept up his interest in other types of livestock, but it was his horses which established him as Kentucky's most important breeder. In 1856 he sent two winners to the Lexington track, and that same year he purchased from Richard Ten Broeck the sensational stallion Lexington. At Woodburn, Lexington proved to be as successful as a stud as he had been a pace setter on the race tracks. A good mare bred to him assured a high-quality foal. During the next half century before the last of the Woodburn stock was sold, the Alexanders and Daniel Swigert produced some of the finest horses in American turf history. Out of no more than 5 percent of the country's foals from 1868 to 1880 Woodburn-bred horses won over 50 percent of the six major American stake races, including four Derby and ten Belmont winners. This same reputation held good in the trotting field. No trotters in the nineteenth century were faster than Jay Eye See and Maud S.

A partial list of Woodburn horses includes Norfolk, Australian, Asteroid, Preakness, Harry Bassett, Jay Eye See, and Maud S. Both of the latter set and held time records. Maud S was one of the finest animals of either breed ever foaled in Kentucky. In 1884 she set a time record of 2.083 ¾ for the mile drawing a high-wheel sulky. This record was never lowered by a trotter drawing the same type of vehicle.

Woodburn was in its first successful phase of breeding thoroughbreds when the Civil War broke out. During four war-troubled years the stud withstood ravages of both the war and horse-stealing forays by the two armies, but in the closing months of the struggle guerrillas threatened the destruction of the stables. Twice the place was raided, and each time prize horses were ridden away. On the first raid Asteroid was stolen and had to be ransomed from the thief in Anderson

County for $250. On the second visitation the vandals stole Norwich, Abdullah, a prime trotting stallion, and several mares, almost $60,000 worth of horses. Abdullah was ridden to death and the other animals were taken beyond the owner's reach.

Robert Aitcheson Alexander's description of the guerrilla menace is one of the most graphic written about these villians. The captain of the second band to raid Woodburn took not only horses but every gun on the place, including Robert Alexander's long rifle which he had brought from Philadelphia.

Woodburn was not alone in its exposure to raids from Confederate and Union soldiers and the guerrillas. John Hunt Morgan's raids into the Bluegrass resulted in several breeders losing valuable horses. One of the horses lost to the Confederates was John Clay's famous mare Skedaddle.

Perhaps loss of horses in the war was more than compensated for by the rich revival of breeding and racing in the gilded age of postwar America. Bluegrass horses came into their own when wealthy eastern purchasers bought Kentucky stock. Many Kentuckians, however, reaped ultimate satisfaction by breeding and racing their own horses. Nothing enhanced the fortunes of a stud like having several major stake winners stabled in its barns. It was here that the new-rich money and railway barons of the East came to buy the horses which gave them personal standing and prestige in the new age of kingly status symbolism.

In these later years the most prominent Kentuckian who renewed interest in breeding and racing was General John C. Breckinridge, who returned from the Confederate Army by way of Europe and Canada. A son of John Breckinridge, he was born and reared at Castleton where horse breeding was a central business. Though not an important breeder and owner, General Breckinridge lent prestige to the Kentucky Racing Association as its president, a position which he held at the time of his death on May 18, 1875. This was the day after H. Price McGrath's colt Aristides galloped home to win the first running of the Kentucky Derby.

Aristides' jovial Irish owner never enjoyed the public distinction of General Breckinridge, but nevertheless he was one of the most colorful personalities of the American turf. He said for lack of 2½ cents he was denied an education. He had sent a dime to Versailles by a wealthy neighbor to buy a spelling book, but the price was 12½ cents and the neighbor came home without it. Whatever Price McGrath lacked in formal education he made up for with his rugged Irish nature and raw experiences in a bare-knuckle competitive society. Before he settled down as a gentleman farmer on a choice spot of Bluegrass between the Georgetown and Newtown pikes in Fayette County, McGrath had courted fortune in the gold rush to California, had flirted with luck in New Orleans where experiences came fast and bitter, and had strained the seams of life in other places. At the outbreak of the Civil War he was as ardent a Confederate as could be found east of St. Charles Street. He organized a company of troops and swore he would bar the Yankees from the levee. General Benjamin Franklin Butler foiled his plan to do this when he captured New Orleans in 1863, and McGrath went north to fraternize with the enemy in his New York stronghold.

Whatever else Price McGrath did in his sporting house in New York, he made a quick and modest fortune at the card tables. It was said he won $105,000 in a single night, sold his gambling establishment, and headed for Lexington and the Bluegrass. There on 420 acres of land he founded McGrathiana. McGrath was a free-handed Irishman who dashed about Lexington in his Jersey wagon drawn by a pair of buggy mules. Out on the Newtown Pike he dispensed hospitality with the lavishness of Dr. Warfield, but not always with the same degree of sophistication. He captivated his guests with an inexhaustible fund of personal anecdotes, and was as masterful with a hand of cards in the Bluegrass as in New York. His guests were filled with bourbon and gossip of bloodlines, track records, and aspirations. It is doubtful, however, that these convivial conversations were ever dampened by references to McGrath's partnership with Calvin C. Morgan in the earthy hemp business.

Despite lack of formal education and family and political background, H. Price McGrath made racing history. His Aristides, a chestnut colt out of Sarong by Leamington, glorified his stable by winning the first Derby. There was irony in this, however, because McGrath had his heart and his money on his second entry, Chesapeake. This favorite brought up the field.

By the 1880's the days of Kentuckians who had come up the hard way in racing were almost ended. Race tracks were being organized in the East by bankers, railway barons, stockbrokers, and politicians. Men like August Belmont, James R. Keane, W. C. Whitney, P. A. B.

Widener, and Milton H. Smith established stables in Kentucky, and sometimes in partnership with experienced Kentuckians they carried breeding and racing to heights undreamed of by the old southern sportsmen. Native Kentuckians like Ben Ali Haggin, John E. Madden, Major Foxhall Daingerfield, A. B. Hancock, and Johnson N. Camden struck it rich in other fields in this golden age and returned home to become major sportsmen. James Ben Ali Haggin topped them all. He was one of the wealthiest Kentuckians ever to engage in breeding thoroughbred horses. Like the Alexanders, he developed a vast estate along the North Fork of the Elkhorn. Here he added to the fabulous Elmendorf Farm, originally developed by Milton H. Sanford and Daniel Swigert. Swigert gave it its Dutch name in honor of his wife's grandmother. Here Colonel Haggin built a great manor house that overlooked the Elkhorn on one side and a spacious deer park among ancient trees on the other.

No medieval duke ever had a finer estate than James Ben Ali Haggin. Not only did he survey broad acres of choice land but he occupied a seat in the millionaires' corner at the horse sales, and his farm and stables produced their share of stake winners at the turn of the century. When the master of Elmendorf drove through the long rows of trees and across the shining meadows he must at times have felt the best part of the world belonged to him.

Across the line in Bourbon County, A. B. Hancock in later years rivaled Elmendorf with his vast Claiborne Stud, and out on the Winchester Pike from Lexington John E. Madden was master of Hamburg Place. Behind its flaming torches, Hamburg Farm produced many important horses, and its master became a highly respected student of breeding and racing. These men, along with more modest neighbors, carried on the Kentucky horse tradition of the early nineteenth century. Now at Spendthrift Farm in Fayette County Leslie Combs II is master of one of the most important breeding establishments anywhere. Stud fees paid for service from the great Nashua amount to almost enough annually to endow a small college. The same is true of the Calumet stallions.

The big farms form a consistent link with the past when the first land hunters viewed the rolling Bluegrass Plateau. They were quick to predict the rise of a rich grazing industry, a prophecy which was fulfilled. In some respects the horse industry has come into conflict with an America which is being crowded for industrial and urban lands. Modern society cannot always be as hospitable to the sport of racing and breeding as it was in its less opulent years.

The Lexington Junior League Horse Show and scores of tiny country fair show rings have within the past twenty-five years brought the horse closer to Kentuckians than have the trots and races. The average man can see himself more clearly mounted on a standard-bred horse or upon a Tennessee walking horse than upon a thoroughbred. Too, it is possible to be an owner of a modest show horse without incurring all the expenses of maintaining the high strung racers.

Breeding and racing horses are only a part of the long Kentucky history of livestock production. Between the dropping of a foal and its appearance on the race track are three full years of conditioning and training, and maybe several changes of ownership. In fact a colt's owner may actually be the least important man involved in its successes and failures on the track. The training is the responsibility of trainers, exercise boys, and jockeys. Since the days of Colonel Ambrose Buford and his brother Scott a long list of trainers have seen their chargers gain glory in stake races. Among these have been Daniel Swigert, Richard Ten Broeck, Major Foxhall Dangerfield, Albert Cooper, William Lakeland, John E. Madden, H. J. Thompson, and Ben A. Jones. These and scores of others have brought promising colts to top racing form, and then devised the racing strategies by which they won.

The man who finally sees the horse to success in a race is the jockey. In the past century and a half almost as many jockeys have gained fame on Kentucky race tracks as there have been statesmen in Frankfort. Isaac Murphy, a Negro lad, was astride many winners in his time. He brought home three Derby winners: Buchanan, Riley, and Kingman. Earle Sande, Don Meade, Eddie Arcaro, L. McAtee, C. Kurtsinger, and J. Winkfield topped their trade in keeping their weight down and their winnings up. Few American occupations exceed jockeying race horses for its peculiar mores and hazards, yet it has its moments of sparkling glory in the winning of a big stake race.

Historically, those functionaries who have played major hands in selling and buying horses have operated well back away from the track. Many an unpromising colt has gone under the hammer to fetch a modest price, but in his racing career showed his heels to a handsomer pack. Horse sales in Kentucky have progressed over the years from jockey ground swaps and sales on court days to semisocial affairs at Keeneland and Tattersall's. If a Kentucky horse breeder of the first half of the century could wander into a modern bidding session at Keeneland he would no doubt get the impression that the auctioneer was crying the sale of Kentucky itself.

Maybe James Harrod was the first person to offer something for sale at auction. Kentuckians have always sold their housewares, land, slaves, hemp, and livestock at auction. Not even political speakings brought people running as did a public sale of land or a stableful of horses. One of the best known early auctioneers was Jerry Delph, son of a Dutch father and a backwoods mother. He was raised to be a blacksmith. Somewhere along the way he learned it was easier to make a living crying an auction than swinging a hammer, and he turned away from the forge and anvil.

In late antebellum years Jerry Delph's chant was frequently heard on the corner of Cheapside in Lexington where he sold farms, droves of mules, horses, and slaves. For thirty-five years this bull-voiced blacksmith cried the property of an extensive host of clients. He sold the last of Robert A. Alexander's Woodburn stock. Though he never left Kentucky to hold auctions, the Dutchman accumulated a fortune from sales.

Delph had as rising competition a colorful lad who like H. Price McGrath was denied 2½ cents' worth of education. What Captain Philip C. Kidd lacked in educational advantages he gained in personal adventures. During three years of the Civil War he rode with Cluke's regiment of Morgan's command. Hardly had the raiders broken their final camp before the young horseman was back in the Bluegrass selling cows, sheep, mules, hogs, and horses. Throughout the Mississippi Valley Captain Kidd was in demand to sell purebred cattle and sheep. Two of his cattle sales yielded the largest sums ever exchanged to that date in a public sale. During his career the captain sold three fourths of the thoroughbreds and trotters brought to auction. The banging of his gavel separated many a promising stake horse from his nursery background and started him on the road to fame at the tracks.

The profession of auctioneer has lost none of its glamour with the passage of time. The big difference lies in the prices paid for horses. George Swinebroad of Lexington has on several occasions exceeded the $100,000 price. Maybe he has befuddled purchasers with his dulcet chatter. Who knows, the next horse brought under his hammer may be another Buzzard, Lexington, Man o' War, or Whirlaway. The wheel of chance whirls as certainly in Bluegrass Kentucky as foals are dropped in the spring and the locusts bloom. At least a Kentuckian can go to the sales on a balmy spring afternoon and vicariously stock his stables with the choice of the yearling crop.

XIV

Green Grows the Mint

The history of distilling whiskey in Kentucky is befogged by the haze of time; the origin of bourbon is even more obscured. Almost anything one might say within reason on this subject would contain an element of truth. The trouble is that long ago bourbon history became involved in two confusing issues. First, who made the first batch and where did he make it? Second, how did it come about that this pioneer used a charred white oak keg? Stout claims have been made for Elijah Pepper, John Ritchie, Henry Hudson Wathen, Jacob Beam, Evan Williams, Jacob Spears, and Elijah Craig. All of these men made liquor at an early date, but which one discovered bourbon? Perhaps none did by himself. Clearly the process of making bourbon has developed bit by bit over the years. This is still an evolving process, in a way, as distillers gather fresh knowledge and skills.

Almost as many claims have been made for the spot where the first distillers saw their white fluid turn amber as are made for trees where Daniel Boone carved his initials on his lonely ramblings. There may be some possibility that the spot was in Scott County on the Elkhorn where that sparkling little stream gathers in the cold outpourings of the Royal Springs. The Craig-Parker mill turned out all sorts of products, and it could be true that the ingenious millers made bourbon whiskey.

Historical speculators have had a merry time trying to explain how the charred keg came into use. Some say the first bourbon maker used a white oak keg which had contained fish, and in attempting to remove fish odor and taste he burned the inside of the keg. The charred keg is explained in Harrison Hall, *The Distiller,* Philadelphia, 1818. Kegs were hand dressed, and splinters were raised. These were singed off with straw to prevent the gathering of undesirable bacteria. That is all there was to it. No fish, no accidental charring. Hall's book was used in Kentucky soon after its publication. No doubt it introduced charring. The charred keg contains much of the secret of converting white Kentucky grain liquor into amber-colored bourbon by extracting certain chemical properties from the raw fluid. Too, there is an outside chance that a bit of tannic coloring from the white oak staves seeped into the liquor during the aging process. It would be strange indeed if this were not so. Maybe the charring was hit upon in the first place in an effort to check the discoloration from the wood. Anyway, aging in oak casks helps give Kentucky whiskey its color, bouquet, and fame.

By the opening of the nineteenth century distillers had popped up in Kentucky along almost every live spring branch. Stills may even have been more numerous than water mills; in fact the two were often associated. There were by estimate 500 stills in operation in 1792 when Kentucky gained statehood, and the number climbed upward to 2,000 just before the outbreak of the War of 1812. The great postwar panic of 1819 severely reduced this number and took out of business many amateur farmer-liquor makers.

Fayette, Scott, Franklin, Jefferson, Jessamine, Anderson, Mercer, Marion, and Daviess became famous distillery counties. From the beginning of the Republic, Kentucky distillers have had trouble with revenuers. If the Whiskey Rebellion in Pennsylvania had succeeded, Kentuckians were prepared to war against the United States Treasury Department. Washington's militiamen, however, changed Kentuckians' minds when they manhandled the Pennsylvanians; men of the Bluegrass uncocked their rifles. Some of them took cover in the hills and coves and became moonshiners; legitimate distillers submitted to the taxing of their products.

If you say you are from Kentucky you are immediately regarded as an authority on both bourbon and white lightning. You may build the finest university in the land on the banks of the Elkhorn, send away the most intelligent crop of young Kentuckians to serve government and industry, grow poplar trees to the sky, build the highest church steeples this side of Hamaan, and "dry up" every county in the state, but Kentucky and bourbon will still be synonymous in the public mind. Long ago whiskey formed one of the three pillars of state fame.

Like Texas, Kentucky has to endure a thousand and one corny jokes about its local fame, but Kentucky's fame centers about liquor and not space. The imaginary colonels' beards smell perpetually of mint, and even their fragile granddaughters' breaths have been emboldened by essence of burley and bourbon. Traditionally every spring branch is choked by a bed of mint, and every handwrought, family-heirloom cherry sideboard is heaped with silver cups and "fixings." One cannot tell outsiders differently, they "know." I once heard Bernard De Voto of "Easy Chair" fame try persistently to shake the steadfastness of an old Anderson County gauger that liquor made in the old days was much better than that made by more modern methods. De Voto had become involved in a national argument over this point and had come to Kentucky to substantiate his wild statement popped off in easy chair style. The old Kentuckian stood his ground. He said modern bourbon is made by more precise methods than that distilled and bottled in earlier years, and the Bostonian went away still unconvinced.

Historically Kentuckians have always made a little run, either at the head of the hollow or down by the millrace. Wherever Scotsmen, Irishmen, or Germans settled and grew an abundance of corn, small grains, and fruit they made liquor of some sort. A Kentuckian likes nothing better than to imagine that in the old days whiskey flowed at flush tide from stills along every creek. He even likes to perpetuate the old and hackneyed expression that his has been a land of beautiful women, fast horses, fine whiskey, and quick pistols. In a promotional meeting of distillers and their distributors, a gathering of Kentucky colonels whooping it up at their annual pre-Derby breakfasts, or a group of visiting scholars in the university, the chatter is the same. Kentuckians, however, are among the most inconsistent people in the Union. They drink heavily, talk even more loudly about liquor, support their schools and institutions to a significant degree from liquor taxes, and vote more than ninety of their one hundred and twenty counties "dry." It is an unusual year when the liquor question is not on a local ballot or before the courts.

Not since the days when the old Washington Temperance Society roared out of the north like the Asiatic cholera and the yellow fever plagues have Kentuckians rested easy. The temperance crusaders came to make sober men out of confirmed drunkards. Early in the 1840's they beset wild and woolly Louisville at the Falls of the Ohio and shattered it under their hammerings. Men sported almost as many white ribbons as they did gold teeth and pistols. Ribbons, however, proved flimsy shields between virtue and an impelling thirst, and many sawdust-strewn floors caught the falling symbols of sobriety. In fact "falling off the wagon" has over a century and a half become a major Kentucky sport.

"Dry" crusades in Kentucky catch up strangely mixed groups of people who are motivated by all sorts of personal impulses. Nothing favors a local bootlegger so much as "drying up" a county. Such a crusade kills off his competition and so long as he watches his step with the local law-enforcement establishment he is in business. Since bootleggers deal largely in state and federally taxed whiskey they haul into dry counties, they keep the rough state and federal revenue officers away. There are no doubt thousands of Kentuckians who are most conscientiously convinced that the way to promote the best objectives of their society is to vote their communities dry.

Indications are that the tug of war against liquor will go on so long as corn sprouts and yeast is viable. This is a way of life in Kentucky. A court docket without complaints against rumrunners, bootleggers, and other dry-law violators would be a bland affair in many counties. A dry community without its well-known local bootlegger or its citizens of high and low estate who smuggle in some wet goods to slake their thirsts would be a museum piece. One could almost say that large numbers of private automobiles going from Lexington to dry counties carry private stocks in their trunks.

If there are inconsistencies in official attitudes in Kentucky toward making and selling whiskey, there are no inconsistencies in the fact that state history of whiskey making begins with the coming of the earliest pioneers. It would be a foolish historian who would attempt to say dogmatically on what date this all began. One thing can be said positively: Daniel Boone did not make liquor between 1769 and 1771, as one enterprising distilling corporation has claimed. Corn and small grains were grown from the beginning of settlement. Virgin Kentucky soils yielded abundantly from the outset. An educated guess is that Scotsmen drifting down the Ohio from western Pennsylvania knew how to make whiskey, and they set to work building stills. This does not overlook the fact that early Irish and German immigrants also had a hand in bringing the art of whiskey making to Kentucky.

A note appears in J. Stoddart Johnston's compilation of the *Memorial History of Louisville,* in an essay prepared by Colonel Reuben T. Durrett in which he claimed that Evan Williams built a small distillery on the corner of Fifth and Water Streets in 1783. The author said, "Here the first whisky was made in Louisville and possibly the first in Kentucky." Colonel Durrett was never a timid man when it came to untangling troublesome knots of local history. In this case, as in many others, he may have had more local pride than cold facts at his command. One can hardly imagine so long a delay after the first settlement of Kentucky in starting a distillery.

Making a good quality of bourbon has long required skill and reasonably good equipment, even though the machinery for distilling spirits is relatively simple, consisting of mash barrels or wooden tanks or silos, a copper boiler nestled in a stone furnace, a worm, a thumping keg through which cold water flows over the coil containing vaporized alcohol, and a receptacle in which to catch the drippings. The process of distilling nearly always required double distillation in order to increase the alcoholic density. The first run was called "singlings" and the second one "doublings."

The skill with which the distiller selected his grain, had it ground, mixed the yeast, mashed it, and finally extracted the alcohol in the still went far in determining the flavor and quality of his products. Perhaps the early Kentuckians never quite duplicated their whiskey in two succeeding batches of mash and cooking runs; that is, before they began the process of sour mash distilling.

Almost as much a point in liquor making as the origin of bourbon has been the mineral content of the water. From the moment the first pioneer discovered ledges of soft limestone beneath the surface of Bluegrass soil he began attributing magical qualities to limestone water. This mineral has supplied calcium which has strengthened spare-built race horses; it has resulted in the production of fine sheep and cattle and the growing of excellent grains, and distillers have boasted from the beginning that limestone water produces good bourbon. Early distillers used raw spring water in making their mash, and no doubt a certain amount of calcium found its way through their stills.

Cool spring water had a great appeal for pioneers. It 'suaged their thirsts, watered their animals, and cooled their milk and butter. No more vivid memory has stirred countrymen turned town dwellers than that of recalling a cool drink of spring water from a nearby limestone pocket. Thus distillers have had a natural explanation for the excellence of their product—it was the water. At an early moment Kentucky claimed a near monopoly on limestone-seasoned bourbon.

There are tales of old gaugers who had such sensitive taste buds that they could readily identify on which side of the Kentucky River a whiskey was made. They could come near telling where the grain itself was grown. Perhaps the truth of modern distilling lies in the fact that raw limestone water plays a small if any part in scientifically controlled distillation of bourbon. Neutral distilled water is used, so say some distillery chemists, else they would find it difficult if not impossible to maintain standards of flavor and quality.

Few if any American industries have drawn so heavily upon a primitive and nostalgic past for inspiration in their advertising ballyhoo. Whiskey advertisers seem to be fond of creating allusions to "old" and "primitiveness" in manufacturing procedures. It sounds far more romantic to present the image of a little still up the hollow than of a modern manufacturing plant. Bourbon drinkers seem to enjoy the illusion that they are imbibing the nectar of an old farm spring bubbling up from beneath an ancient and ragged ledge of limestone. They like to think their liquor was "mashed" slowly the old-fashioned way in archaic tubs and run through the worm of a tiny farm still in small batches, and was "aged" forever in a dusty charred keg tucked away in a corner of the distiller's smokehouse. Even when consumers see the huge industrial and chemical plants in which modern whiskey is distilled, and the great rows of towering bonded warehouses where the United States Internal Revenue Service stands vigilant guard over the aging and bottling processes, the advertisements continue to create the folksy and "unhurried" illusion.

By the opening of the nineteenth century Kentucky whiskey had become a prime commodity in the growing western trade down the rivers. The endless flotilla of flatboats drifting out of Bluegrass streams carried aboard them thousands of casks of bourbon for the New Orleans market. In subsequent years steamboats bore Kentucky spirits up- and downstream, even into competition with Pennsylvania rye whiskey. There were hundreds of farm distilleries which converted grains and fruits into readily salable products. These were the places about which a great deal of folklore of Kentucky whiskey originated. The whiskey maker, like all other craftsmen, kept his "hand" in the business. In 1815 the *Kentucky Gazette* contained a recipe for making sweet and sour mash whiskey.

The Scots physician James C. Crow added further knowledge to distilling. Unhappily the bourbon industry now knows little about Crow's background, even though it perpetuates his name as a brand. He used such elementary instruments as the sacchrometer and the thermometer. He may have introduced the sour mash process of preparing grain for fermentation.

The name of James Crow was perpetuated after his death in 1865 by Colonel Edmund Haynes Taylor's Gaines, Berry, and Company, and then by A. W. Gaines and Company. Old Crow was one of the early branded whiskeys, but more important it was a pioneer in repeating the sour mashing and distilling processes with some degree of precision. Use of sour mash ensured some continuity from one batch of mash to the next.

Like almost every other aspect of Kentucky history the Civil War caused a sharp demarcation between two periods in distilling history. The demand for bourbon liquor shot up phenomenally by 1865. Soldiers of both armies were heavy consumers of Kentucky's favorite product. Civilians at home also tended to drown their anxieties in their cups. Liquor making quickly became big business. A multitude of new brands made their appearance, and so did new faces and names among the distillers. No longer was whiskey making a sideline to farming and milling. Heads of families often brought great prominence to their clans because they were also heads of distilling enterprises, a distinction which was handed down from one generation to the next as an intimate part of family tradition. Distilling companies ranged from the small ones producing a few thousand barrels a year to those which stocked great batteries of warehouses.

None of the postwar distillers was more colorful than Colonel Edmund Hayes Taylor, Jr. He was descended from the Virginia Taylors, and his people had early become interested in the lands of the Jackson Purchase area of the commonwealth. Colonel Taylor started his business career as a Frankfort banker but following the war he organized Gaines, Berry, and Company and in 1868 the W. A. Gaines Company. Then he built the Old Crow and Hermitage distilleries in Frankfort, and almost immediately erected the famous

O.F.C. distillery on Glenn's Creek on the border between Woodford and Franklin counties. By 1886 Colonel Taylor had won worldwide fame for his name and his whiskeys and he retired to his rolling Bluegrass farms to gain an equally illustrious reputation as a Hereford cattle breeder. Wherever bourbon was consumed it was quickly associated with the name of E. H. Taylor, Jr. In fact bourbon was often called "Old Taylor." Old Taylor is still a popular brand.

Colonel Taylor had an unusual interlude in his distilling and cattle-breeding career. In 1917 the Association of Collegiate Registrars visited him in Woodford County; whether they were attracted by bourbon or Herefords is not precisely a matter of record. It is known, however, that they became so enamored of Colonel Taylor's gracious hospitality that they issued him an elaborate diploma asserting that he could at least get into the offices of fifty-eight registrars on the strength of his degree of "Master of Hospitality."

The Old Taylor distilleries located on the line between Woodford and Frankfort counties near the Kentucky River became a show place. Nestled in this beautiful natural site in the glade of Glenn's Creek it gave more the appearance of being a gentleman's deer park than that of an industrial plant. Here thousands of visitors came to marvel at the big spring, to see the fountain, and to revel in mash odors.

If the Civil War boomed the distilling business in Kentucky, the dry crusading during World War I which led to the adoption of the Eighteenth Amendment and the passage of the Volstead Act all but destroyed it. Warehouses in 1919 had reasonably large stocks of bourbon in wood when the great popular market was cut off. A few foresighted distillers' families stocked their private cellars from their warehouses before the fatal day, but other Kentuckians were left theoretically "bone dry." Some distillers picked up their formulas and brand labels and went off to Mexico to ride out the dry spell; others contented themselves with making small runs of "medicinal" whiskey and grain alcohol.

Prohibition years in Kentucky were the heyday of moonshiners. Revenue officers were called upon to tramp up the hollows and over hills in numbers rivaling those of "sang" hunters who sought every sprig of ginseng that grew. They shot it out with the boys, dug mash barrels out of the ground, gathered fruit jars full of evidence, and otherwise made themselves obnoxious to the operators of a traditional home industry. At Golden Pond, between the Cumberland and Tennessee rivers, the wildcatters fed the Chicago rumrunners' pipelines. The "dew" of Golden Pond quickly established its reputation as being some of the best corn liquor available in the country. In the wild forest-covered backlands between the rivers moonshiners had excellent coverage, and water was no problem. The rivers also offered reasonably safe channels of transportation. So popular did Golden Pond liquor become in the Middle West that it came close to replacing the taste for bourbon in the mouths of old topers and helped to create a younger generation of drinkers who had a taste for stout corn liquor.

Thirteen years of prohibition created quite a hiatus in the history of bourbon whiskey. Warehouse stocks disappeared, old brands were almost forgotten, and few young apprentice distillers were trained to carry on. Some of the old distillers ran afoul of the law trying to evade restrictions, some retired, and others drifted away from the state. Thus a Kentucky business and a tradition were interrupted. Nevertheless, the repeal of the Eighteenth Amendment to the United States Constitution brought a quick rebirth of the industry. Old Taylor and Old Crow returned to Glenn's Creek. Across the Kentucky along Benson's Creek Old Fitzgerald again was tucked away to age in its warehouses. Lawrenceburg, Bardstown, Athertonville, Louisville, Owensboro, Lexington, and Camp Nelson were again bathed in mash odors. These were often intermixed with the aroma of burley tobacco steaming in redryers to assure Kentuckians that all was again aright in their ancient land.

Today forty-five distilleries operate in seventeen Kentucky counties. Liquor making involves large sums of money and a vast reservoir of corporate management. There is almost no place left in the industry for little family distillers who put away a small number of barrels of "handmade" contents to age leisurely in rural peace.

This same thing applies largely to the mint julep. By far more mint is consumed as flavoring for iced tea than in juleps. Families of any affluence at all have silver julep cups, but many of them have forgotten, if in fact they ever knew, that these graceful vessels were created to hold real juleps. It is not at all unusual for "dry" religious groups to present julep cups as expressions of appreciation to their deserving members. Maybe the mint julep never was as generally popular with Kentuckians as tradition has it. It is too hard to make. Vague tradition associates this drink more with ceremonial occasions than with straight-out liquor drinking. J. Soule Smith's poetic recipe for making a julep also gave it wide popularity in the 1890's.

Kentuckians, however, cash in on juleps. Derby day would lack luster without someone whooping it up for mint juleps, and financial returns would be slimmer from this grand promotion without them. Whiskey and what passes for mint is served in paper cups at a dollar a throw. (In this case the question becomes wholly irrelevant as to whether one does or does not crush the mint.) Perhaps some of those folks of enough social prominence to get their pictures in the paper during Derby weekend are drinking mint juleps, but their "glasses" sometimes look suspiciously "old-fashioned." A man could come near causing a riot between Derbies if he strolled casually into a Lexington or Louisville bar and ordered a mint julep. The barkeeper would want to throw him out for being a smart aleck.

No matter how "dry" most Kentucky counties are today, the making of liquor in the state is an important industry. It is even more important because the revenue from whiskey provides a tremendously important margin for the support of schools, hospitals, and even in paying the governor's salary. The industry is a heavy purchaser of raw materials and employs large numbers of people. In a way Kentucky and the distilling industry balance each other off. So important are the Kentucky tradition and name that the liquor industry would no doubt suffer if it were deprived of their use

As indicated above, there have always been two types of whiskey makers in Kentucky: the one which did not have to flee on the approach of revenue officers and the one which has lived in mortal fear of official visitations. Somewhere below a cool spring astride a branch a pioneer with a sack of freshly ground corn meal, a dab of sugar, a virulent yeast culture, a pot, a keg, and a copper tube made the first run of moonshine west of the Appalachians. This unsung and nameless frontiersman perhaps had no more in mind than to quench his own thirst, and, if he had any liquor left to treat his neighbor. He may have made a little run to supply a dance and a wedding party with a little "sweetening."

Not until Congress authorized Alexander Hamilton and his tax collectors to dabble in the affairs of backwoods distillers did these little enterprisers realize they were engaged in a commonplace industry that had greater implications than those of making maple syrup or soap. One thing became clear; large numbers of home distillers intended neither to pay liquor taxes nor to quit making the stuff. They were backed in their determination by drinking neighbors who shared their views and dared not expose them. Too, the terrain of much of Kentucky was highly adaptable to hiding moonshine stills.

Within their lights the old Kentucky moonshiners were upright and honest men. They made reputable "family" liquor which they drank themselves. Few if any of them knew anything about chemistry, but they understood almost from babyhood what would happen if yeast was added to a mixture of sugar and corn meal. They understood further the physical principles of applying heat to a pot of ripe mash and running off alcohol. They knew how to build a still, coil a copper tube into a worm, how to regulate the heat of a wood fire, and how to "single" and "double" a run.

In a more vital way moonshiners, members of their families, and their neighbors mastered the art of keeping their mouths shut. Few strangers to eastern Kentucky can fully comprehend the caution with which the mountaineer communicates with outsiders, and even fewer can understand how news travels so fast in the hill and rock-bound region. The old-time revenue officer was up against at least a couple of mean problems: securing safe and reliable information and approaching a still without news of his approach arriving ahead of him. Literally no Americans are more skillful in passing news about than are rural and isolated Kentuckians. They almost seem to send it on the breeze. For short distances at least they could have made pikers out of the pony express.

There were two vulnerable areas in the moonshiner's protective armor. He could not make liquor without a fire and smoke, and the deep mountain coves either forced smoke up in long telltale spirals or trapped it in heavy canopies which refused to be dispersed. Too, it was impossible to run a still under a rockhouse or at the head of a hollow without disturbing the ground, and once a path was made it took years of rain and leaf fall to obliterate it. Revenuers knew this and kept a keen eye out for such trails. They could almost distinguish by instinct between a cowpath and community trail and one which led to a still. Old-timers believed that paths to rigs had a greasy cast.

Nothing could be worse for moonshiners than neighborhood rows. In the face of such disturbances the best thing to do was to hide their stills and lie low. Old hillmen will sometimes point out whole communities which were destroyed by burnings because the people got to tattling on one another. They will also point out smoke-stained places in rockhouses and smack their lips in memory of the fine liquor that was made in those places. Occasionally they will spot a set of barrel hoops or a mutilated metal drum and recall the great tragedy which occurred at that spot early one morning when the revenuers all but came up out of the ground.

In more recent times moonshiners give themselves away in country stores, supermarkets, and wholesale houses. Revenue men learn who is buying large quantities of corn meal, sugar, and empty soft drink jugs. These are giveaways which often lead officers to wildcatters' doors. In more recent years raiding officers have become too mobile and clever for old-timers to risk tending stills, even in the remotest mountain fastness. They cruise the liquor-making country in small airplanes from which they spot smoke and stills with deadly accuracy. Not even those ingenious ones using propane gas tubes can escape detection from the air. Trails still reveal unusual activities on the ground.

Revenue men on foot today are far more lethal than were the old-timers. They can wreak an awful lot of havoc in the hills with their magnum pistols, and few or no moonshiners want to get into a shooting match with them. They prefer to play another kind of game, gambling on getting by with a certain amount of liquor making before their rigs are uncovered. When they leave their stills they hide the copper worms and other key parts, so about all the modern officers find are mash barrels buried in the ground, a pile of empty jugs, and maybe a few bags of meal and sugar. Occasionally the officers come up with the whole still and a good quantity of "evidence" whiskey, but they have to surprise the moonshiner to do so. So long, however, as the wildcatter saves his "copper and his hide" he is still in business, but not necessarily at the same old places.

The saga of Judge Andrew McConnell January Cochran, who presided for a long term of years over the Eastern Federal District Court in Kentucky, during the years of intensive moonshining, is filled with pathos and comedy. Judge Cochran in time no doubt came to know more moonshiners and the details of their involvement with the alcohol tax division of the Bureau of Internal Revenue than anybody else in the United States. An aristocratic scion of a whole string of pioneer families, several of which were represented in his name, he spent his years listening to suppliant mountaineers explaining why they turned to making illegal whiskey. A stern old boy on the bench, the judge extracted both humor and pathos from the procession of illiterate human beings who passed before him. Like his supplicants, Judge Cochran too lived by a stern code and that was to tell the truth. Some men he saw with predictable regularity. He knew that many of them would scarcely be released from federal prisons before they would be arraigned again for the same old crime. Over the years he sent a veritable army of free-ranging hill men away to spend time behind bars. On the other hand, he let many a hardened old sinner off with a stern lecture because he felt he had told the truth and would, within reason, at least try not to get caught again.

Thus Kentucky has lived over the years by a double standard of values. Moonshiners have gone to the penitentiary for avoiding taxes, while their neighbors have prospered from making tax-paid whiskey. The mixed symbols of one aspect of Kentucky life are in the flossy advertisement of "famous old" whiskey made by corporate distillers and black-hatted hillbillies with stone jugs of moonshine slung over their shoulders. So it has ever been below the Ohio.

XV

Like a Shadow on the Heart

New Year's Day, 1900, dawned on a cold gray morning on which many Kentuckians bemoaned the fact that they had eaten and drunk so freely on the evening before. The end of the nineteenth century had come on a note of the sternest possible reality for Kentucky. So far as any penetrative observer could see the state had arrived at a new age of social chaos and confusion.

For the century and a quarter that Kentucky had been in existence some of the events which colored its history were heroic while others reflected failures. The era of pioneering was a proud one. Even the years when Kentuckians had marched off to fight the British and Indians in Upper Canada in the War of 1812 and to fight the British at New Orleans were years when state pride reached a peak. In subsequent years Kentuckians had endured the Civil War with its moral and political destructiveness, readjusting both its society and its economy to the demands of these sterile war years.

Most of the major successes of Kentucky in the nineteenth century were to be evaluated in terms of personalities. There had, however, been institutional failures. No forceful leader had fired public imagination enough to organize and support adequately a really good public school system, though many a gallant crusader had tried to do this. No university at the turn of the century came within gunshot of realizing the promise of Transylvania in 1825. Bigots and misers had starved the old university and the colleges in their formative years.

Thus in 1900 no college or university in Kentucky could claim to be
a great or even promising seat of a high degree of intellectuality. No
truly great scholar, artist, scientist, physician, or creative author then
called Kentucky home. Young Kentuckians seeking more mature professional training left the state to attend older and more reputable
institutions. The proud cultural landmarks to which nostalgic people
referred were in fact poverty-stricken institutions which never matured beyond their academic adolescence.

In fact at the turn of the century no truly significant American
statesman in the service had sprung from the Bluegrass state. There
was an army of political hacks and flowery orators who showered
their moldy encomiums upon fair womanhood and the inexhaustible
beauties of mother Kentucky, and proclaimed the glories of the past
whenever they could assemble auditors. These windy scions rested
their empty heads figuratively on the bosom of fair Kentucky with
gestures as monstrous as was their insincerity. They were bitterly
factional in their political allegiances and grasping and self-seeking in
their personal motives. These men more often than not served special
interests: the railroad companies, the tobacco trusts, the distillers, the
Jockey Club, the schoolbook and insurance companies, and the rising
coal-mining corporations.

There had never been a time in Kentucky when political leaders
could claim less truthfully that they were free to make independent
political decisions in and out of office. Nor was there ever a time
when leaders and people had less fundamental confidence in themselves to find acceptable answers to their public problems. Like the
foolish son in the Scriptures who had left unproductive his talents,
Kentuckians were now defensive. The more they beat their breasts
and boasted of rugged individualism the less of it they demonstrated.
In the latest revision of their Constitution, in their legislative acts
which poured from the General Assembly in ever-fattening volumes,
and in the administration of both public and private affairs they failed
to demonstrate confidence in their heritage of courage and adven-
turousness. The age of McKinley held them fast in its grip. There was
little or no promise of major business and industrial expansion, almost no hope for the reform of unhappy affairs at Frankfort, and
certainly a change in political conditions awaited the passage of many
years. Tobacco trusts helped to hold farmers everywhere in thralldom
by paying starvation prices for raw leaf. Not only were prices of

tobacco low but buying practices were discriminatory. No matter how loudly the little farmer protested and threatened or how angrily he stormed the polls, he sank deeper and deeper into frustration and ruin.

If one undertook to sort out the picayunish details of the miscarriage of democracy in Kentucky in this era he would become intellectually exhausted by the struggle to disentangle the web of evil little personalities, and even more their evil deeds. The age had its personalities all right, but not a single one who might be adjudged with certainty as either selfless in public service or as of top leadership quality. The times, the people, the leaders, and even conditions in the nation made for social failure in Kentucky. The difference between this age and others lay largely in the fact that since 1866 Kentuckians had nurtured a defeatist attitude in many parts of their lives. Too, they had allied themselves with the reconstruction South and its distraught economies. Measured in terms of an agrarian economy there were rich farmers in Kentucky, but there were few or no rich businessmen. Bankers were severely limited in the amount of capital at their disposal and by their thinking in terms of farm mortgages, small blocks of capital assets, and the necessity for concluding credit contracts each twelve months. There were, in fact, no accumulated blocks of capital which would permit credit extension beyond the span of the crop year.

Important capital invested in Kentucky came from outside the state. The railroads were controlled from New York—not Louisville. Rich mountain coal and timber lands had been largely transferred into the hands of corporations and outsiders who had little motivation to preserve these resources for the future. The new masters of the land had invested a quick dollar with the aim to turn an equally quick profit and get out. They cut away the virgin forests in absolute butchery and waste, they used the ignorant mountaineer and the Pennyroyal and Purchase farmers in the most arduous labor to gut their lands and to leave both people and soil impoverished. In the same way the big coal companies moved in. Many of them came as captive organizations of other corporations. Engineers and miners thrust deep stab wounds into mountainsides, they raised grim black tipples to spew dust over everything, they clawed railway spurs out of streamside shoulders, and spoiled virginal highland swales with slum villages, ringed with sulphurous heaps of burning slag.

These were the years described so vividly by John Fox, Jr., in his local color novels. The land about the "Lonesome Pine" was slashed apart and left to bleed and blister in ugly gashes and rocky barrens. Primitive mountain society itself was gathered up and forced into a bedraggled exploitative industrialism which it was not prepared to enter. Men's labor was sold at ridiculously low wages—so low that no historian can say truthfully on the face of the record that Kentucky received any enduring economic returns from their voracious industrial invasion. No doubt thousands of mountaineers suffered irreparable damage in their broken bodies, loss of their lands, the breaking of old family bonds, and the sacrifice of the old individual freedoms. Thousands of men who once held the power of decision over their lives, however modest they were, now found themselves pawns in the hands of the companies. The company stores with their token coins held people almost as much in peonage as if they were Andean peasants. Immediately these were personal losses to individuals, but in the long run, and socially, they were collective losses to Kentucky.

In a broader field Kentucky lumped its agrarian fortunes with the postwar South. It lived, competitively, however, alongside Indiana, Illinois, and Ohio. So competitive was this relationship by the end of the nineteenth century that Kentucky became frustrated in its inability to keep up. The state was satisfied to compare its economic and social efforts with those made by Tennessee, Virginia, and the Carolinas rather than with Ohio and Indiana. Even the United States Census Bureau encouraged this grouping by placing Kentucky into a statistical association with its central southern neighbors rather than with those of the Ohio Valley. Legislators supported hospitals, public schools, and colleges on a southern rather than an Ohio-Indiana scale. Kentucky farmers compared their efforts with Southerners'. Defeatists found southern reasons for their local failures. They said the loss of valuable slave property and the drain of the costs of war, plus the loss of markets, had brought Kentucky its troubles. This was hardly an honest and factual attitude. Lack of aggressiveness and economic confidence had helped produce these unhappy results. Kentucky also found itself in a southern freight zone, and discrimination in the shipment of goods and farm products by rail cost them more than Ohio shippers just across the river paid.

To a large extent Kentucky was politically boss-ridden in almost every area of its life in the opening of the twentieth century. Narrow and literal-minded theologians either controlled the church or disrupted its functions. James Lane Allen had cried out against the bigotry of his age in his *The Reign of Law.* So bitter was the assault of his critics that he went to live in New York. Tight-fisted extraregional capitalists controlled the banks, railroads, mines, and forests. They even reached down to control the country stores and their credit facilities. Politics was dominated by factions wedded to a complexity of self-seeking boss interests. Even the people themselves had imposed upon the state a complexity of negativism in the Constitution they adopted in 1891. Kentucky political activities had about them an external atmosphere of folksiness which made the democratic process in the state seem almost an act of neighborliness but underneath the surface there was always the iron hand of control and power-snatching.

There was no longer a beckoning frontier in Kentucky in 1900 nor was there left much independent human spirit from the old frontier. Individuals were nostalgic and paid lip service to the past but they were largely oblivious to present conditions. The big question for the Kentuckian was, what was the condition of his state?

The Census Bureau reported there were 2,147,174 Kentuckians, 284,706 of whom were Negroes. This figure showed little more than a modest increase over 1890. Reflected in the population count was the fact that Kentucky was becoming more and more the home of native-born sons and daughters. Like a sluggish stream it received only a trifling inflow of people. It was a matter of deep satisfaction to many that there were fewer foreign-born people in the state than at any time since 1840. Now that the Kentucky population was 97.7 percent native-born residents, the boasts about pure Anglo-Saxonism grew louder. Only Virginia, North Carolina, Tennessee, South Carolina, Mississippi, Georgia, and Alabama had microscopically higher rates of nativity. If there were people in Kentucky who were disturbed by being compared with the states lowest down in the census scales, they got little satisfaction from the fact that these states also had the highest rates of illiteracy in the nation. Slightly less than a third of Kentucky's population in 1908 was of school age, and less than half of its children kept up regular attendance in school for the meager five-month terms. The rest of the educational statistics were equally gloomy. The public spent, in all, approximately $5 per capita to educate their children, and did this reluctantly. Indiana spent $13,253,949 to educate 768,872 children as compared with Kentucky's expenditure of $3,710,447 for 734,804 children. In a state which made such a strong profession of religion, approximately only a third of the people were members of a church, and of these one out of every three was a Baptist.

If these were the good old days of Kentucky history, as many people believed them to be, the fact was not reflected in that long and enduring foundation of family stability, the home. There were 437,-037 families to 413,974 dwellings, and only a fourth of these were free of mortgages. The family, however, was a cohesive institution in its personal aspects. Out of 627,316 married couples there were only 1,182 divorces, or 172 for each 100,000 marriages.

Three fourths of Kentucky's population in 1900 was rural-dwelling. The number of farms had increased since 1880 by more than a third, while the size of the farm had shown a steady decrease. A farm laborer earned 80 cents a day and board, or $16 a month. Farm property was valued at slightly less than half a billion dollars, and tobacco was the main cash crop. In 1901 it yielded a modest return of $18,644,931 or an average of about $44 per acre, and even this low income sagged in the immediate future.

These are some of the tedious statistics that give a dependable gauge of Kentucky at the turn of the century. It may have cheered many that the state had one positive figure in its ledger. Distillers produced 30,441,778 gallons of whiskey in 1905, an amount which was increased steadily to 36,441,778 gallons in 1917 and the eve of prohibition. This was almost the only national statistic in which Kentucky excelled, and again it was exceeded by Indiana and Illinois. There were other, and possibly more important, issues confronting Kentuckians at the end of the century than mere statistical rivalry with its neighbors.

In the gubernatorial election of 1899 Kentucky politics was left in a hopeless confusion. Partisans of William Goebel, Democrat, prepared to protest the results of the general election when the legislature met early that year. The nature and validity of votes cast in many precincts were being challenged. A deep rift divided Democrats, and Republicans held a shaky control of state offices. Rampant Democrats straggling outside the fold of public office believed they could invalidate enough votes on one charge or another to unseat the

Republicans in the forthcoming contests, including Governor William S. Taylor, and restore the Democrats to control. This was an audacious course pursued by cold-blooded men who had long held sway in Kentucky politics. Frankfort was in a state of panic. An army of mountaineers had descended upon it immediately after the election determined to keep the Republicans in office, even if they had to do so at rifle and pistol point. The town was thrown into further turmoil by a bloody shooting scrape between Colonel D. G. Colson and Ethelbert Scott in the lobby of the Capitol Hotel. Their dispute had arisen over a disciplinary matter when the two were soldiers in the United States Army during the Spanish-American War. Close on the heels of Scott's murder, on January 30, 1900, William Goebel, one of the Democratic nominees for governor and a chief contestant of the election results, was shot as he and two other men walked toward the statehouse. The shot came from a window in a nearby office building which was occupied by the secretary of state.

Goebel was the son of German immigrant parents who had come from their native land by way of Pennsylvania to northern Kentucky. Trained in the law but more carefully schooled in the devious ways of rough-and-tumble northern Kentucky politics, the young German had embarked upon a legal-political career in Covington. Opposing the corporations and other oppressive forces in Kentucky, Goebel stormed through one of the rowdiest nominating conventions in Kentucky history. By clever strategy and naked power he snatched the nomination from old-line Democrats in the Music Hall Convention in Louisville and then campaigned over Kentucky in a bitterly personal crusade. He proclaimed a deep concern for the common man and promised to clean out Frankfort of entrenched privilege when he reached that place as governor. Opposed to him was William S. Taylor, a colorless Republican nominee, and former Governor John Young Brown, a "gold bug" Democrat with exceedingly conservative commitments to special interests in Kentucky.

That there was need for reform in state government was clear on every side, but whether William Goebel was sincere in his promises was unsubstantiated. Even that part of his record which can be established by the historian is so deeply tinged with emotionalism aroused by his murder that it is almost meaningless. Already Kentucky's fair name was sullied by feudal killings, the Colson-Scott affair, and numerous other crimes. Now a contender for the governorship was cut down in unprovoked murder in the statehouse yard.

Seldom in the history of a state does a single act mark so sharp a delineation in the course of events and color so many attitudes toward the past as did the killing of William Goebel. This incident in large measure marked the end of an era in Kentucky, in both politics and state history. From January, 1900, on Kentucky was to suffer from chronically recurring and bitter partisanism, based largely upon personal hatred, ambition, and factional strife. In the campaign which led to the assassination of Goebel there were not only the deeply emotional and personal aspects but there was a severe clash of larger commercial and corporate ambitions.

For more than a half century Kentuckians have speculated on who killed William Goebel. Half the men past seventy years of age now claim to have either specific recollections of the affair or information passed on to them by insiders. Two men, Henry Youtsey and Jim Howard, served terms in the penitentiary convicted of murder and being accessory to murder. No one, however, was certain that they were guilty. Youtsey was a clerk in the secretary of state's office and was accused of having helped arrange the shooting. Jim Howard was a lanky Clay County mountaineer who was said to have been taken to Frankfort to shoot Goebel. He possessed the singular talents of being an accurate shot with a rifle and of having no qualms against shooting an obstreperous Democrat. He was unacquainted with Goebel, and if he was the murderer he was no more than a triggerman for others. A state of public guilt has prevailed over the years as to whether or not the actual murderer was detected and punished. If it were now possible for the guilty man to step forward and confess the crime it would be difficult to make anyone believe him, because over the years there has grown around the Goebel tragedy such an involved legend of hearsay evidence and gross misrepresentation that the truth would no longer fit into the pattern of public belief.

Almost as though it were a sideshow to a larger attraction, Republican Secretary of State Caleb Powers was thrown in jail in Georgetown as another accessory to the murder, even though he was absent from Frankfort at the moment of the shooting. Four times he was brought to trial, twice he was condemned to death, but he finally gained freedom. Once back in his native Knox County he was elected to Congress and was honored by having a small army of mountain boys named for him.

The intricacies of the tangled skein of politics in Kentucky after 1900 can never be straightened out and presented in a single narrative. There were too many grasping, selfish little people involved in the Goebel affair to make such an accomplishment possible. Democrats like the ambitious J. C. S. Blackburn, J. C. Beckham, Urey Woodson, Phil Chinn, Polk Laffoon, and scores of others had everything to lose if Goebel was defeated. Blackburn especially fanned the flames of discord because his only chance of being nominated to the United States Senate lay in successful control of the legislature and governor's office by Democrats. For the Democratic gang political control of Kentucky itself was at stake. This political alliance was a curious affair. It associated the newcomer who had pushed directly and arrogantly ahead for what he wanted with the old windy spellbinder who obscured his real intentions behind a fog bank of oratory and gross insincerity. It associated the old Kentucky aristocrat with the realistic political hustler from the northern Kentucky hustings. The direct actionists of eastern Kentucky were enleagued with the discontented farmer from the western areas of the state, and all of them with the sophisticated managers of the Louisville wards.

In the campaign William Goebel had promised major reforms to soften the burdens of the common man. His friends said he died with an eloquent plea on his lips that the great common people be protected and that they keep up their fight. Goebel's opponents snorted at this sacrosanct outpouring, saying they even doubted that Goebel was alive and could say anything. The faithful gave evidence of believing these deathbed pleas. After his death they sold thousands of lithographed portraits bearing the dead warrior's immortal words. They erected statues to him, one in the Frankfort Cemetery and the other before the new statehouse. The latter long ago became the butt of pranksters, who periodically smeared it with paint of varying hues. A proposal to remove the statue repeatedly brought defenders rushing angrily into print. Finally a Democratic governor from Jim Howard's Clay County mustered up enough courage to have it moved from the path of heavy traffic to a safer haven on the old statehouse lawn.

Whatever the facts of the Goebel murder may be, they comprise finally an unsavory story. The broader fact is that Kentucky itself eased into the twentieth century with feeble if not corrupt political leadership. It is doubtful that any politician prior to World War I had a broad enough conception or sincere enough determination to allay the troublous forces of unrest which stirred a Kentucky caught in the dilemma of change. These were the stirrings in an age which demanded realistic leadership in public office. More than that the forces themselves cried out for proper identification in the context of the times.

→≫ *XVI* ≪←

A Kentucky Image

"Well, sir," said Mr. Dooley in 1902, " 'tis good to see th' gloryus ol' commonwealth iv Kentucky is itself again." "How's that?" asked Mr. Hinnessy. "F'r some time past," said Mr. Dooley, "they's been nawthin' doin' that'd make a meeting' iv th' Epworth League inthrestin'. Th' bystander in Kentucky has been as safe as a journeyman highwayman in Chicago. Perfectly innocent an' unarmed men wint into th' state an' come out again without a bullet hole in their backs. It looked f'r awhile as if th' life iv th' ordn'y visitor was goin' to be as harmless in Kentucky as in Utah, th' home iv th' destroyers iv American domestic life."

Mr. Dooley spoke hastily. Before the echo of his observations had died away headlines across the country screamed a new outbreak of the feuds in Kentucky, and feudists spilled enemy and bystander blood with equal abandon.

While politician and constitutional delegate bumbled their way into the twentieth century, less uncertain Kentuckians in the mountains were shooting themselves into history and their neighbors into eternity. Gaping wounds opened by the Civil War slights and injuries still festered and erupted. An evil deed committed by guerrillas forty years before was compounded into a deep sense of injury with the passing years. The hurt survived the memory of the precise injury. As in the spawning of bacterial spores, every new spilling of blood generated dozens of new hates until neighborhoods were in open conflict for no

other definable reason than a desire to annihilate ancestral enemies.

Causes of the Kentucky feuds, however, ran deeper. They were
compounds of ignorance, isolation, Old World clannishness, poor
economic conditions, and the failure of the Kentucky political system
to assume its social responsibilities. It would be foolish to isolate any
one thing as a cause of the feuds. Sometimes it was the imagined
slight to a family, the impregnating of a daughter, or a fuss over a
land line, or a sale of timber that actually touched off the shooting.
Many times it was boredom with life itself that drove men to drink
and then to fighting one another. Whatever the causes the Kentucky
feuds played havoc with domestic peace.

The pressing silence of many a haze-shrouded mountain cove was
split by the crack of a rifle which dropped a carelessly exposed enemy
and called for future killing of a dozen or more men. Hatfields from
West Virginia battled with Kentucky McCoys along the Tug Fork of
the Big Sandy until both clans were bled white. Tollivers fought
Martins up and down the Chesapeake and Ohio Railroad in Rowan
County in the 1880's while Eversoles and Frenches ran each other
over the Kentucky River hills about Hazard, and Bakers and Whites
fought to bloody exhaustion in Clay County.

There was scarcely a mountain county which at some time in its
post-Civil War history did not know a major neighborhood tragedy in
which personal grudges and slights had been settled at rifle and
pistol point. The rifle and the shoulder-holstered pistol were regarded
as standard personal equipment, even for some of the colonels in the
Bluegrass. Kentucky school and college youths are still apt to answer
a question about major guarantees in the Kentucky Bill of Rights by
saying first, "the right to bear arms."

It is little wonder that the incipient war between the Hargises and
their neighbors the Cockrills and their kin and countless bystanders in
Breathitt County, 1890-1910, was to become so murderous as to
fasten the adjective "bloody" to both state and county. The American
newspaper press from Jackson to Boston spread the news of Breathitt's evil deeds. Judge Jim Hargis, county judge, merchant, and local
political boss of Jackson and Breathitt County was given almost as
much publicity as General George Armstrong Custer and Sitting Bull.
In some ways perhaps he deserved more. The judge was not only
highhanded as a feudal lord with major local political ambitions but

he also cut a wide swath in state and local affairs. Wherever he went he was recognized as a clever manipulator of men and a hard-bitten chieftain. But as the old boss and his kind lived so they died, and so their reputations have passed under historical scrutiny.

After his election to the county judgeship in 1898 Jim Hargis and his clan were involved in politics, and this involved them in all the affairs of their county. An election dispute arose between the fusionist Democrats and O. H. Pollard, a straight-out Democrat, and this had its bloody consequences. Judge Hargis, however, operated on an even larger political stage. He was one of the main manipulators in the notorious Music Hall Convention in 1899 which had nominated Goebel as a Democratic candidate for governor. In those days in Kentucky the Breathitt County judge strode down the streets of Louisville and through hotel lobbies exultant over the fact that his hand-picked candidate and fellow townsman, Daniel B. Redwine, had been selected as presiding officer of the convention. Jim Hargis knew he could manage the chairman. On one occasion such a state of excitement prevailed that there was danger of the presiding officer's being shot; Judge Redwine jumped up to leave the platform. Jim Hargis was quick to discourage him, and when Redwine whimpered that the delegates favoring P. Wat Hardin for governor would shoot him if he remained, Hargis was said to have replied, "Damn you, I'll shoot you if you leave!"

Thus it was that Jim Hargis and his concepts of the democratic process became known to Kentuckians generally. Back in Breathitt the people had known since 1890 how much turmoil this willful mountaineer could cause. Not only had the Hargis gang killed and intimidated their lesser opponents, they had become embroiled with James B. Marcum, a prominent local attorney and trustee of the University of Kentucky. Judge Hargis and Marcum became so angry at each other that they were charged with disturbing the peace of the neighborhood. Warrants were sworn out against them, but Hargis refused to submit to the arresting officer, Judge Jerry Cardwell, who was also a bitter political rival. He insisted that he would honor a warrant of arrest only from his friend Magistrate Edwards. This stubbornness caused the accompanying constable, Tom Cockrill, to draw a gun, and only the intervention of his brother Jim prevented bloodshed.

The intervention of Jim Cockrill prevented a shooting at the moment, but the Hargises were not to forget that Tom Cockrill threatened to shoot the judge. Drawing a gun on a Kentucky mountain man was no light matter. Judge Hargis reasoned that a serious threat had been made upon his life and that he stood grossly insulted. The constable had taken unfair advantage of him in a moment when he was being presented with a warrant of arrest. Relatives and political henchmen took it upon themselves to avenge the insult. Back of this immediate dispute were smoldering angers growing out of the recruiting and raiding activities in the mountains during the Civil War. One of Judge Hargis' stoutest defenders was Ed Callahan from Crockettsville, and the current candidate for sheriff. Ed was a merchant and log man, and as such he was associated with Judge Hargis in business dealings. He claimed that J. B. Marcum's uncle had assassinated his grandfather in a guerrilla fight before either of them was born. When charges and countercharges were made there was no hope for restored peace—the people from the North Fork of the Kentucky Valley girded for war and bloodshed.

In 1902 the Hargis-Cockrill feud came to an open break. Tom Cockrill and Ben Hargis, Jim's brother, met in a "blind tiger," or bootlegger's stand, and "shot out" a drunken quarrel. When smoke cleared away Ben was dead, and the war in Breathitt had begun in earnest. Hargis henchmen waylaid the Cockrills and their friends the Coxes. An evil day had dawned in eastern Kentucky.

Hardly had Ben Hargis' body been buried when his brother Tige was ambushed at a molasses mill and murdered. Between July, 1901, and November, 1902, thirty-seven partisans of the two factions were killed. Warring feudists concealed themselves in the somber brick temple of justice on Main Street in Jackson and took pot shots at unsuspecting enemies who strolled along the sidewalk below them. The old courthouse was prostituted to foul and bloody use in these days by mountain assassins. Behind one of its windows on July 21, 1902, gunmen waited for their enemies to come within range along the street. The first unfortunate victim was Jim Cockrill, who was killed by a shot fired from the second story of the courthouse. Cockrill fell within a few steps of Hargis Brothers store and within speaking distance of Jim Hargis and Ed Callahan. As he fell the town marshall wailed, "Shot in the back! My God! They have got me this time!"

Curt Jett, a tall, long-legged, high-cheeked, auburn-haired, and blue-eyed deputy sheriff was accused of committing the crime. It was said that he and two confederates had hidden in the courthouse all day, and were taken away that night by friends. There were innocent eyewitnesses such as C. C. Green, an employee of the Lexington and Eastern Railroad, who left Jackson at once to avoid having to testify against the Hargis mob. Unfortunate witnesses became marked men for no other reason than they had looked up when they heard crashing gunfire and had seen a man fall at their feet with his body riddled by bullets.

The five shots which cut to pieces the body of town marshal Jim Cockrill increased the fury of war. J. B. Marcum, defender of Republican contestants in the election of 1901, and Dr. D. B. Cox, guardian of the Cockrill children, were at the top of the list of Hargis enemies. Dr. Cox was the first to go. He was ambushed while preparing to make a professional call.

Subsequently J. B. Marcum was visited by his friend Moses Feltner, who came to tell him of the Hargis plan to have him killed. The trembling Moses told the amazing story that he had been given $35 and a new shotgun to kill his friend and defense counselor. At that time Moses stood charged before the Breathitt grand jury with murder. He was promised freedom if he could get Marcum to go to his office in an unguarded moment so that a Hargis partisan could ambush him.

To prove to the apprehensive lawyer that he told the truth, Feltner took him to the woods and showed him four Winchester rifles which he and three companions had concealed with the hopes they could waylay and murder the lawyer. This discovery of the rifles was frightening, and Jim Marcum was now certain that he would be murdered if he did not leave Breathitt County. He concealed himself in his home and for seventy-one days was a prisoner behind his own door. In the meantime his law practice went to pieces. He prepared to leave Jackson and begin a new law practice elsewhere, but there were unfinished matters pertaining to his office as United States commissioner which he could not leave unsettled. Again his friend Moses Feltner came bearing the ominous news that the Hargis faction had learned of his plans and were waiting for him at the train.

Marcum abandoned his plan to escape, and chose to remain in "Bloody Breathitt" and fight to the last ditch. Business in his law office, he decided, had to go on, and he realized that the most bloodthirsty feudist in the county would not harm a woman or a child. To ensure his personal safety Marcum went about the streets of Jackson with his youngest child in his arms and was accompained by his wife. His enemies lay behind the window ledges of the courthouse hoping that he would appear on the street alone. On one occasion one of the assassins had actually drawn a bead on Marcum, but the baby was in the way, and, too, the child might be hurt in the fall.

Other attempts were made to ambush the aggressive attorney but each time emissaries of the Hargises informed him of his danger. At times riflemen dressed as women watched the Marcum home for an opportunity to shoot their man. One morning Marcum discovered a window shade raised about four inches, and he knew that was a stern warning to stay well back from the windows and doors. For two weeks he did not dare go near the front porch of his house.

James Marcum was well above the average of mountain men. He had some education and his reputation for honesty and fair dealing was highly respected. Yet he was kept a harassed prisoner in his own home by unscrupulous murderers, and without access to the law-enforcing agencies of the county. He finally escaped to Lexington, but with typical mountain nostalgia he later returned to Jackson saying, "If I have to die, I want to die at home."

Jim Marcum reopened his law office in Jackson in April, 1903. He was welcomed home by friends, and it seemed that the "troubles" would abate. On the morning of May 4 he filed papers for clients in a disputed election case which, as always, involved Judge Hargis and his henchmen. If this case was allowed to come to trial the testimony would be damaging to the Hargis faction. On that morning Judge Hargis and Ed Callahan sat in the judge's store across the street from the courthouse and watched Marcum enter the building.

When Marcum had filed his papers with the circuit clerk he walked out the front door. On the way out he stopped to talk with an old friend, Captain B. J. Ewen, a local hotelkeeper and deputy sheriff. While he chatted with Ewen he was jostled by a Hargis henchman named Tom White. White was a no-account loafer who hung about Jackson ready to perform any errand, including murder, for Judge Hargis and Ed Callahan. In passing, White had looked Marcum in the eye with an evil expression. As he walked on, Marcum told Captain Ewen, "I am afraid of that fellow, that is a bad man." A shot rang out at that instant, Marcum's body quivered, his knees buckled, and he fell moaning, "O Lord! O Lord! They have killed me." Ewen looked back and saw Curt Jett coming toward the stricken man with a pistol in each hand. Jett advanced on the dying Marcum and shot him through the head. The pistol was held so close that the powder flash singed the hair and flesh. Captain Ewen fled, leaving the bleeding body to lie unattended in the doorway of the courthouse.

Attorney Marcum had fallen at last, a victim of determined murderers who wished him out of their way. His killing was well planned and its execution was carried out with cold-blooded highland vengeance. Again Hargis and Callahan were miraculously near the scene of the crime. Ed was high sheriff and bound by oath to act, but Judge Hargis would not permit him to appear on the street, so it was said in the Marcum murder trial, for fear he would get hurt. No immediate move was made by officials to capture the murderer or to attend the slain man. For fifteen minutes Marcum's body lay where it had fallen.

Within moments after J. B. Marcum was shot the mountain grapevine telegraph was active. A Lexington *Herald* reporter wired his paper that it was an open secret that Curt Jett had fired the fatal shots. Five witnesses, it was said, had seen the shooting, but the reporter believed they would be afraid to testify. The two weekly papers published in Jackson failed to print anything of significance about the crime; in fact, their reports of the cold-blooded murder would have given an outside reader the impression that nothing worthy of notice had happened.

Mrs. Marcum was grief-stricken. At last the terrible tragedy which she and her husband had feared so long had occurred. She told friends that only that day two local men, Henry Bach and Edward Strong, had tried to warn Marcum of his danger, but they were unable to reach him in time. When news of their efforts became public they, too, were involved with the Hargis "boys" and they quickly denied Mrs. Marcum's statement.

Bloody Breathitt was at the mercy of the murderers and the powers behind them. No arrests were made, and Ed Callahan showed a remarkable indifference toward the crime. Witnesses were badgered by county authorities rather than protected. There was Captain Ewen, a deputy sheriff, who was an innocent witness of the shooting, and one who immediately became a victim of the plot. His $10,000 hotel was burned to the ground by incendiaries who hoped to trap him and his family. Captain Ewen's building was a total loss, for since 1902 no fire insurance company would carry a risk in Breathitt County. There was no doubt as to the origin of the fire; witnesses, as in the Marcum case, saw the firebugs running away from the building. Hargis hirelings had broken into a vacant room and started a fire there.

The killing of Marcum was a heavy blow to Breathitt County, and Kentucky's fair name was placed in an evil light before an enraged nation. Murder after murder occurred along the many creeks of the county, but somehow the ambushing of an ordinary mountaineer along a creekbank did not carry with it such horrible implications as did the shooting of a man in town. This was especially true since Marcum was a prominent lawyer, and his blood stained the door of the courthouse. Citizens of Kentucky were up in arms over the shameless killing. Societies and newspapers were vigorous in their criticism of the mountain community. At Lexington, Colonel "Billy" Breckinridge and his son Desha of the Lexington *Herald* assailed the Hargis gang. Marse Henry Watterson thundered menacingly in the columns of the *Courier Journal* at the skulking evildoers up the Kentucky River. Editorial columns of all the other Kentucky papers were crammed with venomous outpourings against the feudists. Urey Woodson, a guiding force in the Democratic party in Kentucky and a personal friend of Jim Hargis, was extremely critical in his editorials in the Owensboro *Messenger*. Outside of Kentucky the press was angered, and many a Kentuckian's face blushed at the awful publicity his state got.

Days passed and no arrests were made. Ed Callahan made no effort to track down the criminals and it seemed that, unless Governor J. C. W. Beckham acted, the Marcum murder, like that of the three Hargis boys, Dr. Cox, and Jim Cockrill, would go unpunished. Finally Tom Jett, an uncle of Curt's, swore out a warrant for his arrest. Six days passed before a move was made to locate Curt and his fellow in crime, Tom White. Where had they gone? Jim Marcum's sister, Mrs. Johnson, told friends that she met the two strolling nonchalantly down the river hill immediately after her brother had fallen, and Curt had said, "Hargis money killed Marcum; I fired the shot."

Someone recalled that Curt had gone off down the Kentucky River to Jackson's Ferry to visit with his mother in Madison County. Sheriff Woods McChord of Clark County was instructed late in the evening of May 10 to arrest Curt and to hold him in jail. This was a disturbing order, for Woods McChord well knew that Curt was a bad man when he wanted to be and that he was handy with a 'forty-four. The story of Curt's arrest is, however, one of the fine contradictions of all the Kentucky badmen. Curt was mean, and he was quick with his gun, yet in his own way and after his own code he was a gentleman. He wouldn't shoot Marcum when he was accompanied by his wife and baby. A few days before the killing of the Jackson attorney Curt had plunged headlong into the river to rescue a drowning child and had succeeded in doing so in the face of grave personal danger. Once before he had performed a brave deed of lifesaving; yet he would lie in wait for long hours to ambush an enemy.

McChord's posse drove out of Winchester on the night of May 10 in four buggies. They headed for the old Jackson's Ferry above Boonesboro on the Kentucky River. When the party arrived at the ferry they hitched their horses and went the rest of the way on foot. They were now in the rugged palisade country where there were steep cliffs and deep ravines. The Hagin home, to which Curt Jett fled, was far down the river under the cliff, making it difficult of secret approach.

All but two of the party were stationed around the house on guard. Sheriff McChord, accompanied by a deputy, knocked at the door of the tenant-farmer's house; Curt's mother came to the door, and after a moment's explanation they were admitted. Mrs. Hagin led the sheriff to her son's room where he was sleeping. The mother was the very soul of humble but gracious rural Kentucky womanhood, and Sheriff McChord and his deputy were gracious and gallant. They entered the badman's room as calmly as though they were sidling up to the counter in a country store. There was no bluster or show of arms. The sheriff greeted Curt as casually as if he were passing him on a Winchester street on Saturday afternoon, and Curt replied, "Hello, Woods," as cordially as if he were welcoming the sheriff to a love feast.

After an exchange of small talk, the Clark County high sheriff informed the gunman that he had a delicate little matter of a murder warrant to attend to. An observer would have thought that the officer spoke a bit apologetically for having to bring up such a distasteful subject in so pleasant a company. Curt was in his shirt and drawers, leaning lazily on one elbow, and from beneath his rumpled pillow the butt of his pistol protruded. Gently he said to the sheriff, "All right, Woods, I will submit to you; you won't have any trouble with me. All I want is to be treated right and protected."

Curt got out of bed, put on his clothes, reached under his pillow and picked up his gun, twirled it on his forefinger a time or two in good mountain braggadocio manner. The officers of the law stood by entranced with the calmness of their notorious prisoner. Meekly the deputy asked Curt to let him see the revolver, but Curt handed it over to his mother, saying to the curious deputy as if he spoke to a little child, "Oh, you don't want to see it." It was a long-barreled gun that had gone a long way toward earning Breathitt County the unhappy name of "bloody."

Curt Jett gave his word of honor that he would submit peaceably, and the officers knew that a mountain man's honor was a sacred bond which would not be violated. He was allowed the privilege of handing his gun to his mother, and of dressing as leisurely as he pleased without fear he would escape.

On their way to Winchester the sheriff and his posse attempted to get their prisoner to talk. They were curious to hear from Jett some of his experiences with Marcum. It was with some subtlety that the sheriff asked about his marksmanship:

"Oh," said Curt, "I can kill a squirrel."

"With a pistol?" asked the sheriff.

"No," said the gunman, "with a shotgun."

To all questions bearing on the Marcum case the mountaineer was shrewdly silent. In his cell in the Winchester jail Jett displayed a picture of himself holding his pistol. He seemed to be very proud of it. He disliked, however, being on display to a curious public. Where the famous gunman had been genteel and polite to the arresting officer he became peevish with visitors. He snarled at inquisitive visitors, "I'm no sideshow!" Newspapermen asked, "Where were you when Marcum was killed?" and the murderer replied, "What do you care?" Curt bellowed at one gawking jail hanger-on who asked about the Marcum murder, "I don't know a damn thing about it, and don't care a damn thing about it!"

Back in Jackson a mountain balladmaker was composing a gloomy but incriminating recitation of the bloody crime. In the genuine manner of an Appalachian ballader, this one covered the whole gruesome story, and set it to a tune which was reminiscent of "Jesse

James" and "The Wreck of Old Ninety-Seven." To the twanging of many a highland guitar, the historian whined in fine nasal voice:

> It was on the fourth of May
> Half-past eight o'clock that day;
> J. B. Marcum then was standing in the door,
> Of the courthouse of his town,
> Where Curt Jett was lurking round,
> Just to get a chance to lay him on the floor.
> Marcum leaves a wife to mourn all her life,
> And his little children stand well and brave;
> But that little Curtis Jett, Thomas White and others yet,
> Are the men who laid poor Marcum in his grave.
> Judge Jim Hargis and his man Ed Callahan,
> Were across the street, in Hargis Brothers Store,
> Some believe they knew the plot,
> Hence were listening for the shot,
> And saw Jett's victim fall there in the door.

At least thirty-eight homicides, and some commentators have been even more generous in their estimates, were committed in the county. In a damaging open letter addressed to Judge Hargis, Mrs. J. B. Marcum asked about these homicides and the murderers who were running at large. When a murderer did come to trial he usually found his case tucked away safely between charges against culprits for dynamiting the Kentucky River for fish and charges of lowly and petty thievery.

Jackson was in continuous turmoil; henchmen of Jim Hargis were busily engaged in intimidating witnesses and the Marcum-Cox-Cockrill clans. Drunken men shot their pistols into the air throughout Jackson, and especially around the blind tigers, without fear of arrest. Jim Cockrill had been the town marshal, and "that little Curtis Jett had laid him low."

Jackson was without a law-enforcement agency. No man could be found who was foolhardy enough to act as town marshal. More recent Jackson officials said that the state of their health would not permit the strain of the office. An old-timer gave a good reason for this state of affairs. He said he remembered when stores closed at four o'clock in the afternoon because of rowdiness, and within a few moments after their closing a blue haze of gunsmoke hung low over the town.

Ironically it was William Goebel's successor, J. C. W. Beckham, who had to deal with the Jackson "troubles." As governor of Kentucky, Beckham, a Music Hall nominee, was the one man in the state who could influence the procedures of courts and law-enforcement agencies in Jackson. No one will ever know what passed between Jim Hargis and his friend Crepps Beckham. Emissaries were said to have gone back and forth between them, and on one occasion the two met in a Lexington hotel room in secret conference. Jesse Spider, a deputy sheriff and a Hargis yes-man, passed through Frankfort "on his way to Indiana after a prisoner" when the Marcum case was getting under way. He stopped off, so it was said, to pay a "courtesy" call on the governor.

Louisville and Lexington newspapers began to dig into Governor Beckham's pardon record, and before they were through they gave their readers an astounding mass of information which incriminated the chief magistrate's administration. Joseph Raleigh was pardoned by the governor after a Breathitt jury had given him a long sentence for a murderous attack upon a fourteen-year-old girl. Petitions for the release of Raleigh were formulated by Thomas Cope, Hargis' lawyer, and upon Hargis stationery. The pliable governor wrote on the pardon that the crime "was at its worst no more than manslaughter. While this man was reckless in handling his gun there was, nevertheless, no murderous or homicidal intent." A fine bit of moralizing on the part of a state governor. By accident Raleigh's "graduation" from the penitentiary was left off the record book, and for two years the fact was not publicly known, except as the "wronged" Raleigh was seen about his home community. Again petitions, written by the omnipresent Mr. Cope and on Hargis stationery, were presented requesting the pardon or "graduation" of Ezekiel Spencer, gun handler extraordinary from Breathitt, and there was some question about his graduation being made known to an anxious public. In all, Crepps Beckham in three and a half years "graduated" thirty-seven Breathitt County hoodlums to enjoy the regenerative air of their native hills. Among this army of poor mortals who were sorry for their wrongdoings and who craved "another chance" were Curt Jett and Tom White. They had been imprisoned for shooting at a couple of men with some indication that they intended to kill.

Kentucky newspaper editors were active in their criticism of the Jackson clique, and of their friend the governor. They felt that feuding in Breathitt was ruining Kentucky's reputation before the nation. Leading the pack was the Bath *Messenger*. Its straightforward editor wrote with intense feeling: "To think that one little, miserable mountain hole, with a small band of cowardly assassins, who are fortunate enough to have gained control of the offices of the county can disgrace the whole state and dictate to the governor of the whole people is a proposition not entirely without a flash of humor to us who live on the ground and understand conditions." He then struck hard at personalities: "Redwine don't want any troops; all he wants is for people 'to please go away and let him sleep.' County Judge Hargis don't want any troops. Sheriff Ed Callahan can see no need for troops. These are the three officials in whose hands rest the prosecution of the murders of J. B. Marcum, James Cockrill and Dr. Cox . . ."

Other papers were equally vigorous in their condemnation of the "troubles." At Owensboro, far removed from Jackson, the facetious editor of the *Enquirer* said "that good and generous gentleman, Mr. Curtis Jett, is in prison at Winchester, Kentucky, in the effete Blue Grass, when he ought to be breathing the free mountain air of his native heath. He has only killed a man or two or three men, and the law has no business to interfere with his chosen industry." This editor had more to say about Jett, but he was even more pointed in his remarks about Judge Redwine. Even Urey Woodson, a political ally, made serious charges against his friend Redwine.

This was the general state of feeling in Kentucky when Judge Redwine finally got around to holding court to investigate the Marcum murder. On May 26 Curt Jett was brought home from Winchester and Tom White was arrested far back in the hills by state troops who had been sent to Jackson to prevent jailbreaking by the prisoners and their friends. All night a race was in progress between the arresting party and an informant who went to warn White that he was to be taken into custody. This race was somewhat a re-enactment of the famous turtle and hare contest. The mountain informant, sure of his ground, stopped to spend the night while the Bluegrass soldiers plodded on, and the next morning they met the would-be tattler two miles from his destination and an hour late. Struggling back to Jackson with their whimpering prisoner mounted on a very large mule, the troops reunited the murderous pair who had been separated on May 4.

Late in the afternoon the sooty Lexington and Eastern passenger train bearing the notorious Breathitt deputy sheriff Jett puffed into the station over across the Kentucky River from Jackson. Everybody who could get away from his business was on hand to greet the Jackson celebrity-in-irons upon his arrival. Troops lined the way to keep the crowd back. When the famous prisoner came down the steps of the coach it was evident that he had been in a tantrum. He was sullen at first, but before he reached the jailhouse he was joking with his friends along the way. Just before he was to cross through the portals of the gloomy, dirty, vermin-infested Breathitt County jail, three tender young lasses approached and caressed his manacled hands. In a sense Jett was enjoying a homecoming. Once before, at least, he had accepted the hospitalities of this well-known establishment. Curt had escaped, and the sheriff had not gone to the trouble of rearresting him. On this latter occasion a zealous newspaperman followed Jett to his cell, but to his questions the high-strung prisoner replied, "You have got the wrong horse this time, partner. Lots of you fellows tried that on me at Winchester, and I haven't a damn word to say to any of you."

Before circuit court was commenced in Jackson, Governor Beckham ordered several companies of state guard to that place. They were sent to keep peace and to prevent a raid on the jail to release the prisoners. Rumors flew fast and thick. Informed persons claimed that before court was to meet on May 25 the grand jurors were already chosen. They were all said to be men definitely implicated in the murder of Jim Marcum.

Judge D. B. Redwine, "regular political handyman of the Hargis faction," was determined to preside over the trial. Attacks were made upon him, for it was believed that it was impossible to hold a fair trial so long as he, Commonwealth's Attorney A. F. Byrd, and Ed Callahan retained their offices. Pistols were being fired on the streets and around the blind tigers at will. Jackson citizens' nerves were at the breaking point, and when a fisherman exploded a charge of dynamite in the river there was general pandemonium.

When the troop train arrived in the town the population turned out to meet it. Here, at last, was safety if not peace.

The troops marched into the town and encamped. While they drove down tent pegs and disentangled guy ropes, attorneys argued the question of who should serve as "elisor" to take Ed Callahan's place. From the start of the procedure at the courthouse there was high tension. It spread to the troops; devilish veterans of the militia told their naïve fellows horror tales of militia wars. At night more sensitive troopers dreamed of grim mountaineers firing guns of ungodly caliber into their carcasses. Nightly there was screaming and yelling among those raw heroes whose dreams were disturbed by these fantastic assaults. These weird experiences did not help the general troop morale. On top of these nerve-racking experiences there appeared an eerie spotlight on top of the north mountain which looked squarely down on the town. This flashing beam played upon the guard around the jail. Guardsmen who saw it were horrified. Their officers grew apprehensive that conspirators were hidden near by and that by the aid of the light they could pick off the guards. Gatling and Hotchkiss guns were put in position and plans were made to blast away at the light if it reappeared.

News of a raid on the jail spread daily. Citizens were nervous and the slightest irregularity sent them into a community panic. On the night of May 28 a prowler crept up close to a sentry and refused to halt. The sentry fired on him, and the intruder answered back with a shot. A thunderstorm was in progress, and with each flash of lightning the guards fired upon the retreating visitor. They knocked out the glass windows, destroyed two lamps, disarranged papers, and smeared coal oil over the interior of the Jackson Deposit Bank, but the object of their firing escaped. On the north side of the courtyard a sentry fired upon what he believed to be a charging horseman. However, when the clouds rolled away and the morning light crept over the mountains he discovered that instead of downing a bloody mounted feudist and his horse, he had drilled a $40 milk cow from end to end.

Killing the cow and tearing out the front of the bank was rather conclusive evidence to drinking mountain pistol toters that the boys from the "outside" could and would shoot with deadly aim.

At the courthouse the Marcum case dragged along in true Kentucky style. Lawyers could not agree on Ed Callahan's substitute. A grand jury could not be selected, and on top of these troubles Judge Redwine became ill. Down in the jailhouse Tom White grew temperamental, while Curt Jett was stolid and loudly profane. Tom had frequent spells of crying aloud. Through the powerful intercession of

Curt's uncle Jim the sobbing White was permitted to take his mind off of the "troubles," and perhaps to corroborate his stories of defense in spare moments, by sharing a cell with Jett.

Blind tigers in the town were crowded with armed men who argued and quarreled on the slightest provocation. Hargis men were everywhere. They talked too much, and told more than they knew. Newspapermen, among whom was the well-known mountain novelist, John Fox, Jr., were busy taking down everything they heard. They overtaxed the capacity of the clumsy telegraph facilities at the Lexington and Eastern Railway depot. When facts were lacking in the preliminaries of the trial, they wired reams of "color" to their papers.

In daylight Jackson streets were crowded with coarsely dressed, unshaved, and unbathed citizens who had ridden into town astride scrawny mules and ponies soon after sunup to hear the trial. Many of them were drinking but "they warn't drunk!" They were all chewing and spitting into the corners and around the baseboards of the courthouse, under benches, or into the breaks of stair treads. Breathitt County's courthouse had the rancid, nauseating smell of liquor, unwashed bodies, and tobacco-laden floors.

At the dry goods counters, shoe racks, or before the hardware shelves, mountain women stood in gabbing flocks. They were clad in faded and formless calico dresses of home manufacture; sunbonnets with heavy stave hoods dropped sadly over careworn faces, bony legs and calloused feet were encased in coffee-colored home-knitted stockings which in turn were thrust into cheap coarse shoes. These women, "old long before their time," had trod long miles up rough creek trails behind their slouchy husbands or they had ridden astride stubborn mules and clumsy-footed ponies to the county seat.

Down along "Jockey's row" sluggish mouse-colored potbellied mules with heads drooping awaited the return of their drunken masters. "Shingle-tailed" ponies rested on three feet, with one hip thrown out of joint, from jogs up the Kentucky creek beds. Dogs in packs ran among lolling mountaineers. They chased through the courtroom, the stores, and through the streets smelling each other, raising their rough naps, and growling fiercely at canine strangers.

This was the county seat of Bloody Breathitt in May, 1903, and it was the atmosphere in which the law, order, and good name of Kentucky were on trial. Since there were numerous accusations that the case was to be tried on partisan grounds by partisan court officials, at least the petit jury had to be imported from another county. The native grand jury returned indictments against Curt Jett, charging him with the murder of J. B. Marcum, and against his cellmate, Thomas White, as accessory. While the grand jury was making its report, a dramatic scene was taking place at the depot: Thomas Marcum, burly brother of the murdered man and a successful Oklahoma criminal lawyer, was being greeted by grieving relatives. Tom Marcum was on hand to avenge through the courts the heartless murder of his brother.

Each day brought new and bitter attacks upon Judge Redwine by the press. Desha and Colonel W. C. P. Breckinridge, of the Lexington *Herald,* led the pack. Redwine was frightened and confused. At one time he planned to move the trial to West Liberty in remote and inaccessible Morgan County. This announcement brought so much protest that the muddled judge immediately rescinded it and sped a court representative to Magoffin County to secure an impartial panel of jurors.

On the morning of June 2 Judge Redwine read a stirring charge to the grand jury. Before a packed courtroom he declared to the talesmen: "Crime has flourished in this county, and only once in a while is punishment meted out. The victim then is generally a poor fellow without friends, money, and influence. The stigma that rests upon Breathitt County is upon your shoulders. Wipe the stain from the records." He then lamented the fact that the pistol toter and the whiskey seller had victimized the county. It had become the rendezvous of "blind tigers" kept by men who were too mean to live elsewhere in Kentucky. "This is your county," Redwine told the jurors. "If you prove false to the trust and the expectations reposed in you, these crimes will haunt you."

The judge did his task of charging the jury well. He had four fifths of the mouths in the room agape. Men leaned forward to catch every word and to nod approval when the court mentioned the chief causes of crime in their community. Even those who crowded themselves into the windows were intent upon hearing every precious syllable. Every man who entered the room was searched for pistols and knives. Several pocketknives with tobacco-grimed "big blades" were retained by the doormen, and an occasional pistol was taken into custody. Bony knuckles were the only weapons allowed in the presence of the jury. Just as the eloquent judge said these "crimes will haunt you" a sentry going off duty beneath the windows of the courtroom accidentally fired his gun. Pandemonium broke out, and one black-hatted ruffian jerked out a 'forty-four and waved it menacingly at his stampeding brethren.

Men from Magoffin County rode over the steep hills and down the creeks to the Kentucky River town to serve their benighted neighbors as impartial jurors. There were forty in the first contingent, and others straggled in later. Twelve of these men were selected and they testified that they had not heard anything about the crime. Although they lived only fifty miles away they had not even read of the Marcum murder in a newspaper. Defense and prosecuting attorneys were vigorous in their examination of these unread yeomen. One man, Burns Fitzpatrick, caused Commonwealth's Attorney A. F. Byrd to hesitate. There was something about Fitzpatrick which caused the attorney to doubt he would be a good juryman. Finally, however, he was accepted, and the panel was completed.

Witnesses for both the prosecution and the defense were brought in one by one to give their versions of the crime. "Boss" Hargis, however, was permitted the irregular privilege of sitting through the whole trial. Eyewitnesses generally agreed in their stories of seeing Ewen talking to Marcum, and of seeing Tom White coming out of the courthouse and looking Marcum squarely in the eye. They told of hearing shots ring out and of seeing Marcum crumple and fall. They said they saw Jett run out of the side door of the courthouse. One difficulty faced the prosecution; witnesses were hesitant about telling "all" they knew. They were afraid to tell their stories even with troops surrounding the courthouse. The burning of B. J. Ewen's hotel was indelibly imprinted upon their minds, and they feared ambush and assassination.

Blustering defense attorneys tried to establish an alibi to prove that Jett and White were not at the courthouse and that they had no part in the murder. One sullen witness after another gave evidence of having been coached, and nearly every one of them was a Hargis employee.

For four days the lawyers argued back and forth in the case. On June 18 it went to the jury after a stirring plea by the commonwealth for conviction. The twelve Magoffin farmers made their way into the jury room to argue among themselves as to their decision. Eleven of them were for hanging the defendants, while Burns Fitzpatrick was for clearing them. Burns refused to change his opinion and became downright threatening in his manner. Rumors went around that the dissenting juryman was a son-in-law of a Breathitt man and that he boasted of getting $500 and a Winchester rifle out of his trip to Jackson.

From Jackson in the mountains the case was sent to Cynthiana in the Bluegrass for retrial. On July 27 the case was reopened in the court of Judge J. J. Osborne. The prosecution staff was composed of A. F. Byrd, J. Stanley Webster, Tom Marcum, and L. P. Fryer. Defense attorneys were J. D. O'Neal, J. D. Black, Ben Golden, W. T. Lafferty, J. T. Blanton, Thomas Cope, D. B. French, and Judge Noble. This was a fine assembly of legal talent. Some of these men were the best criminal lawyers in Kentucky—an honor which required exceptional skill where the demand for criminal practitioners was heavy. These eloquent barristers were to display their talents before twelve tried and true citizens of Harrison County. Eleven of them were farmers, and the twelfth "went out to the country to sleep every night."

New witnesses were introduced by the prosecution. Miss Emma Clark, who did not appear in the first trial, told of seeing Ed Callahan peeping through the door of Hargis Brothers store at the time of the killing. He had stood clutching his pistol and peeping expectantly in the direction of the courthouse door. Then there was the perspiring proprietor of a blind tiger who said that he heard Curt Jett say at his place that a dog had been killed. Curt had philosophized over a glass of moonshine, "I had to get rid of him and I did the best I could." This was incriminating evidence, and for three days this witness had pretended to be drunk rather than make it known. It was not until he had been "cooled" on a militia "cooling board" that he was sober enough to talk. All other witnesses who found themselves safely beyond the clutches of the Jackson assassins added materially to the evidence against the defendants.

When the defense called up its witnesses at the beginning of the trial, there were fifty-one of them. Perhaps a more bumptious lot of testifiers was never assembled within an American courtroom. Among this crowd were unshaved, unbathed Breathitt County mountaineers. Many of them had come without coats and ties. There were among them men who bore the highly interesting nicknames of "Ratankle" and "Tickle." One of the witnesses was Jim Rose of Clay

City. He had the reputation of being the best rifle shot in the mountains and was a distinguished "Beckham graduate" from the penitentiary at Frankfort. Once he had gone to guide troops to the home of a prosecution witness who lived back in the mountains, but before the party reached the house he began yelling to warn him to escape.

This shabby Hargis rabble had come to Cynthiana to clear Curt and Tom. They had memorized an alibi but unfortunately they had done the job too well, for they had all memorized the same lines. When questions led outside the memorized procedure all of them suffered strange lapses of memory.

Jett and White were at last placed on the stand. Jett was cool and deliberate in his testimony. His very nature, plus his rough-and-tumble experience with inquisitive newsmen, had conditioned him for the grilling of the courtroom. He cast his blue eyes leisurely but observingly over the audience. Even stinging cross-questions did not disconcert him. Tom White was nervous; frantically he crossed and recrossed his legs. His eyes were focused upon the floor, and his voice quavered and broke in his answers. Big Tom Marcum was merciless in his questioning of both Jett and White. Perhaps no other Kentucky criminal trial, not even the great cases in which Henry Clay figured as an attorney, was prosecuted so vigorously. Tom Marcum placed his large body before Tom White and pounded searching question after question at him. White became so badly involved in contradictions that he could scarcely speak. Marcum's last thrust was to damn the cowardly defendant for permitting his brother and White's professed friend, to die without giving him comfort. So stirring and dramatic was Marcum's handling of the prisoner that even the defense attorney, W. T. Lafferty, was unable to speak until he could send to a nearby drugstore for menthol drops. The palliative influence of the drops seemed not to help, for Lafferty was confused and unenthusiastic in his plea.

J. Stanley Webster of Harrison County followed the defense with a bitter rejoinder. He damned the leaders of the Breathitt County political ring by declaring: "In the hereafter, when time shall be no more and the Angel Gabriel shall come forth and blow the final blast, James Hargis and Ed Callahan will read by the red fires of hell the story of the murder of James B. Marcum at the hands of their tool Curtis Jett." These were stirring words with which to send a jury to its private room to reach a decision in a murder case.

As the last juror filed through the door scarcely an individual doubted that they would reverse the Jackson decision. Many people from Breathitt hoped that Jett and White would have to pay the supreme penalty. One juror, Jasper King, however, disagreed with his fellows. It was said that he had a grudge against Lawyer Webster, and the jury was forced to ask for life sentences. This was the end of the Marcum trial. Jett was tried and sentenced to die for killing Jim Cockrill, but the weak-kneed Beckham saved his neck. Judge Hargis and Ed Callahan were then tried at Mount Sterling, Lexington, and Sandy Hook as accessories to the Breathitt murders, but they were finally acquitted.

After the Cynthiana trial life in Breathitt County became more bearable. The troubles, of course, were not ended, but the fact that a case could be transferred to a Bluegrass county for trial was a sobering fact. For James Hargis and Ed Callahan the shabby drama was to be played out with fatal results for both of them.

At the tiny county seat town of Sandy Hook, tucked away deep in the Elliott County hills, Jim Hargis' reign as feudal lord practically came to an end. He returned to Jackson to recoup his fortune in the log and mercantile business. He carried with him a deep worry in this moment of freedom from the charges of accessory to the Marcum murder. His son Beech was a sore disappointment.

On the morning of January 24, 1908, the troubled lord of Breathitt came down from the hills. He walked along Fourth Street in Louisville, a dignified-appearing man of fifty-five. He was as properly groomed as a drummer from the nearby Stewart's Dry Goods House. He was, in fact on a commercial errand himself, he was going to visit the salesrooms of the National Casket Company. His mission was to buy a coffin which would be in keeping with his status in life. Louisville knew Jim Hargis well. Many times he had trudged its streets on political missions. His picture had appeared in local newspapers on several occasions. Mention of his name in connection with the killing of J. B. Marcum had appeared in dozens of stories.

Now times had changed, and on this brisk January morning not all of Jim Hargis' thoughts were on the past. He was going to buy a coffin—not a crude one known to the mountain hardware trade as "a rough box," but a really fine affair with graceful silver handles. He wanted the best casket the big city supply house had to sell.

He walked into the stockrooms of the great casket company and in a commanding yet mellow tone of voice announced to the patronizing clerk: "I'm Jim Hargis, of Jackson, and I don't know that I'm going to die right soon, and I don't expect to, but when I die I want to put myself away in the best style you ever saw." This was the most unusual customer who had ever wandered into the company's showroom. The clerk, although a hardened veteran in the business of selling funeral supplies, was startled. He was courteous and obliging to the point of being obsequious. Many fine caskets were displayed, and finally a choice red mahogany one with shining silver handles was selected. Judge Hargis had selected a masterpiece of the coffinmaker's art. He asked that this $1,500 coffin be stored until he had need of it.

There must have been some presentiment in the Breathitt County feudal lord's mind that death stalked his heels in Louisville that morning. But surely he did not foresee the horrible future that lay before him as he strolled out of the casket company's door into the street again. Within two weeks he was dead—a victim of a wayward son.

Jim Hargis—a feudist who was said to have been involved in the killing of Jim Cockrill, Dr. D. B. Cox, and J. B. Marcum—fell at the hands of his son Beech. He fulfilled the biblical prediction: "Vengeance is mine; I will repay, saith the Lord."

Beech (Beauchamp) Hargis was an only son, and a headstrong one who was given from early youth to drink. His father had been generous and even tender at times with the boy, but not even the judge's closest friends could deny that he had set his son a horrible example. The boy, truly a prodigal son of blood, had wandered off to Honduras as a teamster for a Louisville box company, but in six months he was back in Jackson drinking liquor and sporting pistols in wild mountain style. He was frequently in trouble. At Cincinnati in 1908 he ran amuck of the vagrancy law, and at the time his father and mother paid his fine he was laboring on the city rock pile. His mother, a patient and forgiving woman, tried in her quiet way to persuade her son to calm down and be decent, but Beech was a product of violent family environment. Too long the Hargises had had their way in Breathitt County where bloodshed was almost a way of life.

Shortly after Beech came home from Cincinnati and the municipal workhouse he attempted to raise a row. There were many versions of his tirade; some say the judge whipped him with his cane, some say it was with a rope, and others that the judge hit the boy in the mouth and dragged him into the house. There were subsequent efforts to discipline the son, but none succeeded. The sullen drunken boy became obsessed with the idea of killing his father. He had boasted on the streets that within a week either he or the old man "would be in the bottomless pit of hell."

Beech stole his father's pistol from its hiding place in the store. He brandished the gun at customers in his brother-in-law's drugstore until he was forced to leave. From Dr. Hogg's, Beech went into the large Hargis Brothers general store and seated himself near the front. He overheard his father's conversation with Squire Brown about his failure to reform his son. Beech walked toward his father as the latter criticized him for being drunk, and from behind a counter shot him. Judge Hargis advanced toward the boy, but Beech threw a coat over his father's head and shot him four times more. The great feudist fell at three o'clock, February 8, 1908, a victim of his own son and his own gun. He whispered to the people who tried to aid him, "I'm killed! Oh, Mercy!" Judge Hargis died close by the spots where Jim Cockrill, D. B. Cox, and J. B. Marcum had been murdered.

Jim Hargis, mastermind of the Breathitt County feuds, was dead, but the means and not the news of his death was the only element of surprise. He had been a "marked man" for many years, and he reasonably expected to die a violent death. Three brothers before him lay in the small family graveyard on the Pan Bowl formed by the Kentucky River, all of them having died violent deaths.

This was Jim Hargis' long and unhappy story. As his fine silver-trimmed mahogany coffin was loaded onto a Kentucky Lumber and Veneer Company railroad car for transportation across the Kentucky River to the family graveyard mourners recalled with pitying memory Jim's trials. The coffin was carried to the humble mountain home where the judge was born. Granny Hargis, grief-stricken feudist mother, was once again called on to follow the body of a "warring" son to its final resting place beside three brothers in the family cemetery.

At the Hargis homestead the Primitive Baptist minister, Calloway Cooper, intoned an endless sermon on the hereafter from the standpoint of both eternal salvation and eternal damnation. As primitive brethren huddled about the long-winded preacher and followed him as he lined out that faith's mournful dirges, the Masonic Order of

Jackson lowered Jim Hargis' body into the grave. Friend and foe alike stood about the grave to see him take his final leave of Jackson and Breathitt County. For days afterward Jackson citizens had the unnatural feeling that they were caught up collectively in some fantastic dream. A degree of peace had come at last to the North Fork country. Only Ed Callahan remained behind to answer the final roll call of the feudists.

Grim Kentucky feudists never forgot, and one final anticlimactic chapter was to be written to the Hargis-Cockrill story. In 1908, when Sheriff Ed Callahan stared for the last time on Jim Hargis' face as he lay in his fine mahogany coffin, many troubled thoughts must have run through his mind. He must have recalled the plots which he and the judge had formed. But Ed's grief was not provoked alone by the passing of his old friend and chieftain; he knew that he, too, would someday have to pay the same ghastly price unless he had better luck. There was little hope for better luck when he knew that every move he made was watched by sharp-eyed and vengeful mountain riflemen.

Since 1903 and the death of Jim Marcum, Sheriff Callahan had been extremely unhappy in Jackson. The place was a horrible reminder of his bitter trials and of an anxious life of uncertainty as to whether he would remain free to become another toiling convict in the stinking old hole of a penitentiary in Frankfort. Here the strain of living had grown unbearable and he escaped the torture by moving back to Crockettsville, up the Kentucky River, to get away from the county seat. When he gave up the sheriff's office, the Hargis' right-hand man built a store, and also went into the log business. Rafts tumbled down the Kentucky River bearing his brand, and his raftsmen went armed to ensure their getting through to the big log markets downstream. His store prospered as customers came in from all over Breathitt County. Only one real obstacle stood in his way to complete happiness: who were his customers? It was impossible to distinguish between harmless and innocent mountaineers who came bearing chickens, tied by their feet, and baskets of eggs to trade for spools of thread, cans of chum salmon, and jugs of kerosene, and those who brought pistols in overall pockets to take his life.

No one knew better than Ed Callahan himself that there were dozens of people lurking in the mountains who wished to see him die.

They wanted him to die so badly that they were willing to do the shooting if a halfway decent opportunity presented itself. Ed's life history tells part of the story of why he was such an unhappy object of murderers. He was a grandson of one of the feuding Amys, and as a child he had learned to hate the Strongs, Grandfather Amy's enemies, with complete Appalachian highland bitterness. His grandfather was shot from ambush by a Strong, and as a boy Ed had spent most of his time trying to retaliate against the Strongs for the crime. It all went back to the Civil War and the guerrillas. When Captain Strong was ambushed in 1899 everybody was certain that Ed Callahan had fired the fatal shot. And again, on the banks of the Kentucky River, he was said to have paid off an old Strong debt by killing Jim Deaton.

This latter shooting led to a bitter row with Jim Marcum. Marcum was extremely severe on the defendant Callahan in his trial for murder. So bitter was his attack in the courtroom that Ed Callahan, mountain man, could not forget it. Later, when he peeped through the door of Jim Hargis' store to see whether Jim Marcum had been killed, doubtless he was inwardly happy to see that Curt Jett had paid Marcum's account in full.

When finally the Sandy Hook jury freed him and Jim Hargis from charges of complicity in the Marcum murder, the sheriff dreamed of a life of peace. The Callahans, however, were not born to peace; there was too much hatred in the clan. For sixty years they and their kinfolks had exacted high prices for their abuses. When one of the tribe was shot they killed in return. With them life was one continuous and vicious circle from ambush to courtroom and back to ambush.

The Callahans were people who never exactly looked upon the established courts as effective agencies for settling family disputes with neighbors. Every one of them believed literally that an eye for an eye and at least two teeth for every tooth made an excellent moral formula for quick and decisive justice. Wilson, Ed's son, killed his uncle John Deaton when the latter made a free-handed assault on his father with a butcher knife. Ed Callahan almost lost an arm in the fray. This opened the troubles anew. Now it was Callahan against Deaton to the bloody end.

Callahans oiled their pistols and rifles, and old Ed rode into Jackson "slaunched" over in his saddle at the head of his clan. He stroked his handle-bar mustache as he jogged along; again he was determined that his people should be respected. With half-closed eyes the old sheriff planned the day's campaigning. Once more his tribe was to foregather on that bloody spot, the courthouse square. They were to take up their stand in the upper rooms of the courthouse, and when Deatons strolled below them they were to be shot.

The Deaton clan was wary. They respected the cunning of Chief Ed, they knew by long experience of Callahan marksmanship, and they did not propose to get caught off guard. There was Hargis Brothers store across the way, and from its windows they could fight Callahans on a somewhat equal plane. For days the warring factions terrorized the town, and its main street was no man's land.

Every place he turned Ed Callahan faced an enemy. Long since he had tried to give up the old fights but still he was forced to lead his folks and to be cautious. He could not travel openly and alone. Every move he made was watched by sharp-eyed riflemen hidden on nearby mountainsides. The porch of his home was denied him, and he had to stay well back from the windows of his house and store. It was necessary to build a high fence around the place, and to construct a puncheon-wall lane from house to store. Ed Callahan was a cowed man within his own castle.

In 1909 he grew careless, and an enemy shot and wounded him while he stood talking over the telephone. His body was silhouetted before the window, and the gunman hiding on a neighboring hillside was quick to spot him. Since 1903 many enemies had missed their mark and it seemed that the old sheriff led a charmed life. No one had been able to cut him down; they had hit him, but his wounds were always slight. Early in the morning of May 4, 1912, however, a rifleman broke the charm. Forgetting to be cautious, the storekeeper again stood at his telephone and a volley of shots crashed through the window into his body. One bullet took effect in a knee, another pierced a lung. At last Ed Callahan was to die the death which both his bitter enemies and his intimate friends had died. The rifle had taken up where the courts left off, and without fear of tricky jurors and mistrials its decision was both positive and permanent.

Skilled surgeons from Lexington, Buckhorn, and Booneville worked frantically over the wounded ex-sheriff, but they were unable to save him. Fever and pneumonia completed the work of the rifle. Before he died the hardened old feudist became sentimental. Generously he forgave his enemies. He forgave them perhaps as a matter of intercession with the Lord. "I know that I will die and that soon," gasped the clansman. "I have forgiven my enemies and I want them to know it. I want all of my people to live in peace, pull together and do the best they can. I have been trying to live as I should for the last five years and I have interfered with the business of no other man and I do not think I should have been murdered while attending to my business and at work."

Then, with what may to some have seemed unreasonable optimism, Ed offered solace to his hard-shell brethren by saying, "I believe I will go to a better world and I want my people to live right and meet me there."

As though sounding a valedictory to the old highland disputes, Sheriff Callahan pleaded, "I want my little boy educated. I want to be buried by my dear old mother, she was my true friend and I expect to meet her above."

This last request of the slain man was carried out. He was buried at Crockettsville alongside other sturdy Callahan clansmen. Friends trudged twenty miles over impossible roads to deliver a factory-made casket which they thought good enough for the slain merchant's last journey.

But even while Callahan lay dying his friends were planning revenge—mountain justice, they were certain, would take its positive course. Away in the hills rural silence was disturbed by the thunderous and bloodcurdling baying of Captain V. G. Mullikin's two bloodhounds. They scoured the neighboring hills for the murderer, but the trail was too cold and obscure for them to make a "strike."

At Frankfort, Governor James B. McCreary offered $400 as a reward to an informant who would name the Callahan murderers. All this—Captain Mullikin's hounds and the governor's $400—availed the commonwealth nothing. The crags and deep ravines of the great mountain ridges had once again concealed a feudist's secret. Only God can know who it was that closed the books for good on the last chapter of the bitter feudal war in "Bloody" Breathitt and all but marked the end of a bitterly unhappy chapter in Kentucky's social history.

XVII

Kentucky in Thralldom

If Kentucky opened the twentieth century in political turmoil, its economic situation was no better. Farmers in the dark tobacco belt of western Kentucky revolted against discriminatory marketing practices, starvation prices, low production, and the trusts. What started as organized resistance against prevailing marketing conditions turned into a bitter guerrilla war among the farmers themselves. For three years, 1905-1908, the so-called "Black Patch War" raged in the dark tobacco belt in the western counties of the Pennyroyal. Warehouses at Russellville, Elkton, Hopkinsville, and Princeton were burned by night riders, and with them large quantities of tobacco. The assault against the exploitative tobacco buyers for the large corporations and trusts, both domestic and foreign, had domestic and international repercussions. Involved in serious damages were both British and Italian tobacco agencies, and even some of the nationals of these two nations were caught in the guerrilla fights.

Uncooperative farmers and their tenants were whipped and driven out of Kentucky. They crossed the Ohio River to settle near Metropolis, Illinois. Back in Kentucky they had no recourse to the courts because of the fears of intimidation by the night riders. Newspaper editors in the area dared not raise editorial protests against the outbreaks of violence or the violation of individual rights. Cases which were brought before the local courts resulted in mockeries of the judicial process. Juries and judges were unable to detect wrongdoing, even if the courthouses themselves had been assaulted. It was a waste of time and money to appeal one of these cases to the Court of Appeals or to make an appeal to the governor for relief. The latter official had succeeded to the office in the first place as a result of the monstrous Goebel tragedy and he steadfastly refused to interfere with the will of the "great common people," even in their destruction of domestic peace and constitutional rights. A clever lawyer, John G. Miller, managed to bring suit in behalf of one of the expatriate Kentuckians in the federal court and was successful in creating a legal barrier to further guerrilla activities.

Almost unconsciously, it seemed, Kentucky newspapers carried thousands of inches of news matter detailing the misdeeds of the people. These stories were spread abroad by the news services. Ready-print houses which supplied weekly papers with copy also helped to publicize the Kentucky story across rural America. Civilized people on the outside began to regard Kentucky as a barbaric state. Exaggerated stories were told of Kentuckians' fondness for shooting neighbors and revenue officers. The corn liquor jug, black-hatted mountaineer, and hog rifle supplemented the colonel, pillared mansion, and thoroughbred as popular symbols of Kentucky life. No doubt justice was raped, human life desecrated and destroyed, and Kentucky in certain spots was uninviting to strangers. These were costly notions for a state to have spread abroad about its people.

Thoughtful Kentuckians themselves wondered if their state had not actually slipped backwards into a dark age. Penitentiaries in Frankfort and Eddyville were crowded with evildoers. Every term of circuit court across the state crammed more victims into cells, which were places of medieval horrors. No intelligent effort had been made to classify the criminals who streamed in from the courtrooms. Capital criminals were confined with callow minor and first offenders. Disease, crime, bestiality, malnourishment, and gross mismanagement prevailed. Wardens were untrained for their jobs which they had gained through political appointments, and held by the same methods. They followed the principle that human beings consigned to prison were there to be punished, not reformed. Often the punishment administered in one of the penitentiaries was a greater crime against humanity than was that committed originally by the prisoner. Governors and legislators asked only that the prisons be run frugally and quietly, otherwise they were both indifferent and oblivious to what happened to the souls confined in these hellish islands.

State hospitals for dependent citizens were little better than the prisons. Courts often committed victims to these places to get them off somebody's hands. There were few if any trained psychiatrists and doctors to deal with mental cases. Again legislators and taxpayers were niggardly with funds, and the hospitals they maintained were perhaps better fitted for conditions in twelfth-century Europe than twentieth-century Kentucky. Public indifference came high in the form of maladministration and of ineffective management of social problems. No citizens conducted crusades to bring about improvements, and governors were satisfied to offer no leadership in this field. In this respect Kentuckians in the early decade of this century showed themselves to be enormously self-satisfied with the *status quo* of their society.

The *status quo*, however, was to be challenged. Throughout the South during the closing decade of the past century soberer minds were troubled by the tremendous impact ignorance and illiteracy were having upon the region. Statistics for the South in this field were staggering when compared with the more progressive sections of the country. In Kentucky people awakened to the fact that there was a correlation between educational failures and many of the state's more serious problems. Dedicated leaders before this date had pushed the cause of public education, but their efforts were not always fruitful. The Reverend Thomas U. Dudley of Lexington attended the southern conferences on education held in Virginia and came home each time pleading for improvements of the Kentucky schools. Throughout the South and in Kentucky the story was the same: a frightening rate of illiteracy, low daily attendance, and grudging public support. Massachusetts parents sent their children to school two months longer each year than Kentuckians; they spent $15 million more on almost the same number of children and employed much better-qualified teachers. It was not, however, abject illiteracy which reflected the failures of educational effort in Kentucky so much as it was functional illiteracy that resulted in the deficiencies of the schools themselves.

Education was Kentucky's cross. From the rugged eastern mountains to the fastness of the Mississippi River bottoms money had to be found to build and maintain schools. A high crime rate, a poor political performance, a lack of capital and industry, and the absence of liberality of points of view reflected severe educational needs. It was difficult indeed to persuade a self-satisfied rural population to act when it was unschooled, afraid of taxes, wedded to the idea that to raise more money for public purposes only served the interests of venal officials, and, finally, convinced that what was good enough for the past generation was good enough for the future.

In the face of vast social inertia and selfishness there were courageous souls willing to buck complacency and ignorance with a degree of enthusiasm. John Grant Crabbe, state superintendent of public instruction, dramatized Kentucky's educational needs in 1908 by conducting what he called a "whirlwind campaign." He stirred public opinion through the press, the women's clubs, and in gatherings of all sorts. He hammered away at the idea that more and better educational effort was mandatory if the state was to escape barbarism. Governor and legislator alike felt the impact of Crabbe and his fight, and they were forced to take action. The most important concepts planted in the public mind were that more educational effort would result in better social and economic conditions and that Kentucky's image before the rest of the country would be improved.

A serious handicap in the improvement of schools in Kentucky was the fact that an astonishing number of college graduates had attended institutions of higher prestige outside the state. Whatever the Kentuckian's local pride, it somehow did not include a warmness of affection for some of the local colleges. The law school in the University of Virginia was a training ground for Kentucky boys who studied law. Washington and Lee University rivaled Centre College for Kentucky students, as did Princeton, Harvard, and Yale. Too many doctors, theologians, and degree holders from graduate schools got their degrees outside the state.

There were other facts in Kentucky's educational life to be considered. Examples were cited by superintendents of public instruction of Bluegrass race horses more luxuriously stabled than children were housed in neighboring schools. Kentuckians were taunted for being willing to tolerate such conditions and for standing by to see their state's reputation suffer. The ideas of extended school terms, higher enrollments, compulsory attendance, consolidation of one-room schools, and the dignifying of the teaching profession were all involved.

In an extracurricular way politicians deterred educational advances. Little men grasping at power and local influence served on school boards. Frequently they were but the tentacles of the court-house rings reaching out to gather in all public positions within their control. It was not absolutely unheard of for some of these board members to exact tribute of teachers who accepted their positions as political favors. These leeches, board member and teacher, lacked the integrity and intelligence to comprehend the place of education in a modern society.

Whatever the facts of educational history were in Kentucky prior to the turn of the century, education as an impelling social force in Kentucky life did not become thoroughly established until the eve of World War I. In the slow changes which emphasized this mild revolution, a solidly complacent people making the transition from a listless age of social failure and economic uncertainty were jarred by the demands of the new era of rising social awareness.

However critical the social historian may be of a people floundering in a period of change, he must keep in mind the fact that Kentucky was caught in a moment when the pendulum of progress swung with regressively shorter strokes. Deep-rooted agrarianism was a highly resistant condition. Its basic static condition of social inertness was almost immovable. This was not an agrarianism expressed solely in terms of rural-urban population statistics and ratios; its more fundamental meanings lay in a state of mind. From the banker on Fourth Street in Louisville to the corn-patch farmer at the head of Barren River, the Kentucky mind was cast in the same cautious negative mold of conservative countrymen. For them no adventure should be undertaken which endured beyond the span of a single crop season. All the facts of life and nature were reduced to the lowest agrarian denominators. The rural Kentuckian's sense of joy in life, his human philosophy, his native wisdom, his pathos, loves and sentimentalities were all expressed in the figures of speech and idiom of the soil, and much of it ridge soil at that.

A Kentucky countryman's richest memories were of the days of his youth when he conceived life to be simpler and less subjected to conditions outside of the local neighborhoods. He enjoyed nothing more than recalling the unusual flavor of the foods of his childhood or listening to the endless stories and folklore adapted and colored by the leisurely tribal chroniclers who themselves relived their youth in the spinning of heroic yarns. These homey hearthside historians explained away the quirks of man and nature in the simplest folk vernacular. Their explanations often combined observable fact with mystery and legend. Whether the Kentucky countryman prescribed folk remedies of ungodly mixtures, or explained that he believed lightning never stuck twice in the same place, or that children bore marks of prenatal incidents, science was reduced to the simplest explainable folk terms. So were the Scriptures, a fact which resulted in a later commotion over the subject of evolution.

Kentucky towns in this period were admittedly nothing more than trading villages gathered about county courthouses. Louisville was the only place which exceeded 50,000 population, and much of that came directly from the "country." For a majority of Kentuckians the county seat was the center of the universe. Whether they sought marriage licenses, legal advice, medical care, a fight, or a pat on the back from a patronizing politician they went seeking it at the county seat. There a man could go on court day to get drunk, to gab away the time, or to take the "old woman" to do her trading. He could swap horses, dogs, milk cows, and worn-out farm implements. He could hear a curbside sermon, be buncoed by a hawker of gadgets, or be knocked down and run over by a runaway team. Whatever happened to him, monthly court day was a county-wide gathering which he felt bound to attend. People rode in on horseback, in surreys and buggies, in wagons. They came afoot, and by boat, to congregate in gawking, gossipy, noisy huddles. In early spring they drove hundreds of young mules to traders' row to be sold south, they rode their bony nags up to hitching racks or led potbellied hounds at heel to sell and trade. They came to sell wagonloads of country hams, great mounds of smoked middling meat, barrels of sorghum molasses, bags of dried fruits, homemade chairs, ax handles, walking sticks, bundles of herbs and sassafras roots, and dozens of other country products.

There was limited concern among the crowds with the business before the court. Coming to town on court day was a custom handed down to Kentuckians from colonial Tidewater Virginia. The countryman was interested in the trading, at which he considered himself an expert, in what his neighbors had to say, in cracking broad country jokes, bantering the girls, getting tipsy, listening to patent medicine doctors tout their wonder healing trash, and to politicians declare themselves in the most florid oratory to be honest selfless men who yearned to do public service.

These countrymen came into town from modest cabins, from

sprawling white-painted farmhouses, and from pillared mansions. They came from rolling Bluegrass plantations, from the rich Pennyroyal meadows, from the pinched and eroded knobs and hills. They were swamp dwellers from western Kentucky and mountaineers from the east. Some came intoxicated on corn liquor of their own making, and others came as militant ribbon-wearing temperance men. In religious beliefs they may have been indifferent practitioners, but basically they were literalists and fundamentalists. Among them were the simple Absoloms of plow and furrow who could barely line out the Scriptures by tedious lip movements; there were the preachers, read and unread, the professors, and the pompous colonels. There were even the landed barons whose colonnaded farm entrances led into a world of self-sufficiency and local power. No social distinctions were discernible in the Kentuckian's love of attending court day.

The gregarious rural Kentuckian went with equal zest to picnics, burgoos and barbecues, camp meetings, and the mineral springs. It took only a slender excuse to organize a neighborhood picnic, a family reunion, a community homecoming, or a speaking. There were ways to break rural boredom. Catching a big mess of fish, the maturing of a flock of yellow-legged chickens, the laying by of crops, and even the unrest of farmers were reasons for having gatherings of people.

Protracted and religious camp meetings differed little from other folk gatherings. For ministers and the devout these annual meetings offered spiritual revival and refreshment. The masses, however, were more excited by the social aspects of the extended assemblies. Many a lazy and sultry summer evening was whiled away in conversation and argument, in courting, rude country joking, and comparison of farm experiences rather than by listening seriously to the preachers.

Socially the mineral springs gathered in flocks of Kentuckians who retreated from heat and loneliness for a week or so each year. There was always excitement at the springs. People came to sit and talk, to have social adventures, and to renew old friendships. They went to Dawson Springs, Blue Licks, Olympia, Drennon, and to Crab Orchard, and Graham Springs. They lined the rambling porches of the old resort palaces and talked incessantly of their families, their farming, their successes and failures, their hopes and their doubts. They danced, courted, and ate and drank themselves into a state of self-satisfaction. They reminisced about the good old days that were gone when life about the springs was more exciting, they passed on every shred of gossip, and cussed out or praised every politician in the state. They gave inside information on who controlled the governor and what it took to get a convict pardoned from the state penitentiary, who the next favored candidates would be, and what the President of the United States ought to do.

Whether in town or back-country settlement, Kentucky was overwhelmingly rural, and life for the rural Kentuckian was severely circumscribed and provincial. He had only the most limited knowledge of what was happening about him. What he did know he most likely had learned by word of mouth from tollgate keepers, and from the country newspaper. Often his only source of information was the eternal forum which held forth about the stove or porch of a country store. Few of the large towns had good libraries, and there were none in the villages. Schools had few libraries, and those which existed were largely collections of textbooks gathered by teachers.

Main sources of hearsay news were star mail route carriers, occasional Bible salesmen, peddlers, drummers, and an occasional wayfaring stranger. Communities surrounding Paducah, Bowling Green, Louisville, Ashland, and Lexington were somewhat more favored by being nearer sources of news. A favorite prefatory remark in a country conversation was: "I seen in the paper where they're goin' to . . ."

The course of rural life followed a regimen. People went to bed early in the evening, rose early in the morning, and divided their days with breakfast, dinner, and supper. Time for them was gauged by the movement of the sun. To a large extent the routine of the countryman's life was set by the habits of farm animals. When chickens and cows were up it was time for people to stir. The world of Kentucky before 1920 was one of daylight. Kerosene lamps, tallow candles, and flickering wood fires gave little comfort and light to the night reader and worker. Rural electrification was a long time off in the future. Telephones were curiosities, and only modern patrons living near town had them.

Great masses of rural Kentuckians never heard any form of music except that made on fiddles, jew's-harps, strap organs, and an occasional piano. Many churches were without a musical instrument, sometimes because members of congregations looked on them as evil and distractive things. Church singing was led by a farmer who pretended to know the pitch from a tuning fork. Occasionally choirs of harmony singers were organized to sing the old songs by shaped notes.

From the day the first hunter dragged a deer into a pioneer fort, Kentuckians have liked food in sumptuous quantities. Whether it be a meal at a private dining table or an outdoor dinner, they liked to be surrounded by food in plenty. A rural outdoor church dinner in Kentucky in 1905 might not have competed handily with fancy city food in daintiness or appearance, or in the order of the service, but it was well ahead in flavor. Kentucky cooks at the turn of the century did not know the meaning of calories, let alone staying a generous hand in the preparation of dishes. Reading a contemporary cookbook compiled by church ladies such as *Housekeeping in the Bluegrass* is a gastronomic tour de force guided by a band of knowing gourmands. From the boiling of a well-aged country ham to the tilting of a generous cream pitcher the cooks aimed to pad the ribs and tighten belts.

Not all cooks learned their art from church ladies' manuals. There were thousands of them who never progressed beyond the stage of baking flat heavy biscuits, frying meat in swimming hot grease, and of robbing the coffee bean of every vestige of flavor. Restaurants and hotels teetered somewhere between the delights of the cookbooks and the sag of the flat biscuit–fat meat school. In Louisville and Covington German immigrants gave variety to Kentucky cooking with their Old World dishes. Many a visitor to Louisville was impressed by the local versions of the transplanted Rhineland restaurants.

How much the vital statistics of the time reflected the lavishness of the Kentucky cooks may be a matter of pure conjecture. One thing is certain, however; the faithful sitting by country store stove and on the porches would have argued freely the question on the side of lavish eating. It was only when a man could not eat, they reasoned, that he was in physical trouble. The science of the countryman was never based on precise research, seasoned observation, or experimentation. It was born of folk premises, was suckled by naturalistic arbiters of all things pertaining to rural life, and was adopted and matured by the masses.

Few states in the Union had more country stores or fourth- and fifth-class post offices than did Kentucky in 1900. The concluding decade of the nineteenth century may have brought the boon of rural free delivery to hundreds of thousands of American countrymen, but there was little enthusiasm for it in many parts of Kentucky. There was nothing like a rural postmastership to give a man an honest excuse for opening a country store and taking his leisure in pleasant company. Having a federal appointment also gave a man social and political status.

The stores and their keepers were institutions within themselves, and the storekeeper-postmaster was better informed than anyone else in a community. Not infrequently he read more than half the letters which came to his office for patrons, and wrote replies for them. There was a constant babble of gossip among his customers. They sought credit and revealed their economic plights. In trouble they sought the storekeeper's advice, and the malcontents fussed at him because of high prices for what they bought and the low prices they received for their products. Nevertheless, the stores were places which exercised strong institutional influence over their communities. Not infrequently they were more influential than the churches because they kept open six days of the week. Storekeepers were more active in the formation of local opinion than were the politicians, and many of them were more adept at voter control than were the candidates for office.

If much of rural Kentucky life was centered about the crossroads stores, the unfolding record was recorded by the country newspapers. There were more county weeklies in Kentucky in 1905 than there were counties, and all of these had to hustle to gather enough news to fill their columns. These were largely political organs. For an editor to take a neutralist stand in politics shattered the faith of his patrons. Just as Kentucky countrymen liked to hear one candidate scorch another, they enjoyed reading the inflammatory editorials of the local editor in which both candidates and elected officials were lectured. Editorial blasts were to their readers a vicarious way of speaking their own minds.

There was a tenderer and more human side to the country paper. Rural correspondents kept abreast of the happenings of their communities. For them everything was news whether it was the quirks of nature or the antics of people. If one neighbor sat a drowsy Sunday afternoon away with another, that was social intercourse and news. Weather, crop conditions, illnesses, acts of violence, accidents, and everything else were discussed. Personal libel was unknown, and edi-

244)   *Kentucky: Land of Contrast*

tor and reporter alike were free and uninhibited. They reported events as they happened, with all their human details. Reportorial zeal was exceeded only by the reporters' capacity for being literal-minded. They left out nothing of fact or hearsay, and frequently enriched stories with editorial opinions. No story excited a correspondent more than that of a local wedding. Even death notices and obituaries were assigned secondary places. Brides and grooms did not have to be social leaders to receive space. For the country newspaperman marriage started the cycle of life all over again for two people, and they deserved publicity. Too, this was one way the country editor could give extravagant praise to Kentucky womanhood.

Despite isolated conditions and statistical shortcomings, life in Kentucky in the early twentieth century had its lighter side. Kentuckians liked nothing better than humorous stories and playing pranks. Editors joined them in enjoying this phase of life. They filled columns with outlandish stories, accounts of local antics, and reminiscences of the "old times." Sometimes reporters were hard-pressed for news in a sterile neighborhood and they fabricated humor of their own. They loved to interview the old-timers to get stories which contrasted the times of man. Occasionally an editor went away on a trip and sent back long descriptions of the sights along the way. Once a year he went to the meeting of the Kentucky Press Association, and this was good for another spate of articles on the "outside."

While country correspondents filled columns with their simple little reports, there were flocks of poets who sought space for their tender offerings. These were grass-roots versifiers who, like marsh hens, reacted to seasonal changes. The buds of spring sent them into spasms of love, as did the first trace of color in the fall. When nature had calmed the world in dormancy, there were the memories of boyhood, the joys of summer, and the frivolities of countrymen to inspire the pen. These humble verses may never receive the notice of critics or be embalmed in college anthologies, but they are revived occasionally by nostalgic Kentuckians who recall the old days when life was less frustrating. Occasionally Allan Trout publishes one of these crossroads gems in his highly popular column in the Louisville *Courier-Journal*.

Life in early twentieth-century Kentucky teetered between a condition of rural peace and happiness and the pinch of social and economic reality. Individually hundreds of thousands of Kentuckians lived blissfully uninformed of the internal conditions of their state, while others experienced crises in their lives. The only point in Alice Hegan's simple little social novel, *Mrs. Wiggs of the Cabbage Patch,* was the indifference of most of the people of Louisville to the people of their slums. Collectively the experiences of a rural people clinging to the *status quo* in an age of quick and sometimes violent change, created a mixed image for Kentucky. Changes after the outbreak of World War I came fast for the state, and the old modes of life were altered if not destroyed.

The Warp and Woof
of Kentucky

The writer has ever found Kentucky an inspiration, if not abundant with readers. While the western country still wrestled with the problems of the first frontier, John Filson in *The Discovery, Settlement and Present State of Kentucke* set the stage for historians and contemporary observers alike. In the inflated manner of the late eighteenth century he described the unfolding of the bud which in a short time would blossom a settled society into Kentucky. His rhetorical flourishes were aimed at fetching land buyers and settlers alike to the region to enrich the speculators. The Kentucky which Filson described had been beaten bloody by Indian raids, and still the red menace to the north threatened emigrants drifting down the Ohio to new homes in the West.

On the face of the land there were being traced the first lines of political organizations. Counties were laid out in great sprawling blocks of wilderness, forts gave way to towns, and Indian and buffalo crossings of streams became boat landings and ferry sites. The first political personalities were showing themselves, and the murmurings against the failure of Virginia to govern her western territory properly were growing in intensity. Filson's thin book was a history only by courtesy of title, yet it became an important literary landmark.

Kentucky history has ever had a strong element of destiny about it, a fact which has given it broad appeal. Politicians and schoolmasters alike have had turns at writing it. Old Humphrey Marshall, a flinty Federalist in a rabble of Jeffersonian Republicans, produced on a broad canvas of fact a bitter political diatribe, intimate personal knowledge, and an interpretation in his *History of Kentucky* which became at once a magnificent peep at the creaking processes of creating a new state, a bitter attack on those who had a hand in its making, and a tender memory for the pioneers. His was a final cry of a vanishing political breed; raw young Kentucky was wooed and won by siren republicanism. As years passed in the opening of the nineteenth century there were fewer Federalist partisans to sow the bitter seed of disagreement. In milder tones Mann Butler and Lewis Collins prepared more temperate chronicles which stuck closer to the main narrative of local history. Collins produced the great chronological encyclopedia in which he traced almost day-by-day the rise of the commonwealth from frontier blockhouse to a self-satisfied state.

Other literary men enlivened the annals of the first half century of Kentucky's existence with descriptions of their benighted roles in a new civilization. None was better prepared or more explicit in recording the tribulations of a common man struggling in disjointed times and ill-fortune than John Robert Shaw the well digger. An Irishman who had wandered far from his native heath, Shaw had campaigned across the Carolinas with Lord Cornwallis. He had spent a dreary winter in Winnsboro, South Carolina, before his countrymen marched headlong into entrapment at Yorktown. There amidst sage and pine he found little more than the demon bottle to break the tedium of life. After the war he was caught up in the western tide of emigration and was cast aground in Lexington, Kentucky. There he practiced that useful but hazardous trade of digging wells. At best this was an arduous way for a sober man to earn a living; for an alcoholic it was suicidal. Shaw's book, *A Narrative and Travels of John Robert Shaw,* published in 1807, is a bleeding record of the author having been blasted repeatedly into unconsciousness in the wells of some of the best people in the Bluegrass. When he was not lying unconscious below the ground or recovering from ill-timed blasts, he was fighting the devils of delirium tremens.

With far more dignity, but at little less hazard of authorship, William Littell, like John Filson a Jerseyman, viewed his ambitious neighbors through the eyes of a satirist. In two books, *An Epistle from William, Surnamed Littell* and the *Festoons of Fancy*, he presented the people and their politics at the opening of the nineteenth century in a light vein. Writing the earliest bit of satire in the rising West, Littell used a style of mock heroics to expose the transparent antics of a politically motivated people. He understood alike the foibles of the great and the shoddy. To him the common man and his leaders were as much buffoons as they were dedicated and wise.

No subject was more palatable to contemporary authors than politics and international intrigue. Both flourished in early Kentucky. Rivalries between the young republic and Spain and later the efforts of France to reassert authority over the western rivers were productive of conspiracies and wavering loyalties. Adventurers appeared on every hand. James Wilkinson and his co-conspirators were guilty enough of intrigue to stain at least one full chapter of national and state history. Books such as T. M. Green's *The Spanish Conspiracy* and John Mason Brown's *The Political Beginnings* contained enough charges of misdeeds to darken the reputation of many a Kentucky family sire. Aaron Burr's visit to Kentucky, after the Hamilton duel in 1804, brought the state further worry and stirred ill-will among its people. Henry Clay was attorney for Burr until he was appointed by the Kentucky legislature to a brief term in the United States Senate. Joseph Hamilton Daviess was prosecutor. Some Kentuckians contributed funds to the support of Burr's project, whatever it was. Many of them entertained the colonel in their homes, and none was more hospitable than Colonel David Meade at his Chaumière de Prairie estate in Jessamine County. No Kentuckian, however, became involved in any active scheme to commit treason against the Union. Kentucky's involvement in the Burr conspiracy was largely in social and internal political terms. The Federal Court sitting in Frankfort was unable to convict Burr of any wrongdoing, but the implications of intrigue and treason were strong enough to slightly discolor a chapter of Kentucky history.

While historian, political partisan, and gallant old pioneer strove to write the story of Kentucky's arduous advance through the stages of backwoods beginnings to statehood, the poets were less inhibited in the range of their imaginations. Tom Johnson, Jr., of Danville, for instance, could write his poetry free of all social restrictions. This drunken young Virginian literally staggered into Kentucky from across the mountains and settled in the sedate center of frontier democracy to irritate the populace with his spiteful doggerel. Under the title *The Kentucky Miscellany,* he vented his feelings toward both neighbor and life. Well supplied with his source of inspiration, he gave voice to his true feelings about Danville and Kentucky. Both were anathema to him. ("Accursed Danvile, vile, detested spot," and, "I hate Kentucky, curse the place.") His self-composed epitaph might also have served John Robert Shaw:

> Underneath this marble tomb
> In endless shades lies drunken Tom;
> Here safely moored, dead as a log,
> Who got his death drinking grog.
> By whiskey grog he lost his breath—
> Who would not die so sweet a death?

Other Kentucky poets were intoxicated, but not on Tom Johnson's "whiskey grog." They adorned the literary pages of Kentucky with softer sentiments. In lusty rhyme William Orlando Butler in *The Boatman's Horn* immortalized the ragged Kentucky boatmen who had withstood the perils of the western rivers to thrust open the paths of a national empire. By the Falls of the Ohio, George D. Prentice, Yankee editor and Whig extraordinary, served both his party and the humanitarian arts. As editor of the Louisville *Daily Journal,* this bumptious Yankee plucked the editorial lyre with the cocked hammer of a revolver, and the poetic harp with the gentleness of mother love. *The Closing Year* and *On Revisiting Brown University* brought him recognition. As important was his generosity to fellow poets in giving them space in his paper, no matter how promising or indifferent their offerings. The columns of the *Journal* in time carried as large a volume of poetry as was produced by all the major New England poets put together. No local poet, however, was so promising as the delicate little flower Amelia B. Welby. Amelia often brightened the columns of her patron's paper with her saccharine Victorian sentimentalities which drifted in place somewhere between the rose gardens of Louisville and the lofts of heaven.

In sharp contrast to the precious offerings of Amelia was the thunderous martial poem of Theodore O'Hara. In 1847 he immortalized the Kentucky dead in the Mexican War in *The Bivouac of the Dead.* This still remains one of America's most important martial poems. Parts of it have been engraved on shafts in military cemeteries across the country or have been recited on memorial occasions for the past century.

Poetry is still a Kentucky art with such mature Kentuckians as Robert Penn Warren, Jesse Stuart, James Still, Allen Tate, Elizabeth Madox Roberts, and others contributing so capably to an enduring literature.

Novelists were timid in making their first offerings in Kentucky. Life was too realistic and unsophisticated in the early years for the fiction writer to find readers. Too, there was competition from French and English authors. Robert M. Bird of Philadelphia cast his famous novel *Nick of the Woods* in Kentucky in 1782, and at the moment the last major Indian fight occurred. He visited the state, and much that he wrote in fiction he either saw in fact or heard about at first hand. This frontier novel bore closer kinship to reality than the subsequent writings of James Fenimore Cooper, and Bird's physical settings were drawn in more precise detail.

Mary J. Holmes was long enough in Kentucky to absorb the flavor of the state and its society. As a young Yankee schoolteacher's bride she lived for three years in Woodford County where she gathered the materials to be used as background for her sentimental novels *Tempest and Sunshine, Lena Rivers, Marian Grey,* and *Hugh Worthington.* These stories, set against a romantic Kentucky plantation background, made the author one of the most popular female writers of her time.

The Civil War created a vacuum in Kentucky. Much potential writing talent was devoted to editorializing or too many potential authors were caught up in active strife of the war itself. One of the best pieces of writing to come directly out of the war was Basil Duke's eloquent *Morgan's Cavalry.* More than any other writer he glorified the famous Confederate swashbuckler in print. Describing the experiences of this command, Duke gave his readers vivid literary saddle seats in the harum-scarum raids which upset Kentucky, Indiana, and Ohio. He had intimate knowledge of his subject and the imagination and literary grace to do it full justice.

The war divided Kentucky's history in twain; the "good old days before the war" and the hard lean ones which followed. Never before had Kentuckians viewed their past through such heavy lenses of nostalgia. Everything was changing, and from the point of the sentimentalists not for the better. In time it produced an abundant crop of local colorists, but not until the cobwebs of frustration began to clear. Lexington and Louisville authors recalled the good old days, and they cast the present in the forms of the past. Dean of these was James Lane Allen of Lexington. Like every other southern writer of this age, he struggled during the hard postwar years to earn a livelihood, but he was ill-fitted to teach school, and besides writing tugged too strongly at his emotions. In 1886 he gained recognition as an author with his *Bluegrass Region of Kentucky,* parts of which appeared serially in *Harper's Magazine.* In his early regional stories, Allen put in words the deep nostalgia which gripped many a central Kentuckian for the days before John Hunt Morgan and his men rode away to war.

In a more profound sense James Lane Allen revealed the close affinity between man and land. Even when he struck body blows at the mindless bigotry of local religious leaders he did so from an anchorage in the meadow and furrow. To him the land was the spiritual fountain of the people and the bigots stood between man and nature. Little of this complex author's writings reflected an understanding or sympathy for Kentucky's headlong rush into the twentieth century. His characters clung to the old ways of life as if in blind hope that modernity would bypass the state. Picturing the great folk gatherings on court days about the Fayette County courthouse, Allen described the kind of easygoing society which he and thousands of his neighbors hoped would endure.

The serpent had entered the garden, however, and man has his intellect and spirit to live with whatever else might attract him. Small-minded men struggled mightily to bind the Kentucky intellect with a theocracy as narrow and limiting as that of puritanical New England. In *Flute and Violin* and *The Reign of Law* James Lane Allen talked back to the elders. This was a new experience for them. In the past they had heartlessly crushed their opposition, but now they battled the fierce monster of fiction. In *The Reign of Law* the novelist had set a devastating time fuse which kept on exploding with each new crop of readers.

Shy man that he was, the dean of the Kentucky local colorists moved to New York City away from the local bickerings and away from the land which had inspired him. Only one more of his novels reflected his deep love for the Kentucky countryside and that was *The Bride and the Mistletoe.*

At the Falls of the Ohio an imaginative group of young women writers created a host of characters who would become household names across America. These women ushered in a slight literary renascence in Louisville, which to date had not really produced a single important writer. Annie Fellows Johnston wrote a score or more of books, but her "Little Colonel" stories, like James Lane Allen's *Bluegrass Region,* recalled nostalgically the gentle society of the Old South. She glorified the mellowness of an earlier Kentucky way of life and made her central character the epitome of all the feminine gentility attributed to a bygone age. For the adolescent American girl she set the model of proper behavior.

While Annie Fellows Johnston made the Little Colonel a part of many a household where there was an adolescent daughter, Alice Hegan (Rice) greeted the turn of the century with her story of *Mrs. Wiggs of the Cabbage Patch.* As a mature bit of fiction this novel was a wholly insipid piece of writing, but as a middle-class revelation of social attitudes in Louisville it was a document of enlightment. Mrs. Wiggs, her scrofulous husband Mr. Wiggs, Mr. Opp, and a spavined horse with a name of Rooseveltian proportions, became a sort of American gallery of the slums. The "Cabbage Patch" and "Billy Goat Hill" were set in sharp contrast to the highlands and were places which the Louisville Chamber of Commerce never listed in its glowing descriptions of the city.

Where the Little Colonel set a pattern of manners and demeanor, Mrs. George Madden Martin's Emmy Lou spanned an age for Kentucky juvenile readers. Before her writing career was ended this energetic woman had created many characters who revealed the spirit and the frustration of this vacuous age in Kentucky. They suffered their defeats, enjoyed their little victories, and placed their faith in fundamental human goodness. Mrs. Martin was the dean of the Louisville literary circle, and no doubt was the mastermind who inspired some of their books, including a composite one written about a gentle Louisville female caught alone in a barbershop at midnight.

As Kentucky turned into this century there was at least one woman writer in each of the principal towns who sought to capture the rich market of the emancipated fiction readers. This was an age in which women themselves battled for emancipation on many fronts, and writing was one of the fields in which they could be most self-assertive. Their novels, however, were never as advanced as were the writers' political views. Mrs. Martin, for instance, was a militant suffragette and political reformer who made herself heard, a thing Emmy Lou never could have accomplished.

John Fox, Jr., viewed the primitive Appalachian highlands with cold reality and with rugged masculinity. Graduate of Harvard and Columbia universities and a veteran newspaper reporter of the Spanish-American War, he followed his brothers into the Cumberlands to help exploit the great coal and timber resources. He had the exciting experience of knowing the native hill people before their lives were disrupted by the industrial invasion. The patterns of the old highland frontier had remained virtually unchanged for a century. Human relations were bound by one of the most primitive social codes of behavior in all North America. In much of the area formal education was scarcely known, and the laws of the state were even less regarded. Here were truly children of nature such as John Locke could never have conceived. An outsider required an enormous amount of human insight and shrewdness to understand them. It took even more astuteness to help these people make a cultural and social transfer from their ancient self-sustained pastoral economy to one in which the hard fist of unscrupulous industrialism changed people from free animals of the hills to bonded hewers of the wood of a new era.

Fox was one of the first competent outsiders to write of the Kentucky mountains and their people. He grasped their history readily and sensed the deep chasm which separated them from the people of the Bluegrass and Pennyroyal. The line of social and political differences between the two was as sharply drawn as that between two alien countries separated by impenetrable language barriers. The mountaineer not only had his peculiar mode of speech, his burden of folk superstition and suspicion, but his attitudes toward the administration of justice, the outside world, and the land on which he lived needed special understanding. All of this was bound up in suspicion and ignorance and illiteracy which only the patient observer could unravel and understand. Fox was able to do this. He was able to get inside the mountaineer's mind, to probe his soul, and to reveal his reactions to things and people. With a keen sense of geographical determinism he discerned the sectional barriers which separated Kentucky people. In *The Little Shepherd of Kingdom Come* he treated the attitudes which prevailed in the state during the Civil War. Chad

Buford, the hero, was psychologically incapable of violating the mountain code no matter how persuasive the Bluegrass influences which impelled him to do otherwise.

Though times have changed radically for the Kentucky mountain people, the deep underlying nuances of the Cumberland Plateau society remain basically the same as those described by Fox. He knew the crossings, the fears, and the timidity of the people in the face of changes from the old ways. He knew the hold the past had on the older ones and the uncertainties which gripped the younger ones. His character June Tolliver, in *The Trail of the Lonesome Pine,* outgrew even Fox himself in her desertion of the hills, but the breaking of the ancient ties with her people was fraught with anxiety and tragedy.

Harry Caudill, in *Night Comes to the Cumberland,* has taken up the Appalachian saga where John Fox left off, portraying his region in decades of revolution. He has described the exploitation of man and the resources of his land in gripping terms of heartlessness and waste. Lumber and coal companies and speculators have all taken their toll of the hills. Most of them have given little or nothing back to the mountain society in comparison with the tremendous wealth they have taken from it. More than this, they broke the ancient cycle of direct association with the soil without substituting satisfying new ways of life. Perhaps Fox in his novels did little actually to make the mountaineer conscious of his plight, but Caudill has accomplished this objective with telling effect. He has revealed to the American people as well as to the mountaineers themselves the sins of the exploiters. His clear and sometimes angry prose has hit its mark. Once proud frontiersmen depending heavily upon their personal resources were broken and defeated at their doorsteps. Their sons suffered a second defeat at the hands of the industries which brought the great breaks in their lives and then introduced machines to replace them. Never before has so literate a mountain man appealed to his people in such eloquent prose to take stock of their past and to reshape their future in the light of history.

Jesse Stuart, easily the most prolific of all Kentucky novelists, including Irvin Cobb, has written of the hill people largely from the context of his own life. With a deep sense of attachment to the community of his origin he has examined the central forces of isolated rural life with the insight of a poet. Thoroughly conversant with the mainstream of folkways, he has cast his novels and poetry in a natural frame of reference which is at once as fresh and raw as the hills about him.

Stuart's keen sense of humor, on the one hand, and his profound seriousness, on the other, have enabled him to shift moods. His *Taps for Private Tussey* caricatured the mountaineer in his innermost conflict between impulses of grief and greed. In *Man with a Bull Tongue Plow, Head of W Hollow,* and the fictional autobiographical book, *The Thread That Runs So True,* he reflects the deadly seriousness of the struggle of common people against the frustrating forces which they can scarcely identify and are seldom able to overcome.

In a quieter vein than any of the hill country writers, James Still has opened poetic vistas of a country caught between a century of traditionalism and one of modern progress. His mountain people are drawn to almost precise portraiture, in which he presents a subtle overlay of the innermost facts of their lives. Neither a reformer nor a man who has a deep sense of social destiny, Still has written as an artist capturing the spirit of his surroundings. He has also dealt gently with the conflicts of his people, and even more so with their doubts and failures, yet he never overlooks the harsh realities of the country.

Of an older generation, and from a much more sophisticated background, Irvin Cobb wrote of Kentucky in a deeply reminiscent vein. In *Down Yonder With Judge Priest* he perceived the turnings of Kentucky life, and especially of Kentucky politics. With a journalist's alert sense of what his home people were about, he portrayed them in sweeping transparencies. Sometimes in purplish wrath he lashed out at them as he did at William Goebel in his autobiographical *Exit Laughing.* Most of the time, however, his stories were cast in the same light nostalgic vein in which the old-timers spun their yarns on the Paducah street corners.

Irvin Cobb's keen sense of humor enabled him to capture the easy-flowing careless manner of his characters. His "Judge Priest" stories reflected the folksy qualities of life held in a drowsy thralldom on the back roads and along the Tennessee and Ohio rivers. His Kentuckians in his stories in *Collier's* Magazine compromised the cares of life on terms of their social mores, and accepted them either with a horse laugh or a bitter sob as the occasion demanded. In subsequent

years Alben W. Barkley tapped this inexhaustible fountain of folk
humor to charm a nation, and to record in his book *That Reminds
Me.*

In sharp contrast Elizabeth Madox Roberts of Springfield glorified
the act of pioneering. In *The Great Meadow* she portrayed a
heroic folk movement wrapped in the mantle of virtue and bravery.
Her women characters went forth to meet calculated risks in the
wilderness with the stoicism of Old Testament women. There was a
deep sense of purpose on the part of these intruders into the garden.
They came to claim the land and to plant a civilization with all the
seriousness of crusaders in the past. In *The Time of Man* the people
labored on the hillsides of Washington County in the same way that
Naomi and Ruth gleaned the ancient fields. They were most unusual
Kentuckians because they were not interested in the all-absorbing
subject of politics or lighthearted reminiscences. Their relationships
with the land were starkly spiritual, and their loves, disappointments,
and experiences were tightly bound in the symbolism of man's
eternally laboring under the burden of original sin or on the edge of
succumbing to temptation. She wrote as if there was constantly ringing in her mind a fantasy of life itself.

Nevertheless, it was with profound artistry that this poetic woman
wrote of Kentucky humanity in the throes of subjecting the land to its
will. In a Hardyesque manner her gleaners and herdsmen went forth
to their fields and meadows not only to fulfill their economic missions
but to achieve the fuller spiritual purposes of life as temporary tenants. Their actions were set almost by predestinarian time clocks
which governed their thoughts and relationships. Fundamentally the
lives of many of Miss Roberts' characters were caught up in the nets
of human inadequacies and uncompromising destinies.

Probing deeper into the crosscurrents of Kentucky's past Robert
Penn Warren and Elizabeth Chevalier have dealt with the agrarian
revolt in the field of tobacco culture. In *Drivin' Woman,* Elizabeth
Chevalier portrayed the trials and tribulations of her home people in
the struggle to eke out a living growing burley tobacco. The deep
conflicts which resulted from harsh corporate discriminations and
sagging prices resulted in a minor revolution. Farmers along the
Tuckahoe Ridge in northern Kentucky were bowed down by poverty
in a land which was highly productive. In their blind way they struck

out at the oppressive forces which mashed them literally into their own soil.

Dealing with a more widespread discontent Robert Penn Warren in *Night Rider* gave a more subtle interpretation of the evil forces which enslaved planters of the waxy-dark-fired tobacco of the Pennyroyal belt. The night riders' war went far beyond striking at the corporations and recalcitrant planters. It struck at pinhookers or little speculators who cheated families of the fruits of their labor and others who got out of line. Night riders marauding across the countryside came to attack all wrongdoing, and in time hatreds, fears, and injustices became so intense that no one trusted anyone else. Newspaper editors, judges of the courts, jurors, and everybody else became so intense that no one trusted his neighbor. In Frankfort a spineless governor, thinking more of his political fortunes than the peace and welfare of the commonwealth, showed even less courage than local people. It was with the moral and intellectual conflicts that the novelist concerned himself. Though inwardly his characters knew that morally they should strike out against power gone off the track, they never quite had the courage to take a stand and face angry opposition.

Warren has turned to Kentucky on other occasions for background material and settings for his poems and novels. In the powerful epic poem *Brothers to Dragon* he related Thomas Jefferson to frontier Kentucky through his sister and two nephews. He revealed the horrible sadism of the Lewis brothers in the act of butchering and burning a slave boy as a disciplinary lesson to the rest of their slaves.

In *All the King's Men* and *World Enough and Time* Warren has used the Kentucky background. *World Enough and Time* revived an ever-popular literary theme, the murder of Solomon P. Sharp by Jeroboam Beauchamp. William Gilmore Simms produced a novel around this plot in the 1840's, and time and again it has been used by other authors. Warren used it to probe the morals and political current of social rationality in a Kentucky torn to shreds by a biting public issue. Anne Cook and Jeroboam Beauchamp became something more under his pen than a common woman of Frankfort and a political errand boy. The pair emerged cloaked in robes of a kind of Kentucky chivalry and gallantry. Again the novelist probed the innermost moral fibers of his characters, and at the same time the toughness of the moral fiber of Kentucky society. The trial and execution of Beauchamp and the suicide of Anne Cook brought this episode to a dramatic close. It was to be romantically concluded by burial of the two in lasting embrace in a common grave in Bloomfield. The slab covering the grave bears a long inscription which ensures romantic interest in the tragedy.

In Louisville Isabel McMeekin and Dorothy Clark took up where the older generation of local women writers had left off. In *Show Me a Land,* a highly successful joint writing experiment, they produced a book that gave an imaginative and lively quality to the Kentucky background. Louisville and the state appeared in their books almost as parts of a great western pageant in which the characters came decked in the tinsel and make-believe of actors in a giant folk theatre. They captured the essential and romantic natures of their fellow Kentuckians and presented a world which the romantics hoped had existed once and might again come to exist. Where Elizabeth Madox Roberts and Elizabeth Chevalier's characters were sober and sometimes grim the Clark-McMeekin characters were almost always lively as a river excursion party.

Harriette Arnow created extensive social documents in her novels *The Dollmaker* and *Hunter's Horn.* In these novels she traced the migration of hill Kentuckians to the industrial towns of the Great Lakes crescent. Changing her pace she produced a scholarly two-volume historical work in which she described the rise of civilization in the isolated pocket of the lower Cumberland Valley. These magnificent volumes are more than a detailed and chronological recitation of the lives of rural people, they are revelations of the sufferings, personal sacrifices, and aspirations of the people, many of them to date unheralded in any kind of history. In *The Flowering of the Cumberland* Miss Arnow brings her history to a mature climax in tracing the rise of the valley's cultural institutions. She has dealt with the history of the region in the same degree of depth as did Robert Penn Warren in his novels.

Living in the midst of the Cumberland Valley, Janice Holt Giles has written of the pioneering years of her people in a folksy but penetrative vein. Her concern has ever been with the lives of the people themselves, never pushing them beyond their land and their backgrounds. Like Harriette Arnow, she has been appreciative of their cultural aspirations, and of their triumphs, but her treatment of

these has been in a long continuous level line. The maturing of folkways that were durable in the stern environment of the valley was
accomplishment enough.

Thus Kentucky, a land of fierce contrasts, of bitter rivalries, open
conflicts, sharply divided by history and geography, has ever appeared to its authors as an inexhaustible bed of literary ore. There are
subtleties which divide the people into groups and classes, and which
in many ways set the state apart in an almost impenetrable borderland with borders within it. There is an appreciable span of time and
social maturity between the elegance and sophistication of the membership of the Pendennis Club in Louisville and the periodic lineup of
Kentuckians before the surplus commodity storehouses. The two
worlds have to exist and function within the common enclosure of a
set of political and geographical boundaries, but they can never really
meet, much less understand each other. One stands somewhat
haughty and proud, the other stubborn, sensitive, and uncertain.

In the great vale of contrasts Kentucky authors have found characters in abundance with which to people their books, and situations
enough to form an interminable number of plots. None, however, has
produced the universal Kentucky story, nor has an author yet
fathomed the deep recesses of the Kentucky tradition in the sense that
mother Virginia has been portrayed in the novels of its authors, or in
the biographies of its great men. The Kentucky story and society fall
into parts which no one so far has been clever enough to mold into a
single piece.

→≫ *XIX* ≪←

Visitors Bearing Gifts

Hardly had the last critical viewer of slavery and its insidious effects on Kentucky recrossed the Atlantic or the Ohio before the nation was at war. For four years during the struggle between the sections, Kentucky was almost the only place in the South where visitors could come with fair assurance that they would not be caught in the cross fire of the two armies. Both native and foreigner took advantage of Kentucky's neutrality to gather firsthand information about campaign activities and social and economic conditions in the embattled South. Kentucky was a leaky sieve indeed when it came to gossip and information about the progress of the war. It is doubtful that major campaigns were begun without news of troop movements and plans being divulged in advance.

Soldiers on the move across Kentucky kept diaries and journals, or they wrote hundreds of letters home describing their experiences. Those from the North seemed to think Kentucky was alien ground and this inspired them to describe their feelings with verve. Whether visitors were on their way south or were pushing eastward to the Virginia front, they were usually accompanied by soldiers who crossed Kentucky on their way to do battle. Both William T. Sherman and Ulysses S. Grant came this way, as did Captain James A. Garfield, Phil Sheridan, Braxton Bragg, Nathan Bedford Forrest, and others who became central figures in Civil War history. It took Kentuckians almost a century to become reconciled to the Yankee invasion. Now they point with something approaching pride to the places where Grant crossed the river and where he spent a night while traveling northward along the old Wilderness Road. They have marked the place in Paducah where the great push began up the Tennessee River, and in the neighborhood of Bardstown, Springfield, and Lebanon there are markers designating Don Carlos Buell's route to Perryville to stall the Confederates.

Many a farm boy from north of the Ohio wrote his home folks about the crowded and disorganized conditions in the Union camps around Louisville or described the long drives southward into Tennessee past the river strongholds and to the great climax at Shiloh. These lads were less critical of their accommodations than more sophisticated travelers, but cursed more picturesquely the rough country through which they traveled. Soldiers who found themselves floundering in mountain fastness, wondering if they would ever again reach land level enough to see the sun rise before ten o'clock, had reason to complain.

The interval of military travel was short. When the war ended and railroads were used for something more productive than making "Confederate neckties" by wrapping cherry-hot rails around trees, sightseers invaded Kentucky, coming from north and south. Poverty-stricken country merchants came up to Louisville from the crossroads to stock their pitiful little stores. Sometimes they brought along wives and daughters to see what life was like in Louisville or to wander off to marvel at Mammoth Cave. At the famous cavern they rubbed shoulders with Yankees and Europeans who crawled through the subterranean passages to stare at the domelike chambers. "Fat Man's Misery," the famous narrow passage, humbled all alike, Southerner, Northerner, and European. As post-Civil War travel literature became more voluminous, no other place in Kentucky was mentioned so often as this narrow passage which reminded travelers that the course of life itself was largely one of squeezing by the yokes of crises. In continuous procession people flocked to the cave to sense the thrill of its passages and its diamond-studded ballroomlike chambers. A literary Frenchman, an Oxford University student, a casual English traveler, all were dazzled sufficiently by what they saw to devote several pages of their published journals to the wonders of Mammoth Cave.

Native "scientists" viewed this natural wonder and rushed home to

edify neighbors by publishing descriptions of their adventures. Fortunately these people took time to visit with backwoods Kentuckians
living in the surrounding counties. They viewed Civil War damages
and picked up firsthand accounts of hates and fears of the guerrillas
who plundered Rebel and Unionist without showing favoritism.

Besides the cave, horses, tobacco, and distilling appealed to visitors. Frequently foreigners savored all of these attractions, and many
times through mist-laden eyes they saw things in the cheeriest lights.
There was a certain amount of commercialism in the willingness to
show visitors tobacco warehouses and distilleries, but showing them
horses and stud farms was a matter of pride. Kentuckians have long
felt that to reveal an interest in horses placed them on an equal
footing with many visitors, especially Englishmen. Nothing in the
state brought the native sons into such close kinship with Old World
gentry as their interest in breeding and racing horses. There travelers
from abroad found no boring questioning from backwoods greenhorns and there was about the stables no noticeable self-conscious-
ness of a visitor's superiority. Here was a subject which many Kentuckians could discuss with profound assurance.

Occasionally a European nobleman appeared in the state. In 1910
the German Crown Prince came to visit some of his countrymen in
the Rhineland of Cincinnati and then headed for the Bluegrass. The
local gentry about Lexington spared no pains to entertain him in a
manner to which he was accustomed. Those who were privileged to
break bread with the royal guest considered themselves among the
socially elect.

Not all the visitations in Kentucky were made by outsiders. In
1892 James Lane Allen set out by buggy and train to view his home-
land. He traveled over the ancient route from Lexington to Cumberland Gap. His descriptions of landscape, people, and their homes
reads as though it had been written by a complete stranger—and it
was. The provincial Bluegrass novelist had little social or geographical kinship with the backcountry of Kentucky. He described primitive conditions of society he viewed along the way as though he were
traveling through the Indus Valley. Allen was startled by the primitiveness of the mountain people. For the first time he began to comprehend the gulf between the Kentucky mountain society and that of
the Bluegrass which was so eloquently described by John Fox, Jr., in
his novels.

Where John Fox, Jr., traveled and wrote of life in the hills, scores of later authors published accounts of their visits to the same places. During those troubled years of the early 1930's Theodore Dreiser observed the bitter social and economic upheaval which swept the eastern coalfields into tragedy. This was a moment when a strange face on a coal camp path or on the streets of Harlan, Hazard, Evarts, and Lynch was immediately a suspected one. There Dreiser's literary fame was unsung, he enjoyed no hospitality, and he was subjected to bitter suspicion and distrust. Just as James Lane Allen and John Fox, Jr., had viewed the mountains as a separate Kentucky social world, Dreiser looked upon the eastern coalfields as America's social jungle in which established order of law and society had long since vanished. He was first of many social visitors who came to view this troubled scene, and before the last reformer's travelogue was published the coalfields of eastern Kentucky were branded as places of savagery and bloody violence.

In a less socially militant vein John F. Day took a look at parts of his native section in *Bloody Ground* (1940). This book was inspired by a casual visit to Breathitt County, a region which historically had experienced bloodshed and economic recession. The kind of life the fiery young newspaperman viewed there was as primitive to him as anything the eighteenth-century travelers said they saw in colonial America. Day viewed the country against the backdrop of modern education and industrialization, and he readily sensed that this part of Appalachia suffered from lack of social communication with the "outside" world. Too, he wrote in an age when mountaineers were extremely sensitive about criticism of their country. Privately they knew that most of what the author wrote was true, but his words appearing on a printed page gave their plight a stain of permanence.

Even government employees who have been so bold as to describe backward social conditions in eastern Kentucky have been subjected to the stinging wrath of offended natives. Part of the unhappiness may have resulted from the fact that it was well-nigh impossible to apply the code of the hills to an outside author.

The traveler in the hills often could not see beyond the dramatic and the sordid. In metropolitan Kentucky there was a difference. In Louisville, for instance, certain fundamentals showed above the surface. George Leighton in *Five Cities, the Story of Their Youth and*

Old Age (1936) viewed Louisville from its shabby trash-laden streets
to its proud Pendennis Club. This was in the biting depression days
when Louisville was struggling to find new economic directions. His
description was that of a sprawling city which seemed powerless to
disentangle itself from the past or to fully embrace the future. To him
it was a cluttered, unkempt place reminiscent of the 1850's, except
for the pigs which Madam Stuart-Wortley and Charles Dickens saw
on their visits. But Leighton was not interested in pigs or tobacco-
chewing yahoos who early gave Louisville its rowdy reputation as a
frontier river town. In a bold essay he described Derby eve with its
noisy crowds, the gaudy catchpenny businesses along Fourth Street,
and the men who ran the town.

At Derby time there was the slightly intoxicated gathering at the
annual colonels' breakfast, and the more sedate functions in the out-
lying suburbs. Behind much fanfare there was the history of men who
not only had played major roles in building railroads and banks but
had helped to shape the history of Kentucky itself. Among these were
such powerful personalities as James Guthrie, Milton H. Smith, and
James B. Brown. The latter saw the powerful Bank of Kentucky
come crashing down in the depression of 1930, and with it Louisville
was stunned into economic paralysis. The depression drew a sharp
dividing line in both city and state progress. Never again were the
"old families" to exercise such a decisive hand in public affairs. If
depression weakened Louisville, the subsequent flood of 1937 all
but drowned its hopes for an immediately promising future.

World War II had not long been ended before John Gunther hurried from Nashville to Louisville to try to discover what went on
inside Kentucky. One of the first persons he interviewed was the salty
old editor of the Louisville *Times,* Tom Wallace. The editor had
grown wise and cynical, and he knew much about Kentucky lore.
When Gunther asked him who ran Kentucky he replied, "It doesn't
run—it limps." Mr. Wallace told his visitor that "braggadocio" was
the state's chief distinction, and that the reason Kentucky was so
backward was because it "is infested with Kentuckians." Gunther was
not steered aside by these droll remarks. He felt there was more
romance packed inside the state's boundaries "than in any other
state."

Gunther's search for an answer to his question as to who ran

Kentucky was no more successful than was Leighton's quest for similar knowledge. Many special interest groups had a hand in the job.
The big liquor interests, the Jockey Club, the Louisville and Nashville
Railroad, the coal operators, the Louisville *Courier-Journal,* and a
miscellaneous assortment of politicians could be identified. None,
however, was so colorful as Fred M. Vinson, Alben Barkley, Ruby
Laffoon, A. B. Chandler, and Wilson Wyatt. These men personified
the political force of Kentucky.

Rushing away in as big a hurry as he came, Gunther flung back
over his literary shoulder this judgment:

> Kentucky is the state where a brother of John Keats was a bank
> director, and where ladies may enter the Pendennis Club, the chief meet-
> ing place of tycoons, only by a side entrance; where the WCTU de-
> manded that bathrobes be draped on show window models clad in low-cut
> bathing suits, and where Man-o-War is worth five thousand dollars a time
> at stud; it is the state where the first enameled bathtub in history was
> manufactured, where river towns like Covington give you a wonderful
> glimpse of the sky's the limit river life, and where roast opossum and
> raccoon are still great delicacies.

No doubt Gunther had in mind the serving of these delightful
viands in the dining rooms of the Pendennis Club.

If John Gunther's romantic fling was right, then Harry Shacter, a
public-spirited businessman of Louisville, and Fred Wilkie, a distilling company executive, did much to shatter it in their surveys of
Kentucky. They saw much wrong with Kentucky and set out to bring
about reforms. Not satisfied to take opinions as answers to their
questions they established the Committee for Kentucky to uncover
the cold objective facts about the state. When the report of the committee was published native sons were almost as shocked as their
forebears had been in 1777 when rumors spread that Governor General Henry Hamilton in Detroit would pay bounties for white scalps.
There was no romance, not even a touch of nostalgia, in the committee's final report. One thing seemed clear: it would take more than a
colonel's commission and a broken-down race horse to set Kentucky
aright in the middle of the twentieth century.

Other travelers came to Kentucky as blinded to fact as was John
Gunther. In a gentler manner an Englishman pronounced a sort of
mid-century benediction on the "great visitations" to Kentucky. Sir

Philip Gibbs, tottering between overindulgence of bourbon and the attrition of advancing years, visited Lexington and Louisville as an early wartime lecturer. He came to tell, for a stiff fee, about the horrors of modern warfare. At the close of a long newspaper and writing career in which he had published more than fifty-five books, Sir Philip was ready to view Kentucky in the softest possible light. Local society in Lexington was ready to tolerate even his lordship's piddling lecture, so long as he drank its liquor with gusto, admired Man o' War, and rode about the town to view historic landmarks with a proper appreciation for an "ancient culture." His comments on Lexington were clearly those of a man unduly mellowed by alcohol and cocktail party chatter. If the rest of America's concern for the world crisis was as lighthearted as the patter Sir Philip said he heard in the Bluegrass, then civilization teetered on the brink of calamity.

Sometime after the Civil War Kentuckians discovered that a neat profit could be turned from the entertainment of visitors. Louisville, for instance, carried on a vigorous campaign to make itself a convention town. It invited all kinds of people to the city to kick up their heels, buy its merchandise, and sleep in the the local hotels. The promoters were even so bold as to suggest to the southern country merchants that they come to the Falls to have a good time, and that it would be better if they left their wives behind.

Near the end of the nineteenth century when the old fires of war had burned to soft glowing embers of memory, the Grand Army of the Republic held its convention in Louisville. The city offered every form of entertainment which its promoters believed would gladden old soldiers' hearts. Proclaiming in 1890 style, and for local public consumption, that Louisville was a home of churches, schools, theatres, and art museums, the copywriters created a fine image for the place. More imaginative sons, however, took advantage of the heartbeat of the veterans away from home and the inhibitions of churches, theatres, and schools, and offered them culture of another sort. The kind of art that many an old veteran wanted to learn about was displayed along Green Street and its adjoining alleys. The "bluebook" issued for this occasion was a highly informative guide to visitors and comrades-in-arms. The "book" promised, however, to shatter domestic tranquillity back home for any "Billy Yank" who forgot to toss it out of his coat pocket on his departure from Louisville.

Modern Kentucky is actively engaged in the business of seducing visitors to cross the Ohio and relax in all sorts of ways. Once, not too long ago, some Kentuckians enticed "tired businessmen" to cross the Ohio and unwind in the entertainment parlors about Covington and Newport. There was no known "bluebook" to direct their steps, but somehow word got around, and veritable droves of them found their way to the proper places.

In more acceptable manner the commonwealth spends a generous amount of money to bring the family-type tourist into the state. In a handsome number of state parks Kentucky can offer the visitor luxurious accommodations, a thing that would have completely upset Thomas Ashe in earlier years. Visitors of all sorts pour across the river bridges to seek recreation and entertainment. The parks represent not only recreational facilities but major accomplishments in conservation.

A carload of tourists on a week's visit in Kentucky will yield more clear profit than a medium-sized tobacco crop. They can be sold everything from a plaster model of a red bull to a peacock-adorned bedspread. Tourists will buy bourbon-laden candy, bourbon whiskey, postcards, fishing gear, country hams, and horse etchings. In even greater generosity they will gorge themselves on fried chicken, hot dogs, and country ham.

The modern travelers are not as literate as were the earlier ones. Occasionally an unhappy one dashes off a letter to an editor, but on the whole they come and go without making a record beyond a cash register tab. Kentucky is in the business of selling tourists history in a highly palatable form by showing them the sites where frontiersmen and Civil War soldiers trod. Daniel Boone has become big business, and so have Jefferson Davis, Cassius M. Clay, and John C. Breckinridge. The choicest places of all, however, are those associated with Abraham Lincoln. A good Lincoln spot is a money-maker if it can come within a long rifle shot of being authenticated—and so are a lot that cannot. Some Kentucky communities in the Lincoln country even become involved in neighborhood contentions over the priority of their claims to Lincoln associations.

Earlier Kentuckians might have railed at Thomas Ashe and all the other visitors who spoke critically of the people and the country. No one prior to the Civil War cared how much they bruised a visitor's feelings so long as they did not act downright inhospitably to him. That is not true in modern Kentucky. To ruffle the feelings of a modern tourist is to irritate a cash customer. Such rudeness would be almost akin to discouraging industrial management from locating a manufacturing plant south of the Ohio.

Appalachia

That vast half-moon area that sweeps around the whole pointed eastern end of Kentucky was served from the beginning of time by a lavish natural hand. Mountain valleys and cool north-side coves grew giant trees in an extravagant variety. Ageless patriarchs stretched high to snatch at the sun in its brief pivoting beyond the rocky cliff-lined canyons. Many of the peaks were earliest to stick their heads above floodwaters and glacial paths to form dry land. In deep layers prehistoric plants were compressed into veins of oil and pockets of natural gas, or deep layers of bituminous coal. Thus with timber, coal, oil, and gas the Cumberland Plateau offered a rising industrial America an abundance of indispensable materials.

In time mountaineers hacked away the great stand of virgin timber. For half a century they ran numberless rafts of unbelievably fine logs out on the crest of spring freshets to markets in Ashland, Catlettsburg, Louisville, Cincinnati, Valley View, and Frankfort. Riding down with the sweeping "tides," black-hatted hill men faced endless danger, gulped down hot biscuits, fat meat, and copious swigs of corn liquor. They fought riffle, eddy, and bank squatters with equal ferocity. Hardy as these raftsmen were, they lacked a concept of the great importance of their resources and the engineering skills necessary to exploit them at their places of origin. The big mills that ate up logs the way fattening hogs ate corn were run by outsiders, and one by one these leviathans crept up streams to meet the log runs in order to satisfy their greedy demands for timber to be shipped outside Kentucky and made into profit-yielding products.

Land that was worth little more than a hog rifle, a keg of moonshine, or some other trifling thing now for the first time had a rising value to be set in terms of dollars.

The "foreign lawyer" or land speculator and engineer like Jack Hale in John Fox's novel *The Trail of the Lonesome Pine* prowled the mountains buying rich timber and coal lands for scarcely a fraction of their actual worth. Behind these friendly outsiders who came with "long" deed forms and pocketfuls of cash were corporations who enjoyed more favor in Frankfort than free hill men who had scarcely heard the word "corporation," let alone understood its power and omnivorousness. They had no understanding that on the heels of the engineers railroads would thread themselves up the valleys like giant inching worms. Hazard, Paintsville, Pikeville, Pineville, Whitesburg, Lynch, Irvine, Beattyville, Jackson, London, and Middlesboro would become railroad towns from which thousands of trains would roar away with loads of logs, lumber, and coal. Before this happened great portions of the mountaineer's Eden had passed into outsiders' hands and control, and the native son had become the servant rather than the master of the land.

Occasionally a land speculator or a timber baron took time out from his feverish drive to organize a timber empire to look in wide-eyed wonder at the prodigious virgin forests which lined the coves. They were soul-inspiring sights indeed. Trees that shot up as tall and straight as a fresh-sprung arrow grew to enormous size. Many a chestnut, black walnut, tulip poplar, white oak, and sugar maple all but defied men and short saws in their harvest. Logs of four to ten feet in diameter were not at all unusual. Ship's timbers as long as thirty to fifty feet could be hewn out of the mountain oaks. A single walnut tree often yielded enough furniture wood to furnish a house and to spare. Giant chestnuts yielded lumber, fence rails, stove wood, and crisp brown nuts in endless quantities. Even the most grasping deed-snatcher could hardly wander through this wilderness without having his spirits lifted by what he saw.

With eyes focused more upon the soil than the towering black forests were the mineral speculators who brought "long form" deeds in their satchels to lay hold not only of timber and land but of all the mineral assets of the earth. More often they left the land and tax liabilities in the hands of the original owners, but secured iron-bound possession of the mineral rights. All sorts of people acted as agents in buying these rights. There were the local buyers who threw suspicious landholders off guard, but the experts were the witty, folksy negotiators who came to talk mineral deeds, to spin endless funny yarns, to stay all night, and to pass along the news. Sometimes to lonely mountaineers it seemed worth the unseen and doubtless nonexistent subsurface riches just to break the monotony of their lives so pleasantly.

By 1910 a major portion of the natural wealth of eastern Kentucky had passed to outside ownership. The men and women who had fought wilderness and weather to settle the harsh country were too unsophisticated to understand its potentialities. They did not recognize this fact until it was too late to recover their blunders. The saga of much of the mountain country after 1910 ran like this: "Pap owned the finest stand of timber a man ever set eyes on and he almost gave it away. He done the same thing with his coal lands." "My folks settled this here land where all that coal is coming from, and they let a slick-talking fellow lease it from them for two bits." This author has listened by the hour to mountain men talk about how their folks practically gave their timber and coal away, and how they themselves spent a good part of their lives slaving away in mines to dredge up the coal. Too illiterate to read the "broad or long form" deeds understandingly, or to comprehend the long-range meaning of the leases, they let one act rob them of their heritage. They only saw the meager reward of the moment and heard the sprightly tales of the agent who sat before their firesides and talked about everything but the future economic promise of the coves and the ridges.

After the opening of the twentieth century the mountaineer's economic future swooped down on him like a hawk from his cliffs. Engineers with transits and survey parties located railroads up the creeks. Construction gangs slashed open right-of-ways and gnawed great holes under ridges which were too steep to cross. Tracks were raised high on ledges to lie above the furious spring tides, and bridges towered above the rock-tumbling currents. Hardly had the first locomotive thundered up the gorges before sooty-faced miners were sinking low-ceilinged shafts deep into the bowels of rich coal seams and streams of coal lumps were tumbling into the tipples. For the first time mountaineers could see tangible evidence of the wealth of their land in the great blocks of coal which were sent away to outside markets.

World War I brought revolutionary changes to the mountains. Orders for huge timbers of all sorts sent lumbermen rushing to the coves to fell century-old trees to supply the demand. Fourth-generation Anglo-Saxons dropped towering oaks and tulip poplars to be hewn into waist-high squares for shipment "across the waters," as the ballad singers said, to be laid as doughty keels in British war vessels. Again the smooth-talking agent was abroad in the land, this time buying the magnificent black walnuts with which to make gun-stocks, and the enormous oak beams for naval yards. Lumber was never so much in demand, and the big mills moved farther up the rivers to meet the raftsmen and the short-line log railroads as they brought the virgin timber from the woods. There are still standing in the mountain forests the posts of steer stocks, where blacksmiths shod the oxen that dragged the logs down the steep "snake roads" to loading ramps. Steep mountainsides are still gashed by the trails loggers made in dragging logs to loading ramps.

For many a mountaineer this seemed the age of jubilee; he had sold his land for cash, and now he was selling his muscle for tokens of cash at company stores. His income compared with that of the past was tremendous, but he seldom stopped to think in terms of the real wages he received. Not only did his income seem to be high but he had broken the monotony of his former life in the gregarious company villages. His wives and daughters found it easier to socialize with their neighbors, but often even this was a snare and a delusion because of problems of health, law enforcement, and social frictions. Too, the villager had now severed himself from the land.

The pressure of war demands blinded men temporarily to their actual conditions. Coal trains were ravenous in their demands for coal. A trail of smoke haze above a zigzagging Allied convoy at sea was akin to the new smoky haze which settled over the Cumberland Plateau. The same coal was the source of both symbols of war fever.

Where no structure larger than a double log barn had ever been erected in the highlands and no more complicated engineering feat than the raising of a square rock chimney had ever been undertaken, now giant coal tipples three and four stories high leaned against the rocky faces of the hills. These poured constant streams of coal lumps in a thunderous roar into strings of steel gondolas to be snatched away at the earliest possible moment to fill the maws of industrial furnaces and ships' holds.

Almost overnight the country changed. A lad who had once been thrilled with a cheap homespun cottonade shirt now sported a genuine imported silk one. Feet that had known only rough plow shoes now wore high yellow kidskin slippers. The native son who had lived suspended between corn patch and log woods, and who had never drawn a breath of foul air in his life, now straggled home at day's end with sooty face and hands—a day laborer working for wages.

The coal village shack was not a mountain cabin by any means. There were missing the outhouses which sheltered family cows, horses, and chickens. No hogpens grew the family meat supply. Gone from porch and kitchen walls were the endless strings of dried shucky beans and red pepper, bundles of sage and other dried herbs, and strings of ears of corn laid back for next year's seed. Few or no roofs were covered on hot summer afternoons with boards of drying apples and peaches. There were no more frolicsome sorghum "stir-offs" or apple sulphurings. Company stores were now fountainheads of all human needs.

The old barriers were broken. There were still a few old people beyond the great mining periphery who regarded the stranger as suspect until he made his business clearly known. They still regarded an inquisitive visitor as a threat to their freedom or as an obnoxious sojourner. But in the towns and around the mines there were too many newcomers for the old doubts and misgivings to prevail. Strangers were everywhere, and comparatively the population was growing faster than granny women could heat water and attend to birthings. Truly, foreigners had come down from Pennsylvania, from West Virginia, and in turn from Italy and the Balkans. Up from the cotton South came white and Negro tenant farmers in flight from the plague of the boll weevil. They came to dig coal and to paw out railway lines around the rocky ledges. The surface resources of the land were being way overloaded by the sudden rise in population.

Fortunes for both coal operator and miner in Kentucky rose and fell with the industrial fortunes of the nation. The World War I boom tapered off in the early 1920's and then collapsed in the great depression. The story of coal mining in eastern Kentucky was to be sullied by industrial strife that involved bloodshed with the vengeance of the old feuds and the anarchy of a social jungle. It was difficult to sort out facts from gossip, rumor, and special pleading. The abuses of the armies of deputy sheriffs and company police, of venal public officials, the peonage system of the company store, resistance to organized labor, plain human cussedness, old mountain hatreds, and violent partisan Kentucky politics all played parts.

In time American newspaper headlines capitalized stories of coal-field anarchy. Pistol shot and exploding dynamite charges hidden under the hoods of automobiles took scores of lives. Pitched battles such as that at Evarts or around the coal camps in Harlan and Perry counties were given sensational coverage. Almost around the world the name of Harlan County alone connoted disorder and labor unrest. Actually some of the coal counties had now robbed the old feuding strongholds of their questionable reputations of being "bloody."

All sorts of people flocked into the troubled areas of the mountains in the 1930's to view the chaos and conflict of the region. Heywood Broun, Theodore Dreiser, students from Columbia University and from the Commonwealth College of Mena, Arkansas, all came to see and write about the evils of the economic leviathan that had uprooted man and his institutions and had set going a ruthless tyranny whose main token was the almost valueless coin which miners exchanged for goods at the company stores. Neither native son nor coal operator did anything to lessen the bitter stinging criticism of these visitors. In fact operator and community leader alike organized a vigilante posse to turn back the unwelcome strangers. At Frankfort the politicians did little more than wring their hands and try to figure out how best to keep the peace and the vote. Kentuckians outside the region almost appeared to believe that the strife in the coalfields was closely akin to the Japanese invasion of Manchuria—something completely foreign to the mainstream of life in their state.

The battle of the coal-bearing hills was bitter and fundamental. General of the miners' forces was John L. Lewis, that heavy-browed bull of a man who had sent many an operator's blood pressure shooting upward with his bold demands. Lewis was not a mountaineer with a limited sense of values or a myopic sense of the future. He well understood the depth of the conflict and, even more, labor's future destiny. If the machines promised to supplant the miner in the pits, then the coal itself would have to contribute some kind of guarantee of support to the miner and pay him a set scale of wages in cash. Lewis commanded a large following of loyal supporters, on the one hand, and incurred some of the bitterest industrial resentment in American economic history, on the other. His United Mine Workers erected five elaborate hospitals in the eastern coalfields to care not only for the general health of the miners but for much of the human damage done in the pits. His organizers were looked upon as deadly foes of the old economic order, and wherever they went there was resistance. It was almost impossible to separate social crises, political failures, industrial conflicts, and the failures of the land. Too, it was impossible to remove the ominous threat of the future when machines, not United Mine Workers, would spell the difference between peace and profit. Even the most stupid coal heaver at the head of the cut came to understand that the great mechanical beetles which ran their spike-toothed snouts under and over the seams, and the mechanical loaders which gathered up the coal and loaded it onto cars, could do more work in a few minutes than a man could do all day. Also, the giant shovels and augers which stripped back the earth and bored it out from under the ridges were displacing men, and no matter how well organized the miners were they could not stay the ruinous hand of technology.

More ominous for men who had spent their lives in the pits was the fact that the locomotives which hustled the endless trains of cars away from the mines burned oil. This was true of so many of the industries which once had used coal; new factories used other sources of fuel than coal. Even the rising electrical generating industry used coal to generate a competitive source of energy. It mattered little to today's miner that less than 10 percent of Kentucky's coal potential had been brought to the surface; it was today's car loadings that counted.

The sequel to this story is revealed in the abandoned villages, the great pockets of poverty, the migration of thousands of eastern Kentuckians to other parts of the country, and in the sporadic gestures of state and federal governments and semiprivate organizations to find answers to Appalachia's problems. The span of time between Jack Hale's meeting with June Tolliver in the tangled mountain Eden, as described in *The Trail of the Lonesome Pine,* and the coming of the machine to the hills was relatively short, but the transitions in the country have outrun an age and transformed men and women into sociological and political ciphers of national importance.

By no means is all of Appalachian Kentucky caught in the same vise as the coal miner and his lonely village. Society is as highly stratified in the eastern hills as on the Bluegrass Plateau. There is a constantly growing number of people who have traveled far beyond their native hills, who are keenly aware of conditions beyond Kentucky. Many of them are well educated, and some are highly sophisticated. They are sensitive and perceptive people. Perhaps they take pride in the fact that from their ranks have departed businessmen, teachers, doctors, lawyers, bankers, and others who have brought dignity and prosperity to their adopted homes. Louisville and Lexington would be left poor indeed if all the people of highland origin should desert them. Even Cincinnati, Dayton, Detroit, and Chicago would sense a change if this happened. The pride of these émigrés in their mountain origin has grown with their rising success, and actually much of the boasted rugged mountain independence is to be measured more in the fortunes of these people than by the accomplishments of a majority of those who were left behind.

If there is any one thing which the eastern Kentuckian, at home or abroad, has valued above all else in his cultural heritage it has been his personal pride and what he has pleased to call his individualism. This latter quality he inherited from his pioneer ancestors. He never has, however, stopped long enough to analyze either his pride or his sense of individual independence. He has asserted both at times in the hottest sort of personal furies in which he revealed doubt that either fact was valid. It might be true that the mountaineer's pride was derived far more from the isolative condition of rural provincialism than from distinctive personal accomplishment, or from distinction of ancestry. His individualism was to be measured more in the area of stubbornness and ignorance than in a classic and cultivated sense of fundamental personal dignity, or from a philosophy of life based on clear concepts of individual behavior in a highly rural society. Maybe the so-called individualism of many mountaineers has been no more than resistance to the enforcement of the law which placed limitations upon human indulgences in a primitive social and geographical environment.

Two distinct facts have dealt both personal pride and individualism fierce blows in Appalachian Kentucky. The first of these was the biting depression which necessitated the far-reaching relief measures of the New Deal in the 1930's. Public assistance not only was accepted, it was sought after so vigorously that on one or two occasions political scandals occurred in important national elections. Applications for jobs and for relief ran astonishingly high. The second fact was the impact of direct relief upon the old sense of morals and family integrity. This has been especially true where dependent children and adult disability have been involved.

Harry Caudill, in his *Night Comes to the Cumberlands,* discusses the workings of the welfare state in eastern Kentucky in twentieth-century America. This reads like a journey into phantasmagoria. The old moral contexts in which a mountain man shot his daughter's seducer to avenge her honor have been changed, and the old fires of personal pride in family honor and morality have smoldered and gone out. The very process of human procreation has in staggering numbers of incidents been subordinated to survival on public relief.

Far too much of eastern Kentucky society has become involved in the toils of a social and economic system which was freighted from the beginning with the blight of poverty. Poverty not alone in material things but in the severely limiting facts of education and leadership perspective. The rise of big and mechanized agriculture elsewhere has turned the tiny subsistence mountain farmers into little more than piddlers in the soil. No longer can a hillside farmer, forcing the furrow all the way up a perpendicular slope to the very cliff line, hope to survive. New agricultural techniques, new plant types, and new methods of farm management have not been advantages for the little fellows. Thus strewn along the rock-cluttered creeks and up the coves are thousands of abandoned cabins. Old garden plots, which once fed families, and gullied fields are vine- and bush-bound. Sassafras, redbud, and scrubby oak have again taken over. Beds of perennial flowers fight a losing battle against strangulation. Tumble-down stables are weed grown and old house plots are memorialized only by chimney piles.

In a region which boasts an almost inexhaustible resource of bituminous coal and forest potential the capability of offering human employment to sustain a decent level of personal economy has shrunk each decade since 1930. It is not that coal or timber has suffered a disastrous reduction in consumption or that adaptability of available human labor has changed materially. Again it is technology which has wrought the changes. Machines now operate where once men with pick, shovel, and black powder robbed the coal seams. Behind these leviathans the earth is left gashed and bleeding. Overburden is tumbled down hills to bespoil forest, stream, and civilization alike. Before this barbaric invasion an enormous part of the human host has fled the region. There is still, however, too numerous an army of mountaineers who appear incapable of readjusting to new vocations or of finding jobs in which to make adjustments.

A politically motivated legislature at Frankfort has been timid in the past to take drastic steps to preserve the land for future Kentuckians by enacting workable reclamation laws to enforce repair of the damage done by strip mining. Finally in 1966 adequate legislation to check this desecration was adopted. Constantly recurring floods have blighted the hopes of many places to secure new and less destructive industries, and too many human beings, already benighted by poverty and social frustration, live constantly in dread of recurring flood damage and blighted hopes.

In an even more fundamental way the influence of Frankfort has had an enduring influence over the social and political fate of the highlands. Since the first session of the legislature in the closing decade of the eighteenth century politicians have succumbed to the plea to cut up broad areas of Kentucky into minuscule counties to be named for politicians, and to be ruled and bilked by courthouse rings. From ex-governors down, Kentuckians know they have too many counties. But they also know that laying the ax of statutory destruction to a single poverty-stricken mountain county would raise a hue and cry that would spell political doom to the axmen, not only in the imperiled county but in 119 others. There are at least forty counties in Appalachian Kentucky which have failed consistently to raise enough revenue to sustain their official responsibilities; thus they have looked to the state treasury to supplement their income, which within itself is a kind of public relief.

The argument goes on: how much of its fierce personal pride and individualism and initiative has eastern Kentucky lost? A couple of decades ago a person making a contention that the region had lost its pride would have been threatened with mayhem in angry letters to the editors by enraged sons of the hills. There are still knights who strap on their bucklers at the slightest hint of this fact, but the dragons they ride out to meet are too formidable for them to fell with angry words. There are too many people on the land, too little sane development of regional resources, too little effective use of education, and too remote chances of widespread industrialization which will employ large numbers of semi- or unskilled people to bring the future into clear focus.

Appalachian Kentucky has become a case study for all sorts of people. Sociologists, economists, agricultural specialists, social planners, home missionaries, church workers, local sons, an army of federal officials, members of Congress, and the President of the United States have all visited the region. They have surveyed it, analyzed it, prescribed for it, and expressed, in a great fanfare of publicity, their collective concern. Lyndon B. Johnson sitting on a cabin porch in remote Martin County paying a poor family a folksy visit, Texas and mountain style, gave dramatic point to a pocket of poverty—but could he and Congress cleanse the pocket and ensure it a functional place in the future of America which is driving furiously ahead into an age of even more complex technological advances? Can someone organize an educational and spiritual device by which it can be demonstrated that more than a fierce pride and a misconceived and ill-directed rural individualism will enable people to live on the land? Else much of the main social and economic products of Appalachian Kentucky will continue to be thousands of children begotten and reared in a welfare society which has been allowed to grow too poor and devoid of the inner economic and spiritual capacity to make the people productive even of their own livelihood. The old stereotype of the Kentucky mountain man bears no kinship with the human cipher which now recurs with such frequency in published reports and news stories detailing the woes of Appalachia.

The Garden in Transition

No longer do Kentuckians think of their land as the garden. Time has gone almost too fast for Kentucky in the latter decades of the twentieth century. Changes have come so rapidly and fiercely for the standpat traditionalists that they have come to feel themselves aliens within their native land. The ledger book no doubt stands about equally balanced between desirable and undesirable changes. In the great crusade to supplant the old agrarian economic base with industry the whole social pattern has been uprooted. Though Kentucky farmers speak with loud and often organized voices in public councils, they become less audible in the final decisions made in Kentucky economy. Though the rural home and the yeoman farmstead are still sprinkled generously about the countryside, the fact is that every year the meaning of these once-proud places becomes more blurred. Hundreds of thousands of rural homes have literally melted into the ground. In other areas rural slums of decaying homesteads have often taken the place of the old urban-industrial ones.

No longer is the Kentuckian primarily a rural man in the sense that he is tightly bound to the land and a community. His horizon has been thrust back in seven-league proportions. He no longer has to struggle in mud and rut belly-deep to a mule team to travel about the state. Kentucky has been gashed asunder by super interstate and toll roads. Now one can fish in the Big Sandy one afternoon and the

Kentucky Lake the next. Like a wide-ranging martin the contemporary Kentuckian ventures far afield from his native gourd. No longer are hill men startled at the sights in Lexington and Richmond, nor do they stand in awe of Louisville as being anything more than an overgrown settlement. Most likely they compare it unfavorably with Detroit, Chicago, Dayton, and Indianapolis, where they have worked and huddled in slum communities. They have traveled far and wide in their search for economic security in other parts of the country.

There still remain landlocked pockets in Kentucky, of course, and perhaps there always will be. It is possible, however, to stand in spots that seem completely remote to all modern civilization, where a creekbed road is still the only connective that ties the eighteenth century to the twentieth. Before one can lose oneself completely in reverie of the past, the spell will be broken thunderously by a low-cruising modern jet bomber sweeping in a wing-tilting turning glide preparatory to making a landing at Wright Field in Dayton, Ohio. Or a modern jet passenger plane loaded with Florida-bound passengers sweeps over the ancient pioneer trails in less time than it took hoary old frontiersman to tighten the girth of a pack saddle and to hoist all his worldly goods onto a pack mule.

The bulldozer, the fiercest varmint ever to exist in Kentucky, has gnawed its way deep into the bowels of the state's soil and has made an even deeper gash into its way of life. A frog pond today becomes a subdivision or a shopping center tomorrow. The rolling Bluegrass meadowland spreading out from the very door of James Lane Allen's secluded home in Lexington has been transformed into a warren of monotonous look-alike red-brick houses, winding streets, shopping centers, and traffic snarls. Where once fields of tall hemp, golden tobacco, and rich meadows inhabited by placid sheep, horses, and cattle sustained a civilization, chain stores, funeral homes, filling stations, and apartment houses with their accompanying traffic and confusion now clutter the landscape. On the smiling land where Henry Clay and his ever-industrious Lucretia operated a rich Bluegrass farm, and where their blooded livestock once grazed the broad moors, there are now miles of asphalt ribbons and urban subdivisions.

On the outskirts of Louisville the home of the old pioneer George Rogers Clark has been surrounded and all but overwhelmed by voracious urban Kentucky, consuming all before it in the mad scramble for space to accommodate an ever-growing metropolitan population. A half century ago the term "metropolitan" applied to the average Kentucky city would have been a meaningless affectation. Today it is a fact, and because of its accompanying social and political problems, a distressing fact. One of the most challenging issues in modern Kentucky is that of snatching from the jaws of progress a few of the old landmarks to be preserved as gauges of the history of the state.

Fully half of the native adults in modern Kentucky dream fondly of finding some way to thrust back the curtains of the past and again to associate themselves with the rural soil. Somewhere in the past, they feel, was located the mainspring of the good life—a life of youth, largely untroubled by the neurosis of the urban community. Someday they hope they will return to the country to dream away their remaining years. Yearly opportunities to do so grow more remote. No longer can a rugged yeoman farmer with a stout back and legs, a clean mind, and a willing young wife build a modest house on the land and begin farming with the expectation that he will prosper. Successful farming in Kentucky bears more resemblance to banking, market speculation, and installment financing than to the historic past of a self-sufficient rural economy.

If the bulldozer tosses urban topography about like sand in a child's playpen, then the tractor with all its ingenious automatic attachments has tossed agricultural economy about with a large measure of recklessness. To begin farming successfully in modern Kentucky requires a capital outlay which would have caused earlier Kentuckians to ask "Why begin farming when one already had a lifetime competency?" The horse and mule, once symbols of Kentucky farming, are gone from the land. In many instances so are hogs, cattle, chickens, and sheep. The machinery shed has replaced the barn and the pipelines of rural water districts have outmoded the springhouses.

Since 1940 the state has lost almost 100,000 farms, and the average size of the remaining farms has increased by approximately 35 acres. Steadily the number of farms shrinks, and the average acreage goes up. Too, much of the old conjecture and guess as to what might be awaiting the countryman in the future has been removed.

This is one of Kentucky's most serious breaks with the past. Its people built a good part of their tradition on that comfortable society which flourished in the countryside. Its monuments are the remains of commodious old homes which have outlived their time. Roofs and porches sag, chimneys have crumbled down below gable peaks, yards are weed-grown, and once elegant windows have lost their glass, and tufts of hay often stick out of windows to mark their final desecration. Mounting blocks are buried beneath debris, driveways are obliterated, and the old gate pillars stand nodding in neglect or have tumbled over in final surrender.

These were the homes of a proud rural aristocracy. One can visualize families gathered with kith and kin on the front porches on lazy summer afternoons or posing about bewhiskered heads of families for group photographs which included members of the family, Negro servants, the buggy and mare, and every dog on the place. A more fetching picture is the one of the old parlor, adorned with overstuffed haircloth furniture, a strap organ, and what-not museum displays of family relics and travel souvenirs. Here many a Kentucky lass surrendered her heart. In more somber moments it was where corpses were placed on final display in the family fold.

The great depression of the 1890's opened a rift in this mode of Kentucky life. Migration away from the state disrupted family unity; a decline in farm prices and a rise of urban and industrial centers tempted cheap labor away from the country. In time the old Kentuckians of this way of life died off and the young ones deserted the land. The old aristocracy perished. Kentuckians still delight in hunting for their ancestors among this class. They love nothing better than to reminisce about those other times. They drive out on Sunday afternoons to dig through the weeds in search of familiar landmarks, to review the scenes of their childhood, and to remark on the changes, but at sundown they hustle back to town.

In a land which for a century and three quarters has boasted so stoutly of rugged individualism on the farms the individual is now lost. No matter how much prime tobacco land he owns, the amount of acreage he plants is set for him by a central body, and to cross this authority is costly. The farmer may protest and groan, but he knows that if he tried to farm otherwise he would be lost. Every decade has seen the amount of tobacco in storage increase, and the need for production go down. Many a Kentuckian who thirty years ago believed his farm would go on to the end of time producing tobacco has found his acreage so severely reduced that he has given up hope and abandoned his farm.

Chemists, plant pathologists, and extension agents have all helped in improving farm production and methods, but they have not extended the area's need in production in proportion. It is a common sight nowadays to see great airy tobacco barns standing in shambles atop hills where once there were broad fields of tobacco. No longer are these decaying old structures the scenes of seasonal activity when men lifted up heavy sticks of yellowing ripe burley to swing free in the air until it was cured into a gossamer thin web of gold.

Scientific advances apply to almost every other field crop. An old-time miller who has ground corn meal for almost seventy years grumbles because he can no longer find flinty hard corn which once came out of the patches up the hollows and coves. Farmers now grow high-yield hybrid corn which produces four or five times as many bushels per acre as the old degenerate inbred varieties which had been saved from every harvest year for generations of farmers.

Even the old "shucky beans" which once were strung on threads to form frilly tails to hang against cabin walls as badges of opulence have surrendered to newer types offered each spring by enterprising seed dealers. The old granny woman with her jars and packets of home-grown seeds which were handed down from mother to daughter from the opening of the Kentucky frontier has been carted off to the cemetery or completely submerged by the new era along with all the rest of archaic Kentucky.

In the first place, few modern Kentucky farm wives would have the patience to string beans, dry fruits, or to pack away vegetables in great heaps in cans and cellars for winter use. The chain grocery store with its eternal fresh crop of vegetables and the family deep-freeze are too convenient. No longer do most farm families labor to perform the dozens of arduous tasks of old. Approximately 98 percent of Kentucky's homes now have access to electrical power. Rural electrification lines have followed the most isolated mountaineer to the head of the hollow and tied his cabin into communication with modern America by an umbilical cord of copper wire. Nothing except the automobile has broken the old isolation barriers faster. A humble rural cabin, standing in almost complete dilapidation so that it presents not one touch of architectural modernity, is adorned with a meter box. Television aerials crown Kentucky cabins with halos of modern technology, and washing machines paraded on front porches are status symbols extraordinary. No longer does the woman break her back washing clothes in the branch.

A modern Kentuckian can bring much cultural and historical excitement to his fireside, to say nothing of information about the conditions of his daily life. The weather and news reports have supplanted the almanac and country-store gossip. Frequent reportorial broadcasts keep the most isolated people abreast of the times. Even total illiterates are given a view of the world in which they live. It is no longer possible that a rural Kentuckian would come walking into Lexington saying that he had heard rumors there was a war going on and he wanted "to go to it." Even though the radio and television have offered greater cultural challenge to rural Kentuckians, these media still have to face up to the obligation of doing a better job educationally for their listeners and viewers.

As it stands now, the Kentuckian can bring the features of a simulated Daniel Boone to his children's attention, but by doing so he desecrates the deed and memory of that trusty old hero who helped blaze the way to Kentucky. He, however, never blazed it the way television directors and actors say he did. Red Lick Fork of Station Camp Creek never looked that way even in its most willful moments, and Boonesboro never remotely resembled the television version of its history.

In a land where once the ballad of Old World origin comprised a major source of folk music and entertainment and of emotional release for an intensely rural folk, the hillbilly song of radio and television has blurred if not obliterated the memory of the old classics. No longer do ballad composers and singers keep alive the hoary tales of miscarried love affairs, of murders, local skulduggery, and downright devilry. Instead the phony lads of fancy western duds, electrified stringed instruments, well-greased locks, and corny jokes have taken over. The high adenoidal Saturday night and jukebox performances and the fancy square dance sets have become spectator entertainment rather than a communal affair engaging every bystander.

There remain old speech forms and tonal qualities, but these reflect more the failure of Kentucky to provide adequate educational opportunities than a distinguished Old World cultural legacy. Most of the uncultivated Kentucky speech is just that and nothing more. Some Kentuckians use archaic words and speech forms of early English and Scotch origin, of course, but they have been so corrupted that they are no longer romantic or historical in the true sense. Superstitions and folklore linger on, but this fact is more reflective of human limitations, and sometimes cussedness, than continuity of background culture.

Of the many Kentucky traditional foundations that have been uprooted none is more far-reaching than breaking of the bonds of the old economic past. No one has accepted change less gracefully than the politicians. Many legislators still go on trying to serve the Kentucky of a half century ago; their main objective seems that of keeping peace with rural voters, of gaining a political advantage, and of staying in office. County courthouse rings are bands of reaction. County offices may be equipped with electric typewriters and other fancy equipment and voting machines may be in use in all the state's precincts, but the human element remains largely untouched in its official outlook. The courts have assaulted the ramparts of the legislators in demanding redistricting of the state to ensure more equitable representation. They have made life uneasy for tax commissioners by demanding sharp revisions in property assessments. The automobile and superhighways have knifed distances to pieces. But the courthouses still remain within muleback ride of their patrons and the courthouse rings go on their ways merrily as they have done since the organization of old Fincastle County back in 1774. Even local school superintendents are often accused of showing a keener concern for their political futures than for long-range educational plans. All of these are powerful stumbling blocks in Kentucky's approach to the future, but at that they have not proved immovable. Time itself has a way of running over the reactionary and the standpatter.

The old guards of court and statehouse are confronted with the staggering impact of the twentieth century. For instance, they find it almost impossible to talk back to scientists and social planners who look well beyond the local community and the state in formulating their views. The Spindletop Research Foundation, an organization made up of very unsentimental and unromantic Kentuckians, is fairly capable of gazing into the future with some assurance. What it reports seeing is vastly different from anything the old pioneers saw or even believed possible. It may be true, however, that the Foundation's dreams are no more ambitious. If Kentuckians were now adorning their statehouse with expressive lunettes they would no doubt symbolize a people equipped with electronic computers planning an industrial society far removed from association with the soil or the countryside.

Industrial planners and their machines are blunt in their predictions and dictums. No longer can Kentucky politicians and educators orate their state into a condition of economic and cultural stupefaction and have it remain happy and prosperous. People will have to be fairly well educated just to hold a commonplace job, no matter in which part of the state they now live. They will have to be taught something effectively and to remain constant and faithful in their labors. The new industry shows a remarkable lack of appreciation for the delights of anticipating the opening of squirrel hunting season or the fact that fish are biting in the creeks and lakes. For the first time in Kentucky history the state's leadership is being told that it must deliver something more tangible than glib political promises and faithless performances if Kentucky is to keep abreast of its competitive neighbors.

Somewhat like an anxious mother in search of a son-in-law, promoters of Kentucky become alert when they hear the word "industry" mentioned. Armed with bulging briefcases and elaborate plans, catalogues of facts, and long statistical tables young pioneers of contemporary Kentucky go forth to seduce bankers and industrialists in New York, Detroit, Chicago, Cleveland, or anywhere else that restless management might be induced to locate a new plant in Kentucky. Professional surveyors of industrial prospects have been hired to plot the state. As industriously as the old land surveyors these modern planners have explored Kentucky from the Breaks of Sandy to Mills Point, and have reported on its virtues and its shortcomings in extensive documents. They have stood by to give advice and to help a somewhat naïve agrarian society choose the right industries. Some Kentucky community leaders have been so anxious to embrace the modern industrial age that they have practically promised everything from a corner of the local cemetery to an option on the courthouse square to induce managers to locate plants in which to employ local labor. Thus it is that Kentuckians have had to be alert in separating the good industries from the carpetbaggers who would come and enjoy an extended economic honeymoon, pocket their profits, and move on.

Everything is in a state of change. In January, 1966, the famous old Dixie Flyer, crack train of the Louisville and Nashville Railroad, with a lone woman as its last passenger made its farewell run. For a half century or more this train hauled Kentuckians south to sell goods and Southerners north to spend their money. The grand old lady, grown tawdry and out of date in her latter years, came home to die virtually unsung and unattended. Its last whistle at the final crossing was its dying gasp, and its own bell tolled its passing. No more do Kentuckians congregate in railway stations to say good-by to friends, to socialize, or to pass away a dull Sunday afternoon. Not many depots are left. Trains no longer stop in the smaller towns where as a matter of course in bygone years it was high amusement on Sunday afternoon to "meet the train." The locomotive engineer has ceased to be an envied man and crusty old conductors have either died off or are hanging around waiting to die.

Even though a hundred million tons of freight float on the Ohio River every year, only two old-time packet-type boats are left, the *Delta Queen* and the *Belle of Louisville*. Contemporary Kentuckians are in too big a hurry to fool around with the old and leisurely ways of travel. They think in terms of a few hours' trip to Washington and New York, a dash to Chicago, and less than a day's journey to the West Coast. They have widened the circumference of their travels to the point that a trip to the Orient or to Europe is almost commonplace. They now know at first hand more about national and world geography than they ever encountered in schoolbooks in the old days. How much they know about the history of the places they visit is another matter.

A lack of leisure time, in an age of shorter working days and weeks, is a neurotic manifestation of the times. Only the sentimentalists would have time to listen to favorite old political orators like A. O. Stanley and Edwin Morrow, who took a couple of hours at least to praise Old Kentucky, their mothers, pioneer forefathers, and the voters. No one has time to attend an all-day barbecue, to visit the old resort centers for a week, or to attend a revival meeting of interminable duration. Everybody is in a hurry to get nowhere really. A man speeds up his automobile to pass a line of cars only to whip into the next driveway, or he burns up the superhighways to get home to rest.

Even the colleges and universities are in a hurry. Their administrators and faculties are frantically engaged in planning new administrative organizations and curricular adjustments to keep up with the atomic age, and they have only a limited amount of time to give the present generation of students. Perhaps all this bustle has some positive meaning in the fact that Kentuckians are so busily engaged in anticipating the future that they no longer have time to create fundamentalist rows or to assault their universities for being too liberal. The neurosis of hurry has even caught up with the churches. Ministers and congregations become so immersed in planning and organization that they rob both pulpit and home of much of their purpose.

There are indeed few islands left where some antediluvian Kentuckians can sit and cogitate the wonders of their small world. There are, however, a few country stores remaining which still furnish enough battered chairs, boxes, and benches for the accommodation of the vanishing ranks of wisemen whose minds function best amidst the fumes of tobacco smoke and neighborhood banter. A few remote country courthouse towns still line their squares with benches where less hurried citizens can find a seat and something to whittle on and even spit on the sidewalk without stirring social turmoil. These are the last strongholds of the old civilization; the main thrust of modern Kentucky is in another vein.

One heartening change has caused Kentucky to pause and look backward. A growing sense of conservation of state resources has promoted respect for the land, some for the streams, and some for other natural resources. The federal government set an excellent example when it purchased almost a million and a half acres of land to form the great Cumberland National Forest, now called the Daniel Boone Forest, and other public preserves within the state. Blocks of privately held forest lands have been returned to their virginal condition and state forests have added greatly to the wooded surface of Kentucky. Thus old corners of beauty and natural charm have been restored. Once again some of the earlier animal inhabitants are creeping back, despite the night hunters and poachers.

Spring with its budding enthusiasm again bursts over hundreds of miles of land which once was gutted and abused. The fall months bring a rise of ripening color that again revives the romantic charm of the early mountain, Pennyroyal, and Bluegrass landscapes. Nevertheless, it takes constant vigilance to ensure that this condition will prevail.

In 1966 the Kentucky General Assembly stiffened its spine and enacted a stern strip-mining law which blocked the spoilers and exploiters. If they dig or bore hills and mountains away they have to restore them to their natural contours. No longer can they tumble down great shovel gulps of topsoil and rock to clutter hillsides forever, to block streams, and to impoverish generations of Kentuckians for all time to come. Theoretically at least the state will no longer be disemboweled and left to bleed its poisonous acids onto the countryside for miles around.

With four metropolitan centers studding the outer rim, Kentucky has gone to town. Today its people crusade for all sorts of social improvements which half a century ago might have seemed desirable but not enough so to take active steps to bring them about. Today bookmobiles carry books to readers even in the most remote parts of the state. Cities and towns are beset by challenges to offer their people a better way of life in a new suburbia without destroying all the old landmarks of a past culture. A major fight has become one of preservation of ancient landmarks. The omnivorous automobile with its demand for parking space threatens to iron these into the ground. Already too many asphalt-covered plots exist where once significant buildings stood.

If Kentucky is being physically eroded by the mad push of suburbia, the individual suffers also. The old individualism is being replaced by a rather blank kind of social and communal conformity, and the spirit of what was once a hardheaded old agrarian state is rapidly falling into a pattern of national sameness.

Bibliography

ALLEN, JAMES LANE. *Bluegrass Region of Kentucky*. New York, 1886.

BAKELESS, JOHN. *Daniel Boone, Master of the Wilderness*. New York, 1939.

CAUDILL, HARRY. *Night Comes to the Cumberland*. Boston, 1962.

CLARK, THOMAS D. *A History of Kentucky*. New York, 1937.

———. *The Rampaging Frontier*. Indianapolis, 1939.

COBB, IRVIN. *Exit Laughing*. Indianapolis, 1941.

COLLINS, RICHARD H. *History of Kentucky*. 2 vols. Covington, 1874.

COLEMAN, J. WINSTON JR. *Slavery Times in Kentucky*. Chapel Hill, 1940.

———. *Stage-Coach Days in the Bluegrass*. Louisville, 1935.

CONNELLEY, WILLIAM E., and E. M. COULTER. *A History of Kentucky*. 5 vols. Chicago, 1922.

COULTER, E. M. *Civil War and Readjustment in Kentucky*. Chapel Hill, 1926.

DAY, JOHN F. *Bloody Ground*. New York, 1941.

DICK, EVERETT. *Dixie Frontier*. New York, 1948.

DRAKE, DANIEL. *Pioneer Life in Kentucky*. Cincinnati, 1870.

DREISER, THEODORE. *A Harlan Miner Speaks*. New York, 1932.

DUKE, BASIL W. *Morgan's Cavalry*. Cincinnati, 1867.

FILSON, JOHN. *The Discovery, Settlement and Present State of Kentucke*. Wilmington, Del., 1784.

FLINT, TIMOTHY. *Recollections of the Last Ten Years*. Boston, 1826.

FORD, THOMAS R. (ed.) *The Southern Appalachian Region: A Regional Survey*. Lexington, 1962.

FOX, JOHN JR. *Little Shepherd of Kingdom Come*. New York, 1903.

———. *Trail of the Lonesome Pine*. New York, 1908.

GREEN, THOMAS M. *The Spanish Conspiracy*. Cincinnati, 1891.

GUNTHER, JOHN. *Inside U.S.A.* New York, 1951.

IMLAY, GILBERT. *A Topographical Description of the Western Territory of North America*. London, 1797.

JOHNSON, L. F. *Famous Kentucky Tragedies and Trials*. Cleveland, 1922.

KINCAID, ROBERT L. *The Wilderness Road*. Indianapolis, 1947.

KIRWAN, A. D. *John Jordan Crittenden: Struggle for the Union*. Lexington, 1964.

KNIGHT, GRANT C. *James Lane Allen and the Genteel Tradition*. Chapel Hill, 1935.

LEIGHTON, GEORGE. *Five Cities*. New York, 1939.

MARSHALL, HUMPHREY. *History of Kentucky*. 2 vols. Frankfort, 1824.

MCVEY, FRANK L. *The Gates Open Slowly*. Lexington, 1950.

MICHAUX, F. A. *Travels to the West of the Allegheny Mountains*. London, 1805.

MILLER, JOHN G. *The Black Patch War*. Chapel Hill, 1936.

MOORE, ARTHUR B. *The Frontier Mind*. Lexington, 1959.

MUTZENBERG, CHARLES. *Kentucky's Famous Feuds and Tragedies*. New York, 1917.

NALL, JAMES O. *The Tobacco Night Riders of Kentucky and Tennessee, 1905-1909*. Louisville, 1940.

PERRIN, WILLIAM H. (ed.). *History of Fayette County*. Chicago, 1882.

RAINE, J. W. *Land of Saddle Bags*. New York, 1924.

RANCK, GEORGE W. *History of Lexington, Kentucky*. Cincinnati, 1872.

ROSS, MALCOLM. *Machine Age in the Hills*. New York, 1933.

SHALER, NATHANIEL SOUTHGATE. *Kentucky, a Pioneer Commonwealth*. Boston, 1888.

SONNE, HENRY NIELS. *Liberal Kentucky, 1780-1928*. New York, 1939.

STOWE, HARRIET BEECHER. *A Key to Uncle Tom's Cabin*. Boston, 1853.

TALBERT, CHARLES. *Benjamin Logan*. Lexington, 1962.

THOMPSON, ED PORTER. *History of the First Kentucky Brigade*. Cincinnati, 1868.

TOWNSEND, JOHN WILSON. *Kentucky in American Literature*. 2 vols. Cedar Rapids, 1913.

TOWNSEND, WILLIAM H. *Lincoln and His Wife's Home Town*. Indianapolis, 1929.

VAN DEUSEN, GLYNDON G. *Life of Henry Clay*. Boston, 1937.

Index

ABOUT THE AUTHOR

Thomas D. Clark is Distinguished Professor of the University of Kentucky at Lexington. Born in Louisville, Mississippi, he received his A.B. at the University of Mississippi, his M.A. at Kentucky, and his Ph.D. at Duke University. Since joining the department of history at the University of Kentucky in 1931, Mr. Clark has taught by his own estimate, "almost 20,000 Kentucky students."

Mr. Clark's knowledge of his adopted state is manifold, combining a deep personal familiarity ("I have visited in every county of Kentucky, most of them many times") with the historian's scholarly interest. Among his previous books are *Bluegrass Cavalcade, Frontier America,* and *The Emerging South.* A special interest since 1928 has been the growth of a fine collection of Kentuckiana in the University Library.